THE EVERYTHING®
Pirates Book

Dear Reader,

Anyone who knows us well understands our love of all things legendary, especially if the subject matter is a puzzle with more than a few missing pieces. Pirates are a lifelong fascination for many individuals, who devour reams of historical information as well as the innumerable myths and legends surrounding these renowned sea dogs. And we're suckers for a great myth.

If you love pirates, then you'll no doubt appreciate their rich history, lust for adventure, and never-ending zest for discovering the terminally elusive treasure chest brimming with gold and jewels. What you may not realize is just how long pirates have been around, and how hard the life of a sea robber was. And while this doesn't excuse their crimes by any means, it certainly sheds light on why they chose such a volatile career.

Our study was a journey that took us across oceans of time, sailing in calm waters that pirates so loved and stormy seas that struck sheer terror in the hearts of all who crossed their varied paths. It was a voyage we wouldn't have missed for the world.

Barb Karg

Arjean Spaite

The EVERYTHING® Series

Editorial

Publisher	Gary M. Krebs
Director of Product Development	Paula Munier
Managing Editor	Laura M. Daly
Associate Copy Chief	Sheila Zwiebel
Acquisitions Editor	Lisa Laing
Development Editor	Brett Palana-Shanahan
Associate Production Editor	Casey Ebert

Production

Director of Manufacturing	Susan Beale
Production Project Manager	Michelle Roy Kelly
Prepress	Erick DaCosta Matt LeBlanc
Interior Layout	Heather Barrett Brewster Brownville Colleen Cunningham Jennifer Oliveira
Cover Design	Erin Alexander Stephanie Chrusz Frank Rivera

Visit the entire Everything® Series at *www.everything.com*

THE EVERYTHING® PIRATES BOOK

A swashbuckling history of
adventure on the high seas

Barb Karg and Arjean Spaite

Adams Media
Avon, Massachusetts

For all our touchstones—Ma and Pop, Mom and Dad, our better halves Rick and Jim, Chris Grant, Dan, Matt, and Adam Spaite, David and Mary Ann, Larry and Phyllis, Ellen and Jim, Jim Van Over, Karla, the Scribe Tribe, and especially the Blonde Bombshell. And to all the historians, scholars, and authors who have dedicated their lives to bringing to life the fascinating facts and fiction surrounding the world's most legendary seafarers.

———————

An Everything® Series Book.
Everything® and everything.com® are registered trademarks of F+W Publications, Inc.

Published by Adams Media, an F+W Publications Company
57 Littlefield Street, Avon, MA 02322 U.S.A.
www.adamsmedia.com

ISBN 10: 1-59869-255-0
ISBN 13: 978-1-59869-255-6

Printed in the United States of America.

J   I   H   G   F   E   D   C   B   A

Library of Congress Cataloging-in-Publication Data
Karg, Barbara.
The everything pirates book / Barb Karg and Arjean Spaite.
p. cm. – (An everything series book.)
ISBN-13: 978-1-59869-255-6 (pbk.)
ISBN-10: 1-59869-255-0 (pbk.)
1. Pirates. I. Spaite, Arjean. II. Title.
G535.K18 2007
910.4'5—dc22
2007002582

This publication is designed to provide accurate and authoritative information with regard to the subject matter covered. It is sold with the understanding that the publisher is not engaged in rendering legal, accounting, or other professional advice. If legal advice or other expert assistance is required, the services of a competent professional person should be sought.

—From a *Declaration of Principles* jointly adopted by a Committee of the American Bar Association and a Committee of Publishers and Associations

Many of the designations used by manufacturers and sellers to distinguish their products are claimed as trademarks. Where those designations appear in this book and Adams Media was aware of a trademark claim, the designations have been printed with initial capital letters.

This book is available at quantity discounts for bulk purchases.
For information, please call 1-800-289-0963.

Contents

Acknowledgments

Avast All Ye Scallywags! It has been a fine journey, with occasional rough waters, but plenty of smooth sailing. Better off for the pirating, a pair of scurvy landlubbers such as ourselves have developed a well-earned respect for the seas and all the fine sailors who've crossed our paths. As any fine pirate knows, it takes more than one rogue to complete a project, and *The Everything® Pirates Book* is no exception to the rule. As always, it's our honor to have worked with many fine captains and crew members who helped bring this publication from Davy Jones' Locker to our gleaming mizzenmast.

For starters, we'd like to raise a tankard to the exceptional crew of the good ship *Adams Media* for their support and encouragement. To editor Lisa Laing, whose wily wit and keen professionalism we greatly respect, we offer a chest of gold doubloons (tax free, of course). A wench of unequaled talent is director of product development, Paula Munier. An extraordinary dame who we eternally admire for her exquisite taste in wine, chocolate, and friends, we've set aside a host of emeralds and jewels befitting a queen. Our favorite classy wench of motherly repute is developmental editor Brett Palana-Shanahan. For this fine lady we gift a custom made Jolly Roger she can fly aboard her fully-loaded schooner named *Danica*—which we captured just for her.

We also offer a hearty thanks and a collection of exotic pirate booty to Laura Daly, Sue Beale, Rachel Engelson, copy editor Suzanne Goraj, layout artist and designer Jennifer Oliveira, and proofer Patty Krumholz. We'd especially like to offer smooth sailing and a fine silk waistcoat and tricorn to the *Adams* captain Gary Krebs for giving us the opportunity to present this book.

Above all, we offer our worldly riches to our friends, especially Ellen Weider, Steve Prager, and Jim Van Over, and most importantly, our families, who endured our absence whilst we navigated our way through oceans of never-ending facts, chronicles, legend, lore, and hearsay. Without their love and support no journey would be successful. In particular, we offer our humblest pirate toast to Trudi and George Karg, Jean Collins, and guardian angel Arnold Collins. We also gift cutlasses to our better halves. First mate, Jim Spaite, who spent hours listening to pirate lore and offering support in countless ways, and master gunner Rick Sutherland, whose dead aim research and literary skills kept us happily afloat in all measure of stormy seas. Both notorious scallywags, we dedicate our journey to them, and to all of these fine sailors.

Top Ten Things You'll Learn about Pirates

1. Piracy wasn't just for men. Anne Bonny and Mary Read along with a host of other female pirates were just as tough as—if not tougher than—their male counterparts.

2. Julius Caesar was captured and ransomed around 75 B.C. by Mediterranean pirates, whom he later hunted down and crucified.

3. Pirate crews operated in a democratic fashion, with codes of conduct and each member receiving equal share of plunder.

4. Most pirates died penniless, their high seas adventures lasting only a few years.

5. Pirates continue to roam the oceans of the world in search of riches they can steal, or humans or cargo they can ransom.

6. Piracy began around 3000 B.C. in ancient Egypt and throughout the Mediterranean Sea.

7. Viking pirates often struck intended victims with such speed that by the time defending forces could be assembled, the Vikings were long gone.

8. Modern treasure hunters are still discovering the wreckage of Spanish treasure fleets with cargoes of gold, silver, and jewels.

9. Pirates often flew highly stylized and individualistic "Jolly Roger" flags of their own design.

10. The "buccaneers" made their living smoking and selling beef jerky long before they began plundering ships and sacking cities.

Introduction

▶ WHEN YOU HEAR the word pirate, what image immediately springs to mind? Do you envision a peglegged sea dog dressed in blousy attire, wearing a huge gold earring and sporting a parrot on his shoulder? Do you picture a vile smelly drunkard who shoots pistols into the air yelling "Yo ho ho and a bottle o' rum"? Or perhaps you see a tall spare man enveloped in smoke whirling about his face, whose long black beard fails to disguise his demonic intentions? Fear not. There's no wrong answer. Any of those images are likely suspects when the subject of classic piracy sails into view.

Those unfamiliar with the history of piracy are in for a treat, because there's plenty of it. Piracy began around 3000 B.C., and over the centuries many of the greatest civilizations known to mankind, such as the Egyptians, Greeks, and Romans, fell victim to relentless groups of pirates. Over the millennia, pirates have evolved into efficient sailors, adventurers, and dastardly thieves and murderers, and they've done so with a style and panache that's entirely their own. Pirates, privateers, buccaneers, and corsairs had several things in common. They all shared a love of the sea, the lust for adventure and debauchery, and an obsessive drive for unbridled wealth. Many of the more successful pirates, like Blackbeard and Bartholomew Roberts, didn't live long enough to enjoy their infamy, but that didn't really matter to them. What meant the most was power and the freedom to do anything they pleased, and they'd stop at nothing to attain that goal.

When studied from an objective point of view, the subject of piracy inevitably requires an enormous amount of thought. For the majority of individuals, it's impossible at the outset not to picture pirates as being swarthy drunken sailors who swashbuckle their way across the silver screen. Upon closer inspection, however, one learns that a pirate's life was anything but glamorous and that many became villainous sailors out of necessity.

Then there's the inherent dark side of piracy, which centers on the astoundingly brutal acts pirates inflicted upon all measure of humanity, from men and women to children and slaves. Piracy is not for the faint of heart. Pirates are criminals, and like any individual who brings harm to others, there are accounts that cause one to feel pity and offer great respect to those unfortunate souls who fell victim to unimaginable cruelty. No act of forgiveness can be bestowed upon those who committed such heinous acts. Yet despite their atrocities, pirates remain a popular subject among people of all ages, and that speaks to their irresistible allure.

In this book, you'll find four different types of tips. Pieces of Eight are facts about pirates, privateers, buccaneers, corsairs, and all measure of piracy in general. Shiver Me Timbers are terms relating to piracy, nautical terms, and pirate phraseology. Scuttlebutts are questions relating to various piratical issues, and Sea Rovers are tidbits about various rogues who sailed the seas.

The study of piracy is typical of research into any historical civilization, group, era, and circumstance. On the one hand, pirates and their careers are utterly fascinating and it's easy to have a certain respect for the difficult lives they led. On the flip side, pirates themselves are an enigma. Yes, they were criminals and consummate robbers of the sea. And indeed, more than a few were black-hearted devils. But despite all their exploits, or perhaps because of them, they've fallen victim to romanticized stereotypes of themselves. It's an irony that's inescapable.

In the end it matters little which image individuals conjure up when thinking about pirates. What matters is that pirates and their stories continue to be told and their lives made known to all present and future generations. Pirates are fun, they're frightening, and they're some of the most intriguing historical characters you'll ever meet.

Chapter 1

Ahoy Mateys!

For thousands of years, piracy has been intrinsically linked to maritime history, and for as long as civilized peoples have sailed the oceans and rivers of the world, so have pirates been preying on unsuspecting ships whose cargoes represented nothing less than pure gold to crews of raging rogues. The lore and legends surrounding pirates rival the historic and often atrocious exploits of real-life pirates. Long John Silver may have captured the public's hearts, but it was the devilish Blackbeard and his kind who gave piracy its true immortality.

What Is a Pirate?

There's no escaping piracy in the modern world. Even today, the practice of thievery continues across a wide range of industries including computer software and hardware, music, and motion pictures. Maritime pirates are also in abundance prowling various rivers and oceans from the Amazon to Southeast Asia. But what exactly is a pirate and what do pirates do? By definition, a maritime pirate is someone who without government authorization appropriates goods or money from another party while at sea or who plunders goods on land, having made their approach from an ocean or body of water. The term is derived from the Latin word *pirata*, which literally translated means "marine adventurer." Pirates, with very few exceptions, were seamen who possessed the abundance of skills necessary to sail a vessel, including a working knowledge of a ship's complex sails and its ropes and lashings (called *rigging*), and all things related to keeping a wooden vessel afloat and in top condition (see Chapter 10).

Buccaneers, Privateers, and Corsairs

To understand the evolution of piracy and how it came to be so prevalent throughout history, one must examine the events of each era that enabled piracy to flourish with reckless abandon. From its inception around 3000 B.C., piracy plagued entire civilizations such as those of the Greeks and Romans, and even brought the commerce of several nations to a screeching halt. For 300 years beginning around 789 A.D., the Vikings rampaged the Baltic Seas. Starting in the fourteenth century a new group of pirates, the *Barbary corsairs*, terrorized the Atlantic coast of Europe and the Mediterranean Sea around North Africa. Corsairs were embroiled in a battle between Muslims and Christians and would be hired by either side to attack the other (see Chapter 4).

The Privateers

With Spanish exploration in the fifteenth and sixteenth centuries came decades of wars and riches that proved irresistible to pirates and to economically depleted countries such as England. Queen Elizabeth and her legendary sea dogs literally saved Britain with the riches they commandeered as a result of their "legalized" piracy (see Chapter 6). *Privateers*, as they were called, were pirates who were granted commissions by a sovereign nation and were issued *letters of marque*, which gave them the license to attack any ship that their nation was currently at war with. At face value, this amounted to nothing more than legal piracy, and in truth when privateering ended during times of peace, many of the privateers turned to piracy. On the other hand, it's sometimes argued that privateers weren't pirates at all, but instead men who were simply working for their government much like any military seamen.

SHIVER ME TIMBERS

The term *Davy Jones' Locker* basically refers to someone ending up at the bottom of the ocean. The exact origin of Davy or David Jones is unclear, though he has been immortalized as a type of oceanic demon or the devil himself. Typically, pirates used the phrase as a threat, swearing to kill a man and "send him to Davy Jones' Locker," or as a reference to a pirate near death being in Davy Jones' hands.

The Buccaneers

Starting in the late 1400s, the Spanish took control of areas of the Caribbean and Central and South America. In total, these lands were known as the *Spanish Main*. As part of their own undoing, the Spaniards inadvertently created a new breed of pirates called the *buccaneers*, who are detailed in Chapter 7. Career hunters and tradesmen, these relentless rogues proved to be a major thorn in Spain's side for decades as they plundered Spanish galleons and port cities throughout the Main and beyond into the Caribbean. Among them was one of the greatest buccaneers, an intimidating force of a man called Henry Morgan, whose legendary raids and brutality put him in a class of elite pirates who would stop at nothing to achieve their dastardly goals (see Chapter 8).

Attack of the Scallywags

Over the centuries, thousands of pirates have prowled the oceans of the world, and most of them have been lost to antiquity. An impressive band of scoundrels engaged in such high-profile atrocities that they left their skull and crossbones permanently imprinted on history books, as a result of their highly successful pillaging, their outrageous behavior and antics, or the inhuman cruelty they inflicted upon their unfortunate victims. During the 1700s, the Golden Age of piracy showcased a handful of surly seafarers who rose above the rest to reach legendary status. The most famous among them is without a doubt Edward Teach, a tall, spare man known for his distinctively long beard and rule-by-fear tactics. Few would quickly recognize Teach were it not for his pirate name—Blackbeard.

Though not nearly as prolific as some pirates such as Bartholomew Roberts—or Black Bart, as he is commonly known—Teach perhaps more than any other rogue accomplished what the majority of pirates could never achieve, and did so during a short career that in the end has made him immortal (see Chapter 12). Of almost equal repute for various piratical successes or human atrocities were Charles Vane, Edward Low, Henry Every, Edward England, Calico Jack Rackham, and Black Sam Bellamy. Not to be outdone by their male counterparts, Anne Bonny and Mary Read were just two of the pirate queens who took to the high seas in search of adventure (see Chapter 15). These were the pirates of the Caribbean, and a few of the most famous of all maritime rogues whose scourge of the seas paralyzed even the sturdiest of landlubbers.

PIECES of EIGHT

Statistics for just how many pirates sailed in an area at any given time are extremely difficult to ascertain. Records aren't always accurate, if they exist at all. In his book *Villains of All Nations*, renowned author Marcus Rediker notes that between 1716 and 1718 it's estimated that 1,500 to 2,000 pirates were active in the Caribbean, with numbers increasing to approximately 1,800 to 2,400 from 1719 to 1722.

Becoming a Pirate

In reality, a pirate's life was exceptionally hard and typically short, given the nature of their chosen career (see Chapter 9). Most pirates had no loyalty to any nation or government. They acted entirely on their own device, conducting raids and plundering as they pleased. Contrary to popular belief, however, they weren't entirely lawless individuals. Each pirate vessel had its own *articles*, or codes of conduct, that crewmembers had to sign and abide by if they were to remain on that ship. These articles, which outlined the share of *booty*, or treasure, a pirate would receive, were very specific about the conduct that was expected aboard ship and the punishments a pirate would incur for breaking any rules. Ultimately, the articles were such that pirates ruled themselves in democratic fashion, each receiving equal share in plunder and each having a say in where a ship was headed and who its captain was. Once a seaman signed the articles, he was considered to have gone *on the account*, meaning that he would have to account for his own illegal actions if he were caught, and would be paid only when there was booty to share.

The Pirate Realm

The history of piracy, like that of many other historical endeavors, contains numerous accounts of individuals and their piratical exploits. Given that the majority of pirates couldn't read or write, details of various events were related orally and have over many centuries become highly embellished. So too have "facts," which are often blurred in a mire of hearsay and fictional accounts written by authors of the day. It's fair to say that the majority of traits and adventures that have become an amalgam of stereotypical piracy are a direct result of fiction and accounts such as Alexandre Exquemelin's 1678 work *The Buccaneers of America*.

Thirst for High Seas Adventure

Captain Charles Johnson was credited with the 1678 version of *A General History of the Robberies and Murders of the Most Notorious Pyrates* (or *Pirates*, depending on the version). That was later changed when it was believed that *Robinson Crusoe* author Daniel Defoe wrote the book. Modern scholars, however, once again consider Johnson to be its author. A rich and violent account of high seas piracy, *Pyrates* sparked public interest in the murderous plundering rampages of pirates. So rabid was the general public that in two years *Pyrates* had two volumes and four editions. That interest in pirates didn't wane, and would eventually explode with the 1883 publication of Robert Louis Stevenson's *Treasure Island*. Arguably one of the most famous fictional pirates is *Treasure Island*'s Long John Silver. At times a likable but primarily feared character, Silver walked with a crutch, and had a parrot perched on his shoulder (see Chapter 18).

The Romance of Piracy

In the grand scheme of things, conflicting information about pirates doesn't appear to have had a major impact on the general population, who continue to devour all historical and sometimes hysterical accounts of the world's most famous pirates. The overwhelming image of pirates continues to be that of a romantic rogue, a smartly attired man wielding a sword who swashbuckles his way into the heart of a fragile lovestruck girl. Alternately, pirates are often depicted as swarthy tricksters limping about on peglegs, sporting large gold earrings and bandannas, and carrying ever-present parrots on their shoulders. Still others are tagged as black-hearted devils—smelly, unkempt men who are loaded to the gills with munitions, impervious to drink, and drooling for busty wenches (see Chapter 17).

Call of the Mermaid

There's no denying that the oceans of the world have forever been an enticing and ideologically romantic lure to individuals of all cultures and nationalities. The smell of salt permeating the air, the sound of gently lapping waves, and the sight of crisp sails cutting through an azure sky have enticed many men into becoming sailors. Seamen who turned to piracy often retained this maritime intoxication; wishing to leave naval service for potential riches, they were easily recruited. Other men weren't so lucky—they ended up pirates as a result of being captured or by reluctantly joining to avoid being tortured or murdered.

For the vast majority of pirates, treasure captured from plundered vessels primarily consisted of food and munitions supplies, trade goods such as sugar, spices, or silk, or human prizes consisting of slaves. Rarely did pirates find a treasure chest brimming with priceless baubles and gold, silver, and jewels. But that didn't stop them from trying, or from believing they'd someday retire to a life of luxury. Spanish galleons were cornucopias of wealth. Once their contents were collected and shared among pirate crews, however, the treasure provided rogues only a temporary measure of power. Most pirates didn't save their booty, instead choosing to waste it on gambling, drink, and prostitutes.

SHIVER ME TIMBERS

The term *booty* was a favorite word used by pirates. By definition, booty is used to describe any material goods, money, or supplies obtained illegally either in secret or by force. Given that pirates are basically thieves, booty encompassed their various illegal acquisitions and how they referred to their individual share of goods obtained by a crew.

The Spanish began minting coins in the 1500s. Silver coins were properly called *reales*, but became known as *pieces of eight*. These coins were physically cut into eight pieces to make change. By today's standards, pieces of eight are worth approximately $27. Gold coins, called *escudos*, were popularly known as *doubloons*. Many ships transported gold and silver in the form of bars called *ingots*, a prize that a few lucky modern-day treasure hunters have painstakingly sought and found (see Chapter 19).

Come Sail Away

From a modern perspective, the ships pirates sailed are a feast for the eyes. Some vessels, like the Viking longships, were magnificently crafted with what were at best primitive tools. Galleons, cogs, schooners, sloops, brigantines, and square-riggers were all constructed by shipwrights whose primary goal was to make these ships highly functional for the purpose they served, be it cargo hauling, slaving, or warring. Pirates took great advantage of these vessels and worked hard to plunder and steal them. Once a ship was in their grasp, they typically made modifications within the ship's decks and to its armaments. When raiding an unsuspecting vessel, a pirate crew's attack was swift and unwavering, and among all pirates there was a common strategy of intimidation (see Chapter 10). Pirates would typically offer to *give quarter* to their victims, which allowed them to surrender without harm. But if the offer wasn't quickly accepted, it would be withdrawn and the battle would be a fight to the death.

SCUTTLEBUTT

What kinds of weapons did pirates use?
Most pirates typically used pistols and would generally carry more than one so as to avoid constant reloading in battle situations. They also used axes, daggers, and a shorter, heavy-bladed curved sword called a *cutlass*. These weapons were more efficient for fighting in cramped quarters. They also used chemical warfare by concocting types of grenades called *granado shells* or *stinkpots*.

Raging Rogues

The mere mention of the word "pirate" conjures up a vast variety of imagery and fantasy, all of which surrounds a group of men and women who made their living terrorizing others. Over many centuries, piracy has intrigued, fascinated, and horrified the general population, who continue with their insatiable lust for all things pirate-related. What many don't know is just how long pirates have been around, and how deeply their exploits have affected individual victims, groups, towns, ports, villages, and entire nations and continents. Piracy is a plague that has never been entirely wiped out, and the voyages pirates made have resulted in a treasure trove of history that will either continue to be revealed or remain as elusive as the pirates who buried it.

Chapter 2

The First Pirates

As long as there have been ships navigating the oceans of the world, so have there been pirates who have robbed them of their crews and their riches. Entire civilizations have been marred and sometimes even fallen at the hands of pirates, from the ancient Egyptians to the powerful city-states of the Greeks. Though the dominance of pirates has taken many forms, no era has been devoid of their relentless assaults. No matter their methods or madness, they remain a fascinating part of seafaring history.

Ancient Plunderers

The history of piracy is as rich as the plunder that sea raiders have accumulated over the course of many millennia. When studying history, one doesn't often put into perspective the enduring legacy of piracy, which has been around as long as the civilizations that first set sail across as yet unexplored bodies of water. Some of the earliest seafarers were Egyptians and Mesopotamians who constructed floating vessels and took to the seas around 3000 B.C. These ancient mariners didn't often lose sight of land during their journeys, choosing instead to navigate the Nile, Tigris, and Euphrates rivers. The Phoenicians were another sea-trading civilization whose people lived in the coastal areas of what are now Lebanon, Israel, and Syria.

Growing ancient civilizations were intent on improving their seafaring savvy and technology so that exploration, trade, and warfare could be accomplished on a much larger scale. This would become evident with the rise of the Greek and Roman empires, whose naval fleets over the centuries rivaled each other in glorious fashion. Maritime ambition, however, would always be plagued by piracy in some form or another, as the Mediterranean Sea would quickly become an established shipping route and an irresistible target for pirates.

Mediterranean Marauders

Spanning the coastlines of southern Europe, Asia Minor, and North Africa, the Mediterranean Sea was destined to become a major factor in the economies of many civilizations. As commerce and trade increased beginning in the Early Bronze Age around 4000 B.C., so did riches and technology—and piracy. Cargo-laden ships inspired piratical practices, with sea raiders quickly establishing themselves as a menace to all who had the misfortune of crossing their paths. This was clearly the case for the people and armies of ancient Egypt.

Egyptian Ships

The Egyptians were arguably the master builders of the ancient world, and the craftsmanship of their ship designers, or *shipwrights*, was displayed in their impressive fleets of vessels. Early mariners were ultimately focused on trade, and Egyptian ships were built for transport and cargo. Illustrations show these ships to have been long, elegant, and gondola-like in their curvature. They were designed as *galleys*, which by definition were single-deck vessels powered by sails and oars. The Egyptian vessels were without keels, very light in weight, double-masted, and powered by oarsmen. Later ships would prove to be sturdier in order to accommodate enormous quarry loads and increased cargo, but would continue to retain much of their initial design. The fact that early shipping was navigated through rivers and within view of land was advantageous to pirates, who boldly attacked these ships. Ultimately, Egyptian progress would become challenged by these rogues with the arrival of the *Sea Peoples*.

SHIVER ME TIMBERS

Ancient Egyptian shipwrights were among the earliest known ship designers to build watertight hulls that were made of wooden planks cut from tree trunks and assembled with *treenails* and *pitch*. Treenails are wooden pegs that fastened the planks together. Pitch is heated tar that was applied to the edges of the planks to make the seams watertight.

The Lukka

One of the earliest groups of sea raiders were the *Lukka*. Recorded in Hittite texts, these ancient mariners lived around the fourteenth century B.C. in Asia Minor in what is now the Turkish coast. Despite cultural and political differences with the Hittites, the Lukka allied with them for a battle against Egyptian Pharaoh Ramses II. They also combined forces for the Battle of Kadash in the eleventh century B.C. in what is now Syria. The latter battle ensued over political and geographic boundaries of the predominant Mediterranean powers of the time. After a century, however, the Lukka turned on the Hittites and ultimately contributed to their demise. It's said that the Lukka were one of the tribes that constituted an ancient contingent of pirates called the Sea Peoples.

Who Were the Sea Peoples?

Historians and scholars alike continue to debate and theorize about the origins and exploits of the so-called Sea Peoples who terrorized the Mediterranean's eastern coast during the twelfth and thirteenth centuries B.C. What is known about the Sea Peoples is mostly gleaned from Egyptian inscriptions that describe a battle waged during the reign of the Egyptian king Merneptah in 1208 B.C. According to the inscriptions, the Sea Peoples were an amalgam of migrating tribes, six of which were named: Tjeker, Denyen, Peleset, Weshesh, Shekelesh, and Shardana.

PIECES of EIGHT

As a combined force, the Sea Peoples led maritime invasions in areas along the eastern Mediterranean and later took aim at Egypt during two epic battles, once during Merneptah's reign and again twenty years later during the kingship of Pharaoh Ramses III.

Voracious in their attacks on villages and merchant shipping, the Sea Peoples were maritime raiders on a grand scale. In 1190 B.C., one of the scribes serving Ramses III described the Sea Peoples as a *tour de force* both on land and at sea—a combination of men, women, and children whose numbers grew as they raided and moved through coastal regions. Their seafaring contingent was allegedly a formidable and savage group of warriors who were so feared that "no land could stand before their arms."

Of Unknown Origin

The Sea Peoples' place in history is secured by the historical theory that as a collective force they brought about the collapse of key Mediterranean powers during the Late Bronze Age between 1600 and 1000 B.C., including the Greek and Hittite empires in Anatolia (the Asiatic area of Turkey) and northern Syria. Some scholars conclude that the Sea Peoples were from the Aegean area or Anatolia, were Greek, or were even the original inhabitants of the fabled lost city of Atlantis. One of the prominent theories regarding their formation into a cohesive civilization is that various separate tribes were forced into a southern migration as a result of eroding economic factors, desperation driving them to pillage and piracy.

Attack on Egypt

Egyptian pharaoh Merneptah came to power in 1213 B.C. after the death of his father—the legendary Ramses the Great—and ruled until approximately 1203 B.C. In antiquity, the death of any leader was often followed by a period of panic when civilizations feared being overtaken by neighboring factions. Such was the case after Ramses' death, but an incursion didn't come from the Hittites as might have been expected. Instead, it is said to have been a contingent of Libyans—enemies of the Egyptians—who joined forces with the Sea Peoples. In the fifth year of Merneptah's reign, the Sea Peoples began an assault on the Nile Delta in an effort to block the supply of wheat that Egypt was providing the Hittites. With numbers estimated as high as 5,000, the Sea Peoples attacked, but in the end their efforts proved to be no match for Merneptah's forces.

One by Land, Two by Sea

For the next two decades, the piratical Sea Peoples continued their relentless raids on the east coast of the Mediterranean, liberating any and all goods and capturing men, women, and children who could be sold as slaves. For their efforts, they ultimately controlled entire ports, cities, and surrounding lands. Twenty years after their attempted assault on Egypt, the Sea Peoples once again attacked the Nile Delta. This battle, fought around 1175 B.C. during the reign of Ramses III, is described on the walls of his mortuary temple in Medinet Habu in Thebes (present-day Luxor). The battle against the Sea Peoples depicted in the temple of Ramses III bears striking similarity to the invasion previously fought by Merneptah two decades before, a fact that has led some scholars and experts to believe that there was no second invasion by these seafaring pirates.

Regardless of whether a second battle took place, inscriptions show that Ramses' forces waged an enormous fight against the Sea Peoples and their allied forces. Apparently overconfident, the raiders allegedly sailed into the

Nile Delta unprepared for the battle to come. Their method of attack was swift and they relied on the element of surprise and the use of swordplay at close quarters. While this tactic had traditionally proven successful against less experienced forces, the Egyptians had a distinct advantage in the form of archers armed with bows and arrows. Before the invaders could get close enough to inflict harm, they were cut down and their ships destroyed. Ultimately, the Sea Peoples fought to the bitter end, but were resoundingly defeated. The damage they'd inflicted upon the lands surrounding the Mediterranean, however, was undeniable.

SHIVER ME TIMBERS

The term *bitter end* is often used in modern-day vernacular, especially in regard to a fight or battle. In the nautical world a *bitt* is the post that protrudes from the deck of a ship that is used to secure the anchor rope or chain. The final link of the chain or end of the rope is called the bitter end.

Greek Seamanship

Seamanship and piracy in Greece are bound together in the rich mythologies and recorded realities of ancient Grecian history. With coastlines that constitute more than 90 percent of its borders, few roads, and relatively little agricultural land, the earliest Greeks naturally looked to the sea as a way of life. As a result, Greece would become a pillar of expert seamanship and hub of merchant shipping routes in the ancient world, and it remains so to this day.

At the center of the Mediterranean Sea, Greece was virtually at the crossroads of seagoing commerce and shipping lanes that reached from Asia to northern Africa, and from Italy to the east. It was also directly connected to the Balkan countries to the north. As trading ebbed and flowed throughout the region over the centuries, piracy would also ebb and flow in near-perfect unison. Much of our knowledge of ancient Greece is cloaked in mythology and the fictionalized historical accounts of the Greek poet, Homer. The rise in power and influence of the Greek island of Crete is generally undisputed, and Cretan shipping and trade was extended to virtually all ports in the Mediterranean. On the mainland of Greece, the Mycenaean Greek civilization also flourished and overlapped the Cretan civilization, with trade likely occurring between the two powerhouses.

SCUTTLEBUTT

Who were the Achaens?
In Homer's much debated epic work the *Odyssey*, he describes at length a Greek civilization called the *Achaens*, who were probably mainland Mycenaeans. He further describes the people who inhabited Greek isles as pirates.

Grecian Maritime Power

Ancient coastal communities along the mainland and on the numerous islands of ancient Greece grew into major port strongholds that operated independently of one another, becoming what are commonly referred to as *city-states*, separate territories governed by a single sovereign city. Throughout the Bronze Age, from 4000 to 750 B.C., many of these city-states grew to dominate the seas surrounding their territories and islands, and piracy against foreign vessels was generally regarded as a virtuous undertaking of seamanship and courage. Captured merchant ships and their cargo could be sailed into cooperative harbors, where goods were split with the city authorities and sold at open markets. Crewmembers were often taken and sold into slavery, while wealthy passengers would be held for ransom.

The Menace of Safe Sailing

Seafaring navigation for trade vessels in the ancient Mediterranean world was generally limited to sailing along the coastlines in calm weather, keeping land in clear view. To avoid losing their way in the dark, ships usually anchored close to land or even beached on the shore at nightfall, resuming their journey at daybreak. The coastlines that merchant ships followed were dotted with bays and inlets that presented perfect hideouts and camouflage from which pirates would sprint, in their light and highly maneuverable warships, to attack a potential victim.

Monoreme Pirate Galleys

Some of the earliest boats used by Grecian pirates were variations of war galleys known as *monoremes* that relied on oars for propulsion. The monoreme style of craft is still represented today by the modernized *sweep boats* used in Olympic rowing competitions. The Greek monoreme was built to accommodate oarsman situated in two rows along either side of a boat, each rower handling a single long oar. With as many as forty oarsman, these sleek boats were capable of rapid bursts of speed that could easily overtake wind-powered trading vessels. High fighting decks were built on the front of the boats, or *bow*, and the back of the boats, called the *stern*. Marauding monoremes allowed for quick boarding by well-armed pirates, who could jump directly down onto the decks of their intended victims. This was usually followed by the rapid capitulation of the merchant ship captains and their crews, who were not accustomed to or equipped for hand-to-hand combat.

By around 1000 B.C., war galleys of the city-state navies of Greece were outfitted with fortified bows and battering rams, devices that would quickly change the nature of battle on the open seas. These ships were essentially turned into huge seagoing weapons capable of ramming and debilitating enemy vessels during combat. Often the damage was enough to sink both craft and crew. Because the goal of a pirate is to capture his prey intact, ramming and destroying hapless merchant vessels was pointless. On the other hand, the threat of this new development to pirate fleets was very real, as pirate-hunting naval vessels from opposing city-states utilized the rams against them, destroying their ships.

Stacking the Decks

The monoreme was eventually updated to the *bireme* design, with two rows of oarsmen stacked one deck above the other. With this design, developed and utilized primarily by Greek city-states with relatively sophisticated shipyards, the length of the ship could be cut in half and still retain the same number of oarsmen, thus presenting a smaller target for ramming.

With the success of the bireme, shipwrights continued the concept of stacking oarsmen by designing and building the *trireme*, which included three rows of oars on separate decks located on either side of the ship.

The bireme and trireme designs of the ancient Greek shipbuilders were eventually adopted by subsequent seafaring nations that came into power around the Mediterranean Sea. Centuries later, the Romans, led by Pompey the Great, adapted the bireme model for the naval fleets that would prove to be the undoing of Mediterranean pirates.

The trireme eventually became the classic Greek battle galley, with as many as 150 rowers handling oars up to 15 feet long. With an additional sailing crew of two dozen sailors and another two dozen armed warriors, the trireme proved to be a formidable weapon of war. Often used as escort ships for merchant convoys, only the most foolhardy pirates would dare challenge the size and speed of a trireme battle galley.

Easy Prey

The vessels that Greek merchants used in ancient times were meticulously crafted by expert shipbuilders, although the science of the day presented serious flaws that pirates could easily use to their advantage. Grecian ports and harbors were often relatively shallow, and it was common practice to build vessels with wide beams and flat bottoms that could literally be hauled onto the shore by the crew. Because of the shallow draft design, heavily laden merchant vessels were clumsy and slow, presenting perfect prey for smaller and much nimbler pirate craft.

The nearly intact recovered remains of a Greek trading vessel that has been carbon dated to 350 B.C. is illustrative of merchant ships of the era. About 50 feet in length and 15 feet across, the ship was capable of carrying an estimated seven tons of cargo. Fully loaded, the deck of the ship would ride only 2 feet above the surface of the water, and the single square-rigged sail could provide a speed of about five knots.

SHIVER ME TIMBERS

The word *knot* is common to sailors and pirates alike. A variety of knots are obviously used for a ship's ropes, or *rigging*, but it is also the term used to describe the speed of a sailing vessel. A knot designates a nautical mile, which is the equivalent of 1.2 miles.

Unescorted by protective warships, such vessels would have no defense and no escape from the swift oar-propelled craft favored by pirates of the day. Piracy would continue to tax the patience and commercial aspirations of ruling nations in the Mediterranean Sea well into the era of Roman rule, and into northern Europe, where the Vikings would begin wreaking their own brand of terror and plunder.

Chapter 3

Hellfire and Brimstone

Throughout the Bronze Age and into the Middle Ages, piracy continued to maintain a fearsome foothold in the Mediterranean that would not be shaken until well after the Romans and Byzantines came into power to dominate the entire region. Farther north, along the Atlantic coastlines of Europe, a different breed of seamen, the Vikings, would come into power. Their influence during the Dark Ages would expand the arts of navigation, exploration, and commerce—and piracy, into one of its most frightening forms.

Piracy under Roman Rule

The maritime power of Grecian city-states underwent social and economic declines and resurgences over the last of the ancient centuries, until the Romans finally conquered Greece in 146 B.C. Although Rome's military muscle and political control became dominant in the Mediterranean, Romans relied heavily on the traditional merchant marine trade of coastal countries and provinces surrounding the area. Unfortunately for Rome, relying on traditional marine traffic for commerce and travel would also include fighting the pirates who hounded it.

Roman conquest and the relative stability it brought to the Mediterranean generated a brand new aspect to the marine trade as tourists and passengers began exploring the known world. Businessmen, students, sightseers, public servants, and Romans on vacation began traveling to Mediterranean ports in large numbers, and pirates took notice. Pirates in the Mediterranean were quick to recognize the value of passenger traffic, and prizes from captured ships would soon include captives who were ransomed for handsome profits.

Cilician Stronghold

On the southern shores of what is now Turkey, Mediterranean pirates found the perfect political and economic climate for plying their trade. Cilicia was a rugged, inaccessible, and undeveloped territory that had managed to operate independently from earlier Persian conquests, and continued to do so under Roman rule. Provincial governors often viewed piracy as an integral part of the seafaring trade, and turned a blind eye as long as they collected a share of the spoils.

The Ransom of Julius Caesar

The Greek historian Plutarch recorded that around 75 B.C., Julius Caesar, who at the time was a law student in his early twenties, was captured by Cilician pirates near the port of Miletus, a port city that still exists on the western coast of what is now Turkey. Caesar was apparently highly contemptuous of his captors, and increased the ransom they asked for him of his own accord. Over a month passed before the ransom was paid, and as soon as Caesar was released, he hired ships and soldiers and immediately set sail to hunt down the pirates who'd kidnapped him.

According to Plutarch, Caesar took the pirates to the city of Pergamum and imprisoned them. Caesar then approached Junius, the Roman governor of Asia, and demanded that the scoundrels be severely dealt with. For the Roman authorities, a handful of pirates was hardly cause for concern, and it's likely that Junius would have accepted a ransom from the pirates themselves and gladly released them to go back about their business. Annoyed at Junius' lack of outrage, Caesar returned to Pergamum and crucified the pirates himself. During his captivity, Caesar had promised the pirates that he would find them and kill them, but as the story goes, they mistakenly assumed he knew that kidnap and ransom was all simply an everyday business transaction and didn't take him seriously.

SEA ROVER

There are many versions of the story of Julius Caesar and his capture and execution of the pirates who had taken him. One of the most colorful tales relates that Caesar took pity on his former captors because of their kindness toward him during his confinement. To save them the slow, painful death of crucifixion, he ordered their throats to be slit, and *then* crucified them.

While Caesar's plight is the stuff of legend, and is probably partially fanciful, it does contain enough fact to illustrate the lack of provincial concern for piracy in the Mediterranean and the growing threat to the security of Roman citizens and Roman trade interests. The fiercely independent Cilicians prowled the Mediterranean coastline, attacking and capturing merchant ships at every opportunity and taking cargo and wealthy hostages for ransom. As the boldness and activity of the pirates gained momentum, the Romans were forced into serious military reprisals.

Pompey the Great

While a number of Roman naval expeditions were sent to the coast of Asia Minor over the course of several decades to deal with Cilician piracy, most of them either failed completely or served only to temporarily push the pirates into hiding. In 67 B.C., Gnaeus Pompeius Magnus, known as Pompey, had risen to powerful heights in the Roman military. Although he was greatly feared and distrusted by the Roman Senate, Pompey was given virtually unlimited power and funding to destroy Cilician piracy in the eastern Mediterranean. With this power, Pompey led an enormous armada of warships into the sea and swept the pirate fleets onto the coast of Cilicia.

After a short siege of the last pirate holdout in the port of Coracesium, Pompey arranged a peaceful solution for the pirates and gave them the opportunity to either quit seafaring and move inland or face his wrath. Completely overwhelmed, the pirates capitulated and accepted Pompey's mercy. During Pompey's campaign many thousands of pirates were killed, hundreds of ships destroyed, and scores of ports and harbors destroyed. The campaign lasted only forty days, and piracy in the Mediterranean was reduced to isolated incidents for the next 400 years.

Viking Voracity

During the Dark Ages, the world would come to know a breed of warrior that would leave an indelible mark on both pirate and human history. For 300 years, commonly called *the Viking Age*, Scandinavian men from the cold depths of what is now Sweden, Norway, and Denmark would pillage and plunder the Baltic and Mediterranean Seas and Russian rivers, and even reach as far as Iceland, Greenland, and Newfoundland in the North American continent. A force to be reckoned with, these Vikings, or Norsemen, were known as much for their brutal warring and terror as they were for the culture, civilization, and commerce they brought to the world through the colonies they settled throughout Europe and other continents.

Vikings were pagans who for the most part were skilled traders, craftsmen, explorers, fishermen, or farmers. Harsh weather or poverty are likely what drew Norse pirates from their homeland to the sea and beyond in search of plunder or to areas they could establish as settlements. As their shipbuilding and navigational skills advanced, however, so did their piratical ambitions, and their rule-by-fear tactics would become evident to the unfortunate victims of their assaults, many of whom were killed, captured for ransom, or sold into slavery.

SCUTTLEBUTT

Did Vikings really wear horned helmets?

Vikings often suffer from the same stereotypes that traditional pirates do and they're often misunderstood. When the word *Viking* is mentioned, it usually conjures up images of rabid seafaring barbarians charging boats and shorelines, their horned helmets firmly in place as they ravage all who stand in their way. While the tenacity of the Norsemen cannot be denied, they didn't actually wear horned helmets.

The word *Viking* is likely from the Norse word *vik*, which designates a fjord, creek, or bay. A passionate people, they were polytheistic worshippers much like the Egyptians, meaning they worshipped more than one god. Most important to them was Odin, god of war, battle, wisdom, death, magic, prophecy, and poetry, and Thor, the god of thunder. In an odd twist of fate, the Norse introduced Christianity to Scandinavia sometime in the tenth century A.D., having brought back the religion from the countries they invaded.

The Norse Advantage

The first known Viking attack took place in England in 789 A.D. and was followed in 793 with an attack on the island of Lindisfarne. With its monastery, the island was considered to be not only a source of great wealth, but a sacred place as well. Vikings commonly attacked churches and monasteries given that they were, for the most part, left unguarded, remotely located, and possessed many items of worth including jewels and gold and silver implements or crucifixes. In most cases, they attacked and left so quickly that no defense could even be mounted. At Lindisfarne, the Norse attack was swift and particularly brutal, leaving many dead and the monastery robbed of all its riches.

Viking attacks continued over the years, in Ireland, islands off Britain (the Isle of Iona, the Isle of Man), France, Constantinople (modern-day Istanbul, Turkey), and numerous coastal and inland cities. The terror these Norsemen provoked was undeniable to anyone who could see their distinctive and elegant ships nearing the shore. Hailing from a land beleaguered by fierce cold and limited resources, the Norse were natural warriors whose fighting and plundering skills would have seemed horrifically barbaric to the average coast dweller. Likewise for Norse weaponry, which included heavy double-edged swords or broad battle-axes.

Norse Vessels

The Norse are legendary for their warring skills, but perhaps even more renowned for the incredible ships they built. Vikings developed several types of double-ended *clinker-style* ships, which meant that their frames, or *hulls*, were composed of overlapping planks secured by iron nails, with tarred waterproofing wedged between the planks. Both ends of the ship would curve upward. The later designs would include the addition of a single mast and rectangular sails. Easily recognizable for their long, lean hulls and upward curvature from bow to stern, Viking craft were built for speed, durability, commerce, warfare, and even ceremonial purposes. For their era, these marvels of maritime architecture and efficiency had never before been seen by landlubbers or fellow mariners.

SHIVER ME TIMBERS

A *hull* is a crucial architectural element of all floating vessels. It is basically the frame or body of a ship and serves double duty for a vessel's flooring and walls. The hull provides a watertight surface that is designed to prevent water from leaking into a boat. The Vikings were especially adept at designing and building extraordinarily sturdy and beautiful hulls.

The *knarr* was primarily a merchant vessel capable of carrying heavy cargo up to 15 tons. Over 50 feet long with 15-foot beams in their hulls, knarr vessels were the only Norse craft that didn't rely on the use of oars, instead using only sails. *Karve* ships had 17-foot beams, ranged around 70 feet long, and accommodated up to sixteen oars. These ships were so efficient that they could negotiate waters only a few feet deep.

The most recognizable of the Norse vessels, the stylish *longship*, was a distinctively narrow craft designed for speed, pillage, warring, and exploration. Viking shipwrights perfected the longship's sleek, narrow design that enabled these lightweight boats to negotiate shallow waterways, travel efficiently over open seas, and be easily beached during coastal assaults. Some could even be carried by their crew across land.

The smaller longships were typically around 100 feet long, with a 20-foot beam, elegantly carved prows, and a single rudder and shallow keel. Propulsion was accomplished by the use of around fifty fitted oars along the entire length of the boat. With the capacity to transport approximately twenty tons and about 200 sailors, longships were ideal for Norse pirates intent on quick pillage and plunder.

What are Viking dragon ships?

SCUTTLEBUTT

Some of the more impressive Viking vessels were the large longships, called *drakar*, which means "dragon." With more than seventy oars and a length of over 150 feet, these Norse vessels posed a formidable naval threat given that they were able to carry up to 300 Viking pirates.

Savage Style

Vikings were known for their ferocity as pirates but are perhaps equally known for the stunning longships they constructed and sailed during the Dark Ages. Their vessels were works of art. Easily recognizable with their sleek design and elegant curvature at each end, they immediately evoked fear in their victims, while also serving as fast and formidable attack vessels. Over the centuries, several longships have been unearthed intact, providing historians and maritime archeologists a proverbial wealth of information about the legendary pirates from the north.

Fit for a King

One of the most famous of the Viking ships was found on a farm belonging to the Gokstad family in Sandar, Norway, in 1880. Legend has it that a large mound on their property, known as the "King's Mound," was in fact the final resting place of a Viking king. Instead of leaving the tomb in peace, local residents took it upon themselves to start digging into the blue clay, which eventually revealed layers of pristine wood and moss. Rumors of the excavation quickly spread, and Norwegian antiquarian Nicolay Nicolyasen was put in charge of the dig. Within two days, the stern of a Viking karve ship was uncovered.

A medium-size warship, it was brilliantly constructed from a single tree to a finished length of 76 feet. It was also fitted to accommodate over thirty oars and hold over seventy men. Further studies showed that the grave was dug around 900 A.D. and that the ship was built approximately a decade earlier. What made the Gokstad ship unique is that it housed a burial chamber and the skeleton of a man presumed to be a king or Viking chieftain. Viking burial rituals of the day varied, but it was common for the Norse to be interred with their worldly possessions. The mound also contained three smaller boats, one 21 feet in length and a second vessel over 31 feet long.

Pomp and Circumstance

Twenty-four years after the Gokstad ship was unearthed another Viking vessel was discovered, this one even more spectacular in design. Excavated in 1904, what's come to be known as the Oseberg ship was retrieved from a burial mound in Norway's Vestfold county near the town of Tonsberg. Located on the Oseberg farm, it was carefully removed from the turf and blue clay by archeologists Haakon Shetelig and Gabriel Gustafson.

Both the Gokstad and Oseberg ships were meticulously preserved and are on display in the Viking Ship Museum in Oslo, Norway. The sheer elegance and craftsmanship of the ships, coupled with the items found in the mounds, have given historians a plethora of valuable Viking information that was previously unknown. At the same time, the discovery of the ships gives cause to wonder how Viking pirates could have maintained such ruthlessness yet built something of such exquisite maritime beauty.

The Oseberg vessel was another clinker-style karve ship which was estimated to have been built between 815 and 820 A.D. Amazingly well-preserved, the Oseberg ship is a masterpiece of Viking construction and artistry, an intricately carved ceremonial vessel 71 feet long with a 17-foot beam. Found inside the ship was a burial chamber that contained the remains of two women, likely a Viking woman of high status and her servant.

Medieval Piracy

During the Middle Ages, piracy flourished throughout the Baltic and Mediterranean. After several centuries of Scandinavian maritime dominance, a new age of piracy was born. In the Baltic Sea, a new power emerged in the form of the Hanseatic League, a Germanic guild of naval and merchant ships that worked together to gain riches through extensive commerce and trade while also fighting off the inevitable contingents of pirates. At the same time, pirates were running rampant during the fading years of the Byzantine Empire, which in its prime ruled the Mediterranean for hundreds of years while fighting off the imminent threat of the Islamic religion. With the fall of the empire's primary city, Constantinople, in 1204, the Byzantines suffered at the hands of Italian pirates, who at one time served on Byzantine naval forces but turned to piracy against the empire after a dispute with Venice. By the mid-thirteenth century, with Constantinople again under Byzantine control, many of these Italian pirates were recruited and ultimately turned allegiance, wreaking havoc on their fellow Italian countrymen.

The Black Monk

When staving off the attack of a Medieval pirate, one would hardly expect that seafaring rogue to have been a member of the clergy. Such was the case with Eustace the Monk, a Flemish cleric who spent a part of his youth in a Benedictine monastery before becoming a privateer, pirate, and ultimately a mercenary who sold his services to the highest bidder. Eustace's initial service was to the Count of Boulogne in France, but after a dispute he fled to England and became a privateer under England's King John.

In 1212, the monk-turned-pirate temporarily became an English outlaw when he invaded several villages on England's coastline. Realizing his need for Eustace's services, the King eventually issued him a pardon. Not long after, however, Eustace abandoned the English and once again began service to the French as a mercenary. Three years later, during the Barons' Uprising against King John, the monk protected and transported Prince Louis's French troops during their English invasions to support the rebellious barons.

Sea Rover

Eustace, also called "The Black Monk," prowled the Straits of Dover and the English Channel, where he preyed upon French shipping from 1205 to 1212 while England was at war with France. After successfully capturing the Channel Islands from the French, the islands became his safe haven.

By 1217, still in service to Prince Louis, Eustace engaged in a battle at Dover against an English fleet. This battle would prove fatal, as the English bombarded the French vessels with powdered lime, blinding Eustace and his French compatriots. The Black Monk's ships were boarded and his terrifying reign came to a swift and permanent end when he was immediately beheaded.

A League of Their Own

The mid-1200s saw a surge of maritime activity and piracy in the North and Baltic Seas. One of the seafaring strongholds at the time was the Hanseatic League, which comprised German seaports including Hamburg, Lübeck, Danzig, and Bremen. Realizing their combined maritime potential and the safety of traveling in numbers, this league of merchant ships and naval vessels became a powerhouse whose ideological trade monopoly made them a natural anti-piracy group. Prior to the League's formation, Baltic trade routes were largely controlled by the Scandinavians, but as the decades passed, the League became more powerful, the guild incorporating many port cities whose naval and economic cooperation helped protect their ships from Baltic pirates.

SHIVER ME TIMBERS

The Hanseatic League used to great advantage a single-masted, round-bottomed ship called a *cog*. Typically built out of oak, with a single rudder in the stern, high sides, and a square-rigged single sail, these ships would become the blueprint for all future sailing and warring vessels.

The Victual Brothers

From the late twelfth century until the mid-fourteenth century, the Hanseatic League was plagued by a group of privateers and pirates called the *Victual Brothers*. This maritime guild was first formed in 1392 during a battle for Scandinavian dominance between the Danish Queen Margaret and Sweden's King Albrecht of Mecklenburg. As Stockholm was under siege from the Danish navy, the Victual Brothers were organized from a group of privateers to provide food and provisions to the beleaguered city. Quickly developing into a strong naval force, the guild ultimately proved to be a thorn in the side of the Hanseatic League, sacking and pillaging coastal towns along the Baltic Sea. By the late 1300s, the Victuals attacked the northern Hanseatic city of Bergen and several other cities in the next few years. As a result, their piratical dominance and relentless raiding effectively brought a halt to maritime trade in the Baltic and threatened the very existence of the Hanseatic League.

By 1394, the Victual Brothers took over the Swedish island of Gotland and its main city, Visby. With Denmark, Norway, and Sweden now united under the guidance of Queen Margaret, steps were taken to rid the Baltic of the piratical guild of pirates once and for all. An army sent to Gotland in 1398 proved fatal to the Victual pirates, as Visby was destroyed and the guild removed from the island. Many of the disbanded Victual pirates continued to prowl the Baltic under the name *Likedeelers*, and would plunder coastal towns for the next forty years. One of these more notorious pirates was Klaus Störtebeker, who after a three-day battle with a Hamburg warship in 1401 was finally captured and executed along with his crew. Meanwhile, in the Mediterranean, a new breed of pirate was born—the much feared and ruthless Barbary corsairs.

Chapter 4

Barbarians at the Gate

For several centuries, the Barbary pirates were the very definition of terror on the high seas as they pillaged northern Africa's Mediterranean Sea and even north along Europe's Atlantic coastline. Ruthlessly adept at plundering passing merchant ships, the Barbary pirates often acted as a united political and military force, with enough influence to demand ransoms and tributes from the most powerful nations. At various times from the fifteenth to the seventeenth centuries, Spain, France, Portugal, the Netherlands, and even the fledgling United States paid exorbitant fees to appease the demands of Barbary pirates.

The Barbary Coast

The Barbary Coast of northern Africa ran along the Atlantic and Mediterranean coastlines of what is now Algeria, Morocco, Tunisia, and Libya. Named after the Berber people who inhabited the region, the Barbary Coast and Barbary pirates are often incorrectly credited as being the namesakes of the English word *barbarian*. Although the similarities are noticeable, *barbarian* has its roots in ancient Latin and the terms are unrelated—although it's certain that victims of the Barbary pirates would have argued otherwise.

Much of the north African region is arid and devoid of profitable natural resources. Commerce and wealth were invariably brought into the country through the many seaports that dotted the coastline. Piracy was the most straightforward avenue for acquiring trade goods, meeting the needs of the city populations, and feeding government coffers. In fact, piracy was actually strongly encouraged and handsomely rewarded, and local governors and Muslim leaders called *potentates* created dynasties that spanned generations by offering protection to pirates for a percentage of the trade value of stolen goods and ships. The cities of Tangiers in Morocco, Algiers in Algeria, and Tripoli in today's Libya were the centers of power throughout most of the Barbary Coast history, giving refuge to great numbers of pirate fleets and amassing enormous wealth in the process. During the sixteenth and seventeenth centuries, the Ottoman Turkish Empire gave political support to most of the major Barbary Coast regions, taking a percentage of profits in exchange for the protection of its military might and influence.

The Corsairs

The Barbary pirates were generally referred to as *corsairs*, who were roughly the equivalent of the privateers of Europe and the Americas. Islamic corsairs were given license to raid the ports and merchant ships of all the countries of Christian Europe. As with privateering crews, the corsairs usually signed onboard pirate ships for a percentage of the profits, and most of the Barbary pirates took up the profession out of their own free will. The primary difference between privateers and corsairs was that although they both regularly took the crews and passengers of their victim ships captive and held them for ransom, the corsairs would invariably sell unransomed captives into slavery.

Renegade Pirates

Contrary to popular belief, many of the most notorious and successful Barbary pirates began their lives as European sailors who found their fortunes among the pirates of the Barbary Coast. Nearly all of these expatriated pirates converted to Islam, preferring to prey on the ships of their former countries under the auspices of Muslim sultans and potentates. These converted Christians were often the most despised, the most feared, and the most ruthless of the Barbary pirates, and were known as the *renegados*.

SCUTTLEBUTT

Who were the renegados?
The *renegados* were European seamen who converted to Islam and preyed on European merchant ships in the company of the Barbary pirates. The term renegado resulted in the English words *renegade*, meaning traitor or turncoat, and *renege*, meaning to go back on one's word. The renegados were invariably feared and reviled by their former countrymen.

Dutch Descent

It's probable that the majority of renegados sailing with the Barbary pirates were men of Dutch descent who began their seagoing careers as privateers. A Dutchman who went by the Anglo-Islamic name Suleyman Reis De Veenboer is well noted in history as having been made an admiral of the Turkish navy in 1617. Although he was an expatriated Dutch citizen, De Veenboer was careful to avoid attacking Dutch merchant ships. Most of his crewmembers were also Dutch, and it's estimated that several thousand of the Barbary corsairs were from Holland and other European countries. In 1620, De Veenboer engaged in a sea battle with eight of his pirate ships against ships from Holland, France, and England. De Veenboer was struck by a cannonball that shattered both of his legs, a fatal wound that ended the life of one of the most infamous renegados.

The Barbary Galley

The Barbary pirates learned much about open water seamanship from renegados such as De Veenboer and the experienced Europeans who sailed with them. The design of the traditional Barbary Coast war galley used in the Mediterranean had its roots in the monoreme vessels of the ancient Greeks, with a long sleek hull design and rows of oarsmen on both sides of the hull. Artillery was usually built into the bow of the vessel and aimed forward so that cannon firing was possible only when the entire craft was pointed directly at the opposition. The practical benefits to this design were that the ships were normally in firing position while presenting the smallest possible target to the enemy, and the oarsmen were unimpeded by armament along the sides of the ships.

In the relatively calm waters of the Mediterranean, foreign merchant vessels that were powered primarily by wind and sail were at a distinct disadvantage to the oar-powered Barbary sea galley—especially during a flat-out sprint. With oarsmen for propulsion, the galley could go from a standstill in the water to top speed in a matter of moments, and easily over- take most sailing vessels. The galleys favored by the Barbary pirates would carry over fifty pirates, with about half that number manning the oars. Although Turkish naval ships invariably used slave labor to man the oars of warships, the corsairs' ships were usually democratically operated and, as a matter of practicality, were simply too small to carry a single sailor who was not fully prepared to engage in combat. The pirates generally manned the oars in shifts.

SHIVER ME TIMBERS

The term *corsair* can refer to two different things. Pirates along the Bar- bary Coast are often referred to as corsairs. The small, fast vessels that these pirates usually employed to chase down and plunder their prey were also known as corsairs.

The favored battle tactic of the Barbary pirates was to swiftly sweep up behind fleeing ships, heave grappling hooks and ropes aboard to hold the ships together, and then clamber aboard the vessels from the back end. Few merchant ships had crews who were trained in hand-to-hand combat, and virtually none could afford the luxury of a contingent of trained fighters whose job was solely to provide protection. The outcome of most encounters between merchant ships and Barbary pirate galleys was invariably a swift victory for the pirates.

Europe under Siege

The European renegados were influential in expanding the operating boundaries of the Barbary pirates and brought a great deal of open-ocean sailing experience to the corsair fleets. While the Barbary sea galley was the perfect vessel for close shoreline attacks and short forays into the Mediterranean, it was no match for the high winds and rough waters of the Atlantic. The Europeans taught Muslim crews how to handle heavy, square-rigged merchant ships, and how to outfit them for many months at sea.

SEA ROVER

Miguel de Cervantes Saavedra, author of the novel *Don Quixote*, was captured at sea by Barbary pirates in 1575. Because he was thought to be a man of some importance, an exorbitantly high ransom was demanded for his freedom. After he spent five years in captivity, the Catholic Order of Trinitarians paid for his release and he was returned to his family in Madrid in 1580.

Although slavery along the north African coast is generally considered to be an ugly but undeniable historical fact, the enormous traffic in white slaves taken from the European continent is often overlooked. There are no clear records of the number of slaves who were captured or held by the corsairs, but educated estimates made between the years 1600 and 1800 put the number at over 100,000—some as high as over a million.

Villages and port towns along the coasts of Portugal, Spain, France, and England were regularly raided by Barbary pirates for the express purpose of taking captives to be sold into slavery. Although many ships' passengers were held for ransom and released when the ransoms were paid, many thousands of Europeans were captured and sold into slavery, never to be heard from again. In many seafaring communities along the European coast, normal fishing activities were often brought to a complete halt by virtual blockades of Barbary pirate vessels lurking within sight of land, waiting to pounce on any vessel careless enough to sail within reach.

Murad Reis

One of the most notorious renegados to sail with the Barbary pirates was Jan Janszoon Van Haarlem (usually called Janszoon), who was born about 1575 in the town of Haarlem, near Amsterdam in Holland. Little is known of his early life, other than that he married a Dutch woman and had a child with her in 1596. About four years later, Janszoon became a seaman; and during his travels, he made his way to Cartagena, Spain, where it appears he converted to Islam and married a second wife with whom he had several children.

PIECES of EIGHT

With De Veenboer's approval, Janszoon soon took command of an Algerian pirate ship, and became one of the most successful captains in the fleet. He assumed the Muslim name Murad Reis, and established his own small fleet of eighteen Barbary pirate ships. He then made the port of Salee in Morocco his base, from which he terrorized shipping in the Mediterranean Sea and along the Atlantic coast.

Janszoon sailed for many years as a privateer with letters of marque allowing him to attack and plunder Spanish merchant ships. Historians note, however, that Janszoon overstepped the boundaries of his letters of marque and sailed to the Barbary Coast, opportunistically attacking ships of all nations. When he attacked the Spanish, he flew the Dutch flag, and when he attacked merchant ships of other nations, he flew the Turkish flag. In

1618, his own ship was captured by Algerian Barbary pirates, and Janszoon was taken to Algeria. To his good fortune, he was recognized by the admiral of the Fleet of Algiers, who just happened to be fellow Dutchman and infamous renegado Suleyman Reis De Veenboer.

A Brave Bluff

Unlike De Veenboer, Janszoon continued to attack ships of all nations during the 1620s. One of the more ignoble tales regarding Jan Janszoon van Haarlem relates that his pirate crew began stalking a Dutch merchant vessel sailing off the coast of southern Spain with the intention of plundering her. When the Dutch ship suddenly ran up a red flag to signify that no quarter would be given and turned to sail directly toward the pursuing pirates, Janszoon feared that he'd been tricked by a heavily armed privateer and quickly fled for safety. The Dutch consulate in Algeria later revealed that the Dutch shipmaster was really a peaceful trader who'd simply pulled off a courageous bluff.

Janszoon's Villainous Voyages

Janszoon apparently made several journeys along the European coastline. On one occasion in about 1623, he sailed into the Dutch port of Veere to resupply his ships. The Dutch government at the time was under treaty with Morocco, and Janszoon flew the Moroccan flag to establish diplomatic immunity. While he was in port, the Dutch authorities brought Janszoon's Dutch wife to the docks in an effort to lure him into leaving his Barbary Coast ways and bring him back into the service of Holland, but their well-intentioned plans completely backfired. Janszoon remained unswayed, and several adventurous Dutchmen actually signed onboard his crew and sailed away with the pirate ship.

In 1631, Janszoon again sailed into Atlantic waters to the southern coast of Ireland. In a raid that still resounds in Irish history, over 100 men, women, and children of the small town of Baltimore were kidnapped and sold into slavery. None of the victims would ever return to Ireland, and the attack virtually destroyed the community. There is other evidence that Janszoon's pirates made raids as far as Iceland, seizing the cargoes of fishing vessels along with the fishermen. In one instance, Janszoon's fleet captured over 400 inhabitants from Iceland, all of whom were sold into slavery on the Barbary Coast.

Records of Jan Janszoon van Haarlem become scarce after the year 1641. One of his sons, Anthony, who grew up in Morocco, is well recorded to have married and traveled to New Amsterdam (now New York City) in America where he purchased large tracts of land in what is now Manhattan, Brooklyn, and Long Island. It's thought that his infamous father provided Anthony with a sizable fortune, although the final fate of Janszoon and any wealth he retained is unknown.

The Barbarossa Brothers

Arguably the most famous of the Barbary corsairs were two brothers who served the Ottoman Turkish Empire, and whose adventures left an indelible mark on pirate history. The Barbarossa brothers were born on the island of Lesbos in Greece in the 1470s to a native woman who had married a retired Turkish soldier. The oldest brother, named Aruj, became a corsair as a young man and was captured by members of the Catholic Knights of Rhodes, whose historic objective was to provide protection to Christians in the Mediterranean region.

$\mathfrak{S}$EA $\mathfrak{R}$OVER

Aruj was enslaved as a galley hand until he was ransomed by an Egyptian prince in 1505 and transported to Alexandria. Reunited with his brother, Hizir, and backed by the Egyptian prince, the brothers began raiding trading vessels.

Along with gaining fame and fortune along the Barbary Coast as a corsair against Christian merchants, and particularly the Spanish, Aruj became well loved and respected for his kindnesses toward Muslims in need. To his fellow Muslims, he became known as "Baba Aruj," or "Father Aruj," which translates to *Barbarossa* in French and Spanish. After Aruj lost an arm during a battle with the Spanish, he and his brother made the ships of Spain their primary targets. In 1516, Aruj took exception to the apparent lack of enthusiasm with which the Sultan of Algiers supported their hatred of the Spanish, so he led a corsair fleet into the port of Algiers, murdered the sultan, and had himself proclaimed sultan.

Aruj continued to lead the Barbary corsairs against the Spaniards until he was finally killed in battle in 1518. His brother Hizir took his place, his name, and his title, and officially joined forces with the Ottoman Turk Empire against the Spaniards. With the help of the Ottomans, the corsairs of the Barbarossas helped foil the imperialistic aspirations of the Spanish in the Mediterranean for nearly fifty years, and in doing so became heroes who are revered to this day.

Barbary Wars

For the next 300 years, the Barbary pirates remained a formidable power in the Mediterranean, but their dominion finally came to an end. During the early 1800s, the United States launched two major naval and land campaigns against Algiers, Tunis, and Tripoli that effectively ended the harassment of shipping and piracy by the Barbary pirates. Aided by the English and the Dutch, the city-states of the Barbary Coast were bombarded into submission, and the practice of capturing and enslaving Christians was brought to an end. Algiers would become a French colony in 1831, and Tunis followed in 1881. Tripoli became an Italian colony in 1911, and Europeans would hold power in North Africa until the middle of the 1900s.

PIECES of EIGHT

The Barbary Coast was effectively divided and absorbed into the governments of Morocco, Libya, Algeria, and Tunisia, and the once relatively unified Barbary pirates were reduced to mostly insignificant, independently operating groups of criminals.

Divide and Conquer

While the Spaniards had limited success in their attempts to subjugate the Mediterranean, their faith in an Italian explorer in the late 1400s would expand Spain's holdings into the Western Hemisphere and help to make Spain the predominant power in Europe for the next 200 years. That explorer was Christopher Columbus, and his discoveries would bring unimaginable wealth to Spain, change the face of the world forever, and add some of the most colorful and incredible chapters to the history of plunder and piracy.

Chapter 5

The Spanish Main

In the late 1400s, the Spanish began exploring and then settling the lands of Central and South America, as well as the islands of the Caribbean basin, all of which eventually became known as the Spanish Main. This resulted in riches that sent pirates flocking to the area hoping to share in the plunder that the New World provided. Whether attacking Spanish treasure galleons or ports of the Spanish Main, the lure of the gold, silver, and gems that Spain was reaping was more than enough to capture the attention of not just pirates but entire nations.

The Reign of Spain

The reason so many pirates spent the majority of their careers pursuing the Spanish is intrinsically linked to Spain's discovering and conquering the New World. This began in 1492 when Christopher Columbus landed on an island in the Caribbean. As a result of finding great riches on his first foray, Columbus made return voyages to the Americas three more times, traveling to present-day Cuba, Haiti, Dominica, Puerto Rico, and Jamaica, and along the coast of South America (see Chapter 7). With great haste, Spain established colonies and began exploring the new lands. In time, the Spanish would control most of South America and the Caribbean basin. As the wealth of natural resources of the area was discovered, Spain found itself increasingly challenged over its right to control its new territories.

Treaty of Tordesilla

For many years, Portugal had controlled the Indian Ocean and all trade with the East. As Spain began sending out explorers and discovering new lands, Portugal became concerned that its monopoly would be threatened. Both Spain and Portugal were Catholic countries, and in June of 1494, Spanish-born Pope Alexander signed the Treaty of *Tordesilla*. Written by the Pope with help from Spanish and Portuguese officials, the treaty drew a line through the middle of the Atlantic Ocean, granting Portugal the right to everything east of the line and Spain control of all areas west of the line. This treaty may have pleased Spain and Portugal, but it naturally upset all the other European seagoing nations, and it was only a matter of time before they did something about it.

African Enslavement

As Spain began colonizing the new lands, there was much difficult work to be done. At first, many prisoners and indentured servants were sent to the west to build settlements and work the plantations, but this didn't turn out as well as the Spaniards had hoped. The intense heat and unfamiliar tropical diseases took their toll on the European workers and it quickly became obvious that a different solution was needed. In 1510, as a means of solving their problems, the Spanish began slave trading. Ships were sent to Africa and returned laden with black slaves. These slaves were accustomed to sweltering heat and had immunities against many tropical diseases. Unlike prisoners and indentured servants, who could eventually earn their freedom and leave the Spanish plantations, slaves were the property of plantation owners and were expected to work for them for life. As more and more areas were settled, additional slaves were desperately needed. As a result, Spanish slave ships were able to make a hefty profit from their African slaving excursions.

SHIVER ME TIMBERS

Slave ships, or *slavers*, were often referred to as *blackbirders*, and it was usually difficult for captains of the blackbirders to assemble their crews, given the high mortality rate caused by the intense heat of the African climate and tropical diseases taking their toll among sailors serving on slave ships. Despite the dangers, many merchants became very rich from *blackbirding*, the pirate term for slave trading.

Native Riches

The earliest Spanish explorers had primarily sailed to and from various islands around the Caribbean. In 1519, Hernán Cortés led a party of approximately 600 soldiers on an expedition that landed on the shores of modern-day Mexico. Cortés and his men headed inland through the jungles and into the mountains of Central Mexico. As they traveled, they obtained food and other necessities from the natives they met, and in doing so received what would be highly valuable information about the country and its rulers—the *Aztecs*.

When Cortés spoke with the Mexican natives, he also learned about the gold, silver, and jewels that the Aztecs mined and used to make jewelry and statues. Eventually, rumors also reached the Spanish about another wealthy land located in the continent south of Mexico. These lands were inhabited by an indigenous people called the *Incas*. Spain quickly decided that they wanted to extend their New World holdings to include those prosperous empires. Wasting no time, Cortés set about conquering the Aztecs, with Francisco Pizarro overcoming the Incas a few years later.

The Fall of Montezuma

The Aztecs were an agricultural people who designed impressive buildings and crafted intricate jewelry. They were also a warring civilization who could be very cruel, often performing human sacrifices in the temples they erected. Ruled by the mighty Montezuma, they forced the natives of the country to pay them tribute. In addition, the Aztecs had schools, government, and laws that they enforced with corporal punishment. Within two years of Cortés' arrival in Mexico, he and his men successfully captured Tenochtitlán, the capital city of the Aztecs. At about the same time Montezuma had been stoned to death by a contingent of Aztecs who turned against him. These events gave the Spanish complete access to untold amounts of gold, silver, emeralds, and other jewels that would prove utterly irresistible to pirates. With such great prizes now within their grasp, the Spanish set their sights on the Incas.

Peruvian Plunder

The Incan Empire was located in Peru, and much like the Aztecs, the Incas were master crafters and builders who had set up a governmental system that collected tribute from its peoples. Like the Mexican lands the Aztecs had ruled, Peru was a wealth of gold, silver, and valuable minerals. As word of the wealth of this land made its way to the Spanish settlers living in Central America, plans were made to overcome the Incas and add Peru to the list of Spanish holdings. In 1532, Francisco Pizarro left Panama and headed for Peru with a group of around 200 soldiers. He soon captured Incan leader Atahualpa, and murdered the majority of his men. Pizarro then moved farther into the country, and in 1533 overtook the capital city of Cuzco, murdered Atahualpa, and "liberated" all the wealth stored in the city.

Just as the Aztecs had fallen, so did the Incas succumb to Spanish invaders. Spain now controlled the majority of South and Central America, all of the territory's gems, minerals, and precious metals, and the land in which these riches were mined. So much gold and silver was being mined in South America during this time that the Spanish established mints and began converting the metals into coins. Once news of Spain's assets and untapped treasures spread, the stage was set for a piratical clash that would last for centuries.

PIECES of EIGHT

Unlike Montezuma, Atahualpa did not believe Pizarro and the Spaniards were gods or divine beings. When Pizarro entered Peru and told Atahualpa that he and his people would need to surrender and convert to Christianity, Atahualpa sent back word refusing the Spanish presence in his land saying he would "be no man's tributary" and asking "how do you know your god created the world?"

New World Territories

With the acquisition of the Central and South American lands, Spain effectively controlled the entire area that was to become known as the Spanish Main. Originally, the term Spanish Main was used to indicate the portion of the Caribbean basin that ran along the northern coast of South America, and the islands close to the shore. At that time, the Spanish had divided the area into three different regions, one of which was known as *Tierra Firma*, meaning "mainland." This area covered Venezuela, Columbia, Panama, and the offshore islands.

The second region was called New Spain, and this encompassed present-day Mexico and its surrounding areas. The final region was known as the Viceroy of Peru, and it covered the Pacific coast of South America and Ecuador. Later, the French and the English began referring to all of the Spanish holdings in the Caribbean, the Gulf of Mexico, and Central and South America as the Spanish Main.

The Spanish Galleons

The riches that the Spanish were garnering in the New World needed to be transported back to Spain. This required ships that were capable of making long voyages across the ocean, carrying huge cargoes while also possessing the means to protect themselves from pirates. The *galleon* (from the Old Spanish word *galeon*) was built to meet these needs, basically those of a cargo-bearing warship, and combined the best design elements from two other Spanish ships. The first was a *caravel*, a large but narrow double or triple-masted vessel with a flat stern and lanteen sails.

SHIVER ME TIMBERS

A *lanteen* sail is a triangular sail, which is suspended on a long arm, also known as a *yard* or a *yardarm*, that is set at a forty-five-degree angle to the ship's mast. The lanteen sail allows a vessel to *tack*, or maneuver toward the direction the wind is blowing.

The second vessel Spanish shipwrights used for inspiration was a *carrack*, a light but fast ship with a sturdy hull, a high-rounded stern, and either three or four masts. Shipwrights made use of features such as the caravel's fixed rudder and the carrack's solid hull design and created a galleon that weighed about 400 tons and could carry between twenty and forty cannons (see Chapter 10).

Rough Sailing

The lure of treasure contained within a Spanish galleon was so great that few pirates or privateers could forgo the chance to capture one. The cargo of these galleons varied, but typically they transported silver, gold, coins, gems, and silks. The capture of a large galleon, which to pirates were the Concordes of the sea, could provide a pirate with wealth for the rest of his life. As such, galleons were in constant danger when returning from the New World, both from pirates and from the vicious storms and high seas of hurricane season. Ironically, the modern-day benefit of those hurricanes is that many galleons sank in bad weather, taking their treasure to the sea floor with them and providing treasure hunters a virtual candy store of priceless artifacts.

The Treasure Fleet

The Spanish couldn't do much about the rough weather, but they soon decided that they needed to do something about the raiders who were pillaging their treasures. As a result, they began building larger galleons capable of carrying not just treasure but more guns and munitions, and plenty of soldiers to fire them. At one point, they even began carrying passengers. Regardless of their cargo, the larger ships continued to be threatened by pirates, so the Spanish finally began sailing their galleons in convoys.

PIECES of EIGHT

From the mid-sixteenth to the early eighteenth century, large fleets, or *flotillas*, of ships would band together in a show of mutual protection, leaving Spain and traveling en masse to the Spanish Main. Once they arrived at their destination, they would split into groups, each group traveling to a specific section of the Main to collect stored treasures that were waiting for them in warehouses.

After the ships were loaded with their intended cargo, they would meet in Cuba to once again band together and complete their journey home. While this helped the Spanish successfully transport more of their treasure back to Spain, pirates soon became adept at attacking the ships when they were sailing in smaller groups, or even attacking the mule packs on land that were hauling riches to the warehouses. The treasure fleets continued to operate for almost 200 years, dying off only when silver had devalued and inflation became rampant in the mid-1700s. After that, treasure was once again shipped back to Spain on individual warships.

The Huguenots

With France being a Catholic country during the sixteenth century, the notion of them defying the Pope's edict and being the first country to actively challenge the Spanish right to the New World and its riches may have seemed unlikely, but that's precisely what happened. During this time, while Spain was busy plundering the New World, they were continually at war with France. In France religious unrest was becoming the norm, setting the stage for later religious civil wars. The Protestant French, known historically as Calvinists but frequently called *Huguenots*, had no ties to the Pope and no reason to follow the Treaty of *Tordesilla*. With Spain and France warring, the French would consider such raids acts of warfare—not piracy—and therefore would not intervene.

SCUTTLEBUTT

Who was Jean Fleury?

Italian privateer and pirate Jean Fleury was a Huguenot who sailed for the French. Fleury's capture of two Spanish ships in 1523 triggered the Huguenot plunder of treasure ships, a practice that would continue for the next forty years. Despite Fleury being captured and executed by the Spanish in 1527, the Huguenots proved to be a huge source of opposition to the Spaniards.

Sitting Targets

The Huguenots were naturally interested in capturing Spanish galleons. After the Spanish instituted their treasure fleet, the French continued their attacks on vessels, but it became much more difficult to accomplish their felonious tasks. After Jean Fleury was captured during an attack in 1527 and hanged as a pirate, the French privateers realized that while ships were becoming more and more difficult to capture, Spanish port cities were much easier targets. This changed the Huguenots' strategies significantly. As long as they timed their raids correctly, the Huguenots would be able to capture much of the Spanish treasure before it ever reached the treasure fleet. This plan of action paid off handsomely as they proceeded to attack ports in Puerto Rico, Havana, and Cartagena (modern-day Colombia), collecting an impressive amount of pirate booty.

Fort Caroline

As the religious civil war in France continued, many French Protestants found themselves exiled. In 1564, a group of them settled on Florida's coast, calling their new home Fort Caroline. Unlike most settlers whose ambition was to work the land, this group was comprised of soldiers and tradesmen who planned to use the area as a base from which pirate raids on both Spanish ships and Spanish ports could easily be conducted. Unfortunately for the French, the Spanish were growing tired of the Huguenot pirates, and they decided it was time to settle the score.

Master and Commander

In April of 1562, King Philip II sent Spanish nobleman Pedro Menendez de Avilles to the territories of the Spanish Main. Menendez was named the Captain General of the Spanish fleet, and his mission was to catch any pirates he could and deal with them ruthlessly. Menendez and his brother owned several merchant ships and he was very familiar with both trading and security. He made immediate recommendations that the port cities should be fortified, and that armed ships be on patrol in the Caribbean to protect the ports and ships while they were there.

Sea Rover

Menendez soon learned that the French who had initially been pursuing his ships were shipwrecked farther down the coast. He then set sail after the shipwrecked crew, and when he found them, he killed them all. With the destruction of Fort Caroline accomplished, the French Huguenots were basically stopped from further terrorizing the Spanish, and Philip rewarded Menendez by making him Governor of Havana.

Another of his recommendations was that Spain set up a permanent settlement in Florida, and use it as a base in order to fortify itself against French incursion. In 1565, Menendez returned to the Americas, bringing troops, money, and ships in order to establish a stronghold in Florida. Upon his arrival, he sailed past Fort Caroline and noticed that it appeared heavily fortified, so he sailed farther south and started a settlement at St. Augustine. He remained at the new colony with about 500 of his men, and had his ships continue sailing south. Shortly after, he observed French ships from Fort Caroline following his ships as they traveled south. Menendez immediately took his men and marched on Fort Caroline, attacking the remaining French and quickly murdering them.

Hell Hath No Fury

It may have seemed that Spain had finally risen above being terrorized by pirates and threatened by nations attempting to dip into their New World treasure trove, but that wasn't the case. Little did Spain know that the English were preparing to step in and become the next group to challenge their dominance—and unlike the French, the Brits didn't have a problem taking prisoners. As a nation, their privateers, pirates, and most especially their queen would prove to be indomitable foes who would stop at nothing to save their flailing economy.

Chapter 6

For Queen and Country

France was not alone in her desire to possess the riches of the Spanish Main. England and the Netherlands also wanted a piece of the New World, and their motivation to do so was fueled by their hatred of Spain. After the death of Mary I, the Protestant Queen Elizabeth I came to power, and her conflicts with the Catholic King Philip of Spain eventually ended in warfare. But even in times of peace between the two countries, Elizabeth was quietly backing piracy—under the guise of privateering.

Uniting Two Kingdoms

Mary I, who came to be known as "Bloody Mary," reigned over England from July 1553 until her death in November 1558. Mary was the daughter of the infamous King Henry VIII and his first wife, Catherine of Aragon. Despite being deemed illegitimate after her father divorced her mother, and therefore losing her status as heir to the throne, she eventually regained her father's favor. In doing so, Henry had Mary and her half-sister Elizabeth added to the line of succession behind their half-brother, Prince Edward. However, the Act of Parliament that added the two women to the line of succession didn't legally alter either woman's status as illegitimate.

The Terror of Bloody Mary

Henry VIII died in 1547, and his only son, Edward VI, became king at the age of nine. Knowing that he was of ill health and was unlikely to live long, Edward's advisors had him remove both of his half-sisters from the line of succession in his will. But because this wish directly contradicted an Act of Parliament, and because he was a minor, the exclusion was not upheld. Edward ultimately died at age sixteen, and Mary became Queen of England and Ireland.

PIECES of EIGHT

Edward was the first British monarch who was a Protestant. Mary returned the country to Catholicism, using whatever means she felt necessary. She removed all of Edward's religious proclamations and replaced them with laws regarding heresy against the Church. Under her heresy laws, Mary had hundreds of people burned at the stake, and it was these executions that earned her the nickname Bloody Mary.

A Marriage of Convenience

In 1554, Mary wed Philip II, King of Spain and son of the Holy Roman Emperor Charles V. Philip didn't love Mary, but wed her for the political reason of adding England and Ireland to the growing list of countries that he ruled. Mary, on the other hand, apparently fell in love with Philip. When she announced that she was pregnant, Philip, who felt he'd done his part to ensure the ties between the two countries, returned to Spain to deal with matters there. As it turned out, Mary apparently had a false pregnancy, and died childless in 1558. In her will, Mary decreed that Philip was to be her successor to the throne, but the will was ruled to be illegal, clearing the path for Elizabeth I to assume the monarchy in November 1558. Philip tried one more method to regain control of England by attempting to marry Elizabeth, but she declined his proposal. This action pleased her subjects, who had not been happy with Bloody Mary or Philip during their short reign.

Birth of a Queen

Elizabeth, like Mary, was the daughter of Henry VIII, although her mother was Anne Boleyn, who is best known for having been beheaded by her dear husband. Like her half-sister, Elizabeth was eventually declared an illegitimate child and removed from and later readded to the line of succession. A Protestant, she'd been placed under house arrest when Mary took the throne and returned England to Catholicism, but she was released by Philip when he thought Mary was pregnant. As soon as Elizabeth became queen in 1558, she returned England to the Protestant rule begun during Edward's reign. While many of her subjects were pleased with this decision, the clash between Catholics and Protestants would continue throughout Elizabeth's tenure, and would eventually lead England to war against Spain. It also led Elizabeth to authorize piracy against the Spanish, sometimes legally under the guise of privateering and sometimes illegally but "unofficially" approved.

Elizabethan Elite

As England saw Spain growing stronger and stronger financially, the queen felt the need to appropriate some of the wealth of the Spanish Main for herself and her country. During her reign, England and Spain were often at war; even when they weren't, fervent religious issues made their peace an uneasy one. Taking her cue from the successes of the French Huguenots, Elizabeth set out to build a group of loyal *sea rovers* or *sea dogs* who would plunder wealthy Spanish ships and return the majority of the riches to England, an act that would significantly boost England's sagging economy.

Letters of Marque: The Privateers

Elizabeth, like other rulers, could issue letters of marque during times of war. These were commissions, licenses, or other documents that authorized the holder to attack enemy merchant ships in the name of the government that had issued the letter. This enabled governments to use private ships to obtain the goods and wealth of an enemy country. Because these were private ships, the bearers of the letters were called privateers. Letters of marque existed as early as the eleventh century, and continued to be used until they were outlawed at the Convention of Paris in 1856.

SHIVER ME TIMBERS

A *letter of reprisal* was an uncommon type of privateering commission. These letters allowed the holder to seize goods from a ship in order to right a wrong that it was felt could not be corrected in the legal system. In this unusual circumstance, the commission would be valid in times of peace as well as during wartime.

Legal Piracy

Privateering amounted to legal piracy. It gave the bearer of the commission the right to board any ship and seize its contents and sometimes the ship itself. A privateer would return a set amount of the plunder, usually around one-fifth, to the issuing monarch or government, and the rest they could keep for themselves. On paper, they were supposed to attack only enemy vessels that were named on the commission and only attack during times of war. If the privateers were captured, the enemy government was supposed to treat them as prisoners of war, and not as pirates. The reality, however, was very different.

Privateering was a good way to earn riches, given that privateers were often not content with attacking only enemy vessels. Instead, they would often attack any vessel not from their own country. The rulers of the issuing governments were supposed to punish privateers who stepped outside the boundaries of their commissions, but it was hard for a nation to turn down a share of the wealth simply because it came from a country they were not at war with at the time. As a result of these practices, captured privateers were often treated as pirates—not prisoners of war—and were quickly executed. Within the pirate realm, the distinction between privateer and pirate was a fine line, and one that was often crossed.

Rise of a Master Slaver

Elizabeth had several seamen whom she utilized as privateers during times of war, and whom she financially backed so that they could continue their expeditions during times of peace. One of the earliest and most famous of this elite group of sea rovers was Sir John Hawkins, who began his career as a slave trader and eventually became a national hero. As a young man, Hawkins, like his father, was a merchant trader. Unlike his father, he decided that illegal trade with Spain would be more profitable than following legal channels.

In 1562, Hawkins took a ship to Africa and filled it with around 300 black slaves, some of whom he pirated from a Portuguese slave ship. He then transported his human cargo to the New World territory of Hispaniola (see Chapter 7) and sold them for a hefty profit. This angered the Spanish, who wanted a monopoly not only on the riches coming out of the Spanish Main but also on the items being sold to the colonists who'd settled there. Back in England, Queen Elizabeth was pleased, and subsequently provided financial backing for Hawkins to make a second voyage, even authorizing him to use one of her warships as his flagship. That voyage took place in 1564, and after taking 400 slaves from the coast of Africa, Hawkins once again sailed back to the Spanish Main to sell them. This time he encountered problems, given that the Spanish had now forbidden their colonists to trade with him. Hawkins managed to sell or trade all of the slaves, however, and returned to England with yet another tidy profit for the queen and his other investors.

Sir John Hawkins may have been known as a national hero in England where he built hospitals and improved the navy's ships, but in the Caribbean he would be remembered for torturing and murdering men, as well as burning entire cities to the ground.

On his third expedition, which took place in 1567, Hawkins was joined by his cousin Francis Drake. Together they managed to secure African slaves to sell, but upon reaching San Juan de Ulúa (present-day Veracruz, Mexico) they were met with serious hostility. This time the Spanish were ready for them, and they immediately attacked Hawkins and his men. In total, Hawkins lost three of his five ships, including the queen's warship, and all but Drake and about fifteen of his men. Because of the incident, it had become painfully obvious that Spain was unwilling to allow colonial trade with the English. Hawkins then joined the British navy, and later became a national hero when he served as chief administrator of the navy during the defeat of the Spanish Armada. In honor of his bravery and service, Queen Elizabeth knighted him in 1588.

Drake's Gold

Sir John Hawkins retired as a sea dog after his third voyage, but his cousin Francis Drake was more than willing to continue where Hawkins left off. Following his return from Hawkins' failed third voyage, Drake began planning his own expeditions in order to exact revenge upon the Spanish, and even though he would become famous for being the first man to successfully circumnavigate the world, he remained dedicated to his hatred of Spain. In England, he would eventually become a British national hero, but he would forever be known to the Spanish as *El Dragón*, the Dragon.

Nombre de Dios

Located in modern-day Panama, *Nombre de Dios*, which translates to "Name of God," was one of the principal treasure ports of the Spanish Main, where gold and silver that had been brought in by ship and by pack mules from Peru and Bolivia would be collected and stored until ready for shipping. Twice a year, Spanish galleons would arrive, collect the wealth that had been stored in warehouses, and transport it to Spain. In 1571, Drake spent some time in Nombre de Dios, carefully watching and concocting a plan. In 1572, he again returned to the area with a strategy for plundering the port.

SCUTTLEBUTT

Who was James Rouse?

Captain James Rouse was an English privateer who was also operating in the Caribbean during the late sixteenth century. He met up with Sir Francis Drake, and they combined their forces in order to take the port of Nombre de Dios in 1572.

Drake and Rouse's attack on Nombre de Dios started well, but things soon went sour largely as a result of a huge thunderstorm that impeded their attack on land. To make matters worse, Drake was shot in the thigh during the attack and began bleeding profusely. When his sailors finally forced open the doors to the storehouse, they found that the Spanish ships had left just weeks earlier, and the storehouse was empty. The expedition was a complete failure, but Drake was not discouraged. Instead, he spent time exploring the inland areas and making small raids upon the coast.

In March of 1573 Drake met a group of French Huguenots, and together they planned a raid on mule caravans bound for Nombre de Dios. This attack was successful, and made much sweeter by the fact that each of the almost 200 mules was carrying approximately 300 pounds of silver. Drake then returned to England with a huge plunder and knowledge that El Dragón had begun his scourge of the Spanish.

Capture of the Concepcion

While Drake had been waiting for his chance to attack the Spanish mule caravan, he'd climbed up a mountain ridge that had given him his first view of the Pacific Ocean. At that moment, he immediately set his sights on someday sailing across the Pacific. Four years later, he left England on the ship *Golden Hind* with the intent of sailing around South America through the Strait of Magellan. Nine months later he made it through the Strait and proceeded up the coast of Chile, raiding Spanish settlements and ships as he went.

PIECES of EIGHT

In March of 1579, Drake took his greatest prize ever, the *Señora de la Concepcion*, a heavily armed ship filled with gold and silver from Peru. Drake cleverly used a ruse of disguising his ship as a slow-moving merchant vessel. The captain of the Spanish ship was completely fooled and Drake and his men were able to take the ship and its enormous treasure with ease.

After successfully capturing the *Concepcion*, and knowing that the Spanish would be watching out for him, Drake headed straight for England. Almost three years after leaving, he returned to present Queen Elizabeth and his other backers with their share of the riches. The queen was very pleased with "her pirate" and his haul, and knighted Drake on the deck of his ship.

The Fury of El Dragón

In 1585, war broke out between England and Spain, and Sir Francis Drake sailed off to the New World once again, where he raided the ports of Santo Domingo and Cartagena (present-day Dominican Republic and Colombia). He also captured a Spanish fort at San Augustine in Florida. As a result of this raid, King Philip decided to repay Elizabeth, in no small measure, by invading England. Drake heard about the King's plan and boldly sailed into the Spanish port of Cadiz, where he captured six ships and destroyed more than thirty others. This single attack cost the Spanish a year-long delay in starting their invasion.

Spain attempted their invasion of England in 1588. Now a vice-admiral in the British navy, Drake chased the Spanish Armada up the English Channel, capturing a galleon and its crew. He then organized ships to fire on the Spanish, causing them to break formation and head back out to the open sea. The following day, Drake was part of the Battle of Gravelines, a heavily mounted English attack that drove the Spaniards away from English waters, and aided in the eventual defeat of the Spanish Armada.

Sir Francis Drake continued his seagoing career until his death in 1596, following an unsuccessful attack on San Juan, Puerto Rico. His cousin Sir John Hawkins, who'd accompanied him on this particular voyage, had died from natural causes while onboard only two months earlier. In appropriate fashion, both men were buried at sea.

SHIVER ME TIMBERS

The word *fathom* is a nautical term used to describe the measurement of the depth of water. A fathom is 6 feet and was originally conceived as the distance of a sailor's outstretched arms from fingertip to fingertip. A weighted line of rope with knots spaced 6 feet apart would be dropped over the side of a ship in order to gauge depth.

The Tumultous Walter Raleigh

Sir Walter Raleigh was another of Elizabeth's revered sea dogs, one with whom she would have a tumultuous relationship. Besides being a soldier and a sailor, Raleigh was a poet who at one time had studied law. Driving his seafaring and piratical ambition was the desire to discover and colonize new lands. In 1584, he attempted a voyage to North America, and although the voyage failed, he did conduct some pirate activity while he was attempting the trip. In 1585, he organized a trip to take some 300 colonists to Roanoke Island off the coast of Virginia, but Elizabeth would not allow him to go on the voyage, so Sir Richard Grenville led the journey in his place. The first Roanoke colonists returned to England when they ran out of provisions, but Raleigh later set up a second colony that modern-day scholars and historians continue to debate because the colonists all mysteriously vanished without a trace in 1588.

Queen Elizabeth knighted Raleigh for his service in Ireland, but he consistently fell in and out of the queen's favor. At one point, he even married one of Elizabeth's maids without Elizabeth's permission and was sent to prison in the Tower of London for a time. During another expedition he attempted a trip to South America to find the fabled city of El Dorado, but returned empty-handed. In an effort to regain favor with the queen, he eventually returned to privateering.

After Elizabeth's death in 1603, James I outlawed privateering, and took away several of Raleigh's offices. Raleigh was then convicted of treason in a conspiracy plot against the new king, and subsequently spent thirteen years in prison. After he was released, he led a gold-hunting expedition to Guyana, but en route to their destination Raleigh's partner on the trip led an attack on a Spanish settlement. At the time, King James was attempting to negotiate peace with Spain, and when Raleigh returned from the failed trip, he was beheaded for his part in the attack.

Sea Rover

Raleigh's half-brother, Humphrey Gilbert, was another of Elizabeth's privateers. He was interested in settling the New World and looking for the Northwest Passage, a strait he believed ran through Canada, connecting the Atlantic to China. He made a trip to America in 1583, claiming St. John's Island for England, but his boat disappeared during a storm on the return voyage and he was never heard from again.

Elizabeth's Sea Dogs

While Hawkins, Drake, and Raleigh are probably the best known of Elizabeth's troop of legal pirates, they weren't the only ones. Elizabeth had a number of seafarers in her group of trusted and proven sailors, men who were willing to plunder for England either under her letter of marque or with her hidden approval and backing. Besides Humphrey Gilbert, some of the queen's renowned sea dogs included Martin Frobisher, Richard Grenville, and Richard Hawkins, the son of John Hawkins.

A Fool and His Gold

Martin Frobisher was the son of a very prominent English family. In 1553, at the age of eighteen, he went to sea and was captured by a native chief in Guinea, West Africa, and imprisoned by the Portuguese. After being released from his incarceration, Frobisher turned pirate and spent the next fifteen years plundering from the Spanish. During one journey, while sailing past Greenland he discovered what he mistook to be a strait. Believing that he'd found the Northwest Passage, he returned to England, bringing with him a sample of gold-flecked rock. The queen and several others invested in Frobisher's newly started Cathay Company, and he obliged by harvesting and bringing back to England tons of the gold-flecked ore. Unfortunately the ore turned out to be *pyrite*, or "fool's gold," and several of Frobisher's backers suffered terrible losses.

Frobisher was later sent to guard the Irish seas; he also made several piratical voyages. He fought hard during the war against the Spanish Armada, and the queen later knighted him for his accomplished efforts. After the war he made several voyages with John Hawkins, but died in 1594 from wounds he sustained while trying to help the French Huguenots who were under siege in Brittany.

Grenville's Last Stand

Richard Grenville was born in 1541 in Cornwall, England. From an early age he had a terrible temper, which was put to good use when he fought against the Turks in Hungary in 1566 and helped Humphrey Gilbert quash rebellions in Ireland in 1569. Because of Gilbert, Grenville found his love of navigation and the seas, and was soon joining sailing expeditions. In 1584, he delivered the first group of Raleigh's colonists to Roanoke Island, and successfully plundered a great store of treasure from Spanish ships while en route to England. He sailed back to Roanoke the next year, only to discover that Francis Drake had already taken the discouraged colonists back to England. Grenville instead continued on with his trip, sailing to the North Atlantic islands of the Azores and pillaging several Spanish towns whose inhabitants he captured and cruelly treated.

In 1591, Grenville joined Lord Thomas Howard, who was leading a group of the queen's ships back to the Azores to capture more Spanish treasure galleons. But Spain's King Philip learned of their plans and sent a large squadron of Spanish warships to meet them. The English were forced to retreat, but Grenville's ship was the last to exit the harbor and he was surrounded.

For more than twelve hours he fought, before his men surrendered his ship against his wishes. He died a few days later from wounds he received in the battle.

Like Father, Like Son

Richard Hawkins was the son of Sir John Hawkins, and as a dutiful son he carried on his father's privateering career. In 1588, he commanded a ship in the fight against the Spanish Armada, but his greatest ambition was to sail around the world, combining piracy and scientific experimentation along the way. With that goal in mind, Hawkins began a voyage in 1593, passing through the Strait of Magellan. Shortly afterward he raided a Spanish settlement in Chile, and soon came under attack by several Spanish ships. After a fierce battle, he surrendered with the agreement that his men would be returned to England. He then spent three years in a Peruvian prison before being transferred to a Spanish prison. Eventually he was ransomed by his stepmother and returned to England, where he was knighted by James I and served as a vice-admiral in the British navy. Hawkins died in 1622 after a long career.

SHIVER ME TIMBERS

The phrase *hand over fist* is commonly used to describe rapid financial success. In fact, it originated from the actions of a skilled sailor climbing or pulling in lines of ropes. This action required grabbing a rope one hand at a time or one hand after another. Proficient sailors mastered this hand over fist technique.

Saving Grace and Face

Privateering and pirating made a huge difference to the economy of England. When Elizabeth became queen, her revenues were one-tenth of the revenues Philip had in Spain, and his military budget was a hundred times greater. Spain, thanks to its plunder of the Aztec and Inca Empires in the

Americas, was the European superpower of its day, and that just didn't sit well with Queen Elizabeth. Ultimately, her decision to back privateering provided England with a much needed source of revenue.

PIECES of EIGHT

Queen Elizabeth's share of the booty that Sir Francis Drake brought back from his voyage around the world was enough for her to pay off the entire national debt. Drake received £10,000 himself, which made him an extremely wealthy man in the 1500s. Drake's crew, on the other hand, received not a single pound.

Dutch Devils

When James I succeeded Elizabeth as the head of England, political dynamics changed significantly. Unlike his fiery predecessor, James was interested in pursuing peace with Spain. In order to accomplish that goal, he banned privateering in 1614, and the age of "legal piracy" in England came to an abrupt end. But just as the English had followed the French in raiding Spanish treasure ships years before, the Dutch would take over where the English left off. For decades, the Dutch had a good relationship with the Spanish, but as time passed, that relationship disintegrated.

The Dutch would, in fact, become a painful thorn in Spain's side. In 1624, Dutch privateer Pieter Schouten led three ships through the West Indies, ransacking towns on the coast of the Yucatán and capturing a Spanish galleon. Roche Braziliano (also spelled Rock or Rok) was a cruel Dutch pirate who sometimes roasted his prisoners on a spit like pigs. Not to be outdone, in 1628 privateer Pieter (Piet) Heyn led an expedition of thirty-one ships to Matanzas, Cuba, where he captured an entire Spanish treasure convoy. Heyn was fifty-one years old at the time of the raid, which yielded a huge profit for both himself and Holland. The victory also helped keep the desire for Spanish gold and the bounty of piracy in the black hearts of pirates the world over.

Passing the Buck

Throughout the fifteenth and sixteenth centuries, it seemed the Spanish would never be entirely free of war or the contingents of privateers and pirates who were in constant pursuit. With the Dutch now setting their sights on a share of Spain's riches, word spread throughout the pirate community and, as a result, pirates everywhere became more empowered and more determined. By the mid-seventeenth century, piracy would only grow stronger as a group of pirates known as *buccaneers* took center stage in the never-ending war against Spain.

Chapter 7

The Buccaneers

During the sixteenth and seventeenth centuries, Spain continued her military and economic monopoly in Central and South America. Gold, silver, jewels, and abundant trade goods provided incredible wealth that turned Spain into the richest country in Europe and funded heavily armed and nearly impenetrable convoys of treasure fleets. But Spain's economic successes would soon attract a new breed of individualistic opportunists to the Caribbean, so-called buccaneers, who would test Spanish supremacy to the limits.

Setting the Stage: Piracy in the New World

Christopher Columbus' discovery of the New World would trigger an incredible economic boom for Spain that would reshape the power structure of virtually every nation on the European continent. The subsequent plundering of the New World would also completely destroy virtually every civilization that had existed for thousands of years in the Americas. While the conquest and demise of the Incan Empire in South America and the Aztecs in Mexico are well-known, the first New World civilizations to be conquered and destroyed by the Spanish were the native tribes that had originally welcomed Columbus. Columbus had first set foot on islands in the Bahamas and Cuba, but the island now shared by Haiti and the Dominican Republic was where Columbus first placed the Spanish flag.

Columbus claimed the island for Spain in 1492 and named it *Espanola*, or "New Spain." Soon after, the name would be Anglicized to *Hispaniola*. To Columbus, the island paradise offered forested mountains and large river valleys peopled by the peaceful and generous Taino Indians—the perfect targets for easy conquest. Most importantly to Columbus, the natives wore ornaments and jewelry made of gold that they'd gathered from the valley riverbeds.

PIECES of EIGHT

Columbus' historic discoveries in 1492 coincided with the increasing influence of a brand-new discovery in communications—the printing press. By 1497, Columbus' travel notes had been translated and distributed throughout most countries in Europe, and hundreds of privateers and pirates flocked to the Americas after reading his tales.

After a few months on the island, Columbus set sail for Spain to proclaim his new discovery, leaving behind a small contingent of thirty-nine Spaniards. These remaining seamen proved to be abusive to their Taino hosts, forcing women to work as servants and concubines. The Taino eventually retaliated by killing the sailors and destroying their encampment. Columbus returned to Hispaniola in 1493 with 1,000 Spanish troops to establish the first settlement of Isabella, and to explore and exploit the island. The Taino Indians were hunted down and either slaughtered or enslaved to work the gold fields. It's estimated that several million Tainos had inhabited Hispaniola when Columbus had first arrived. Within twenty years, through enslavement, murder, and disease, the Taino population would be reduced to less than 50,000.

The remaining Taino Indians learned to avoid the Spanish at all costs, and fled into the forests and mountains. The seeds of hatred for the Spaniards had been firmly planted in the hearts and minds of the natives, and that hatred would become a common link with the hunters and adventurers who would eventually join them to become a painful thorn in the side of Spain's dominance of Hispaniola and the Caribbean. Through the Taino Indians, a breed of individualistic outlaws would learn the art of preserving meat, and through that art, those outlaws would adopt a title that would strike terror in the hearts of Spanish settlements throughout the New World—the *buccaneers*.

Caribbean Spanish Colonies

Native Indians were enslaved to work the gold fields and to supply labor for farms and plantations. Labor was also supplemented by indentured servants who traded years of unpaid servitude for passage to the New World. But the gold fields were soon depleted, and agriculture proved difficult in the rough terrain. With Hernán Cortés' conquest of Mexico and Peru in 1521, new gold revenues were opened up, and Spanish colonists set their sights on richer pickings.

Spanish Departure

By the mid-1500s, Spanish settlers had largely abandoned Hispaniola, leaving their livestock to the wilderness of the island. With the native population decimated by slavery, slaughter, and European diseases, the cattle, sheep, and pigs belonging to the colonists flourished and multiplied. The port city of Santo Domingo remained under Spanish control on the southern coast and thrived on shipping, but the rest of the island was virtually deserted. Similar scenarios continued throughout the coastal and island communities of the Caribbean, with scattered, strategically located port towns serving the Spanish fleets. Many settlements were left to the few remaining Spaniards, and they eventually became interspersed with various seamen and refugees from other nations.

The Boucan *of Hispaniola*

From the mid- to late 1500s to the early 1600s, the northern coast of Hispaniola became sparsely populated by intermingled descendants of the Taino Indians and Spaniards, runaway slaves and indentured servants, and marooned sailors and seamen. Learning the art of survival from the native Indians, these people would form the first foundations of New World piracy. The Spanish had driven many French citizens from their homes on several islands in the Caribbean, including St. Kitts. These misplaced Frenchmen found a new home for themselves on the island of Hispaniola and joined the rest of the growing mix of hunting survivalists.

SCUTTLEBUTT

How did the boucaniers learn to smoke meat?
The native Taino tribes taught the hunters how to use a *boucan*, a wooden frame of green sticks and boughs, and how to smoke meat on it. The Taino called this method of cooking *barbicoa*, which is the origin of the word *barbecue*.

The hunters residing on Hispaniola island soon became known as *boucaniers*, the name derived from *boucan*. The boucaniers would kill wild cows and pigs, then cut the meat into thin strips and dry and preserve it over smoky fires. Eventually the name boucanier was Anglicized and became *buccaneer*, a word whose meaning also changed to mean "pirate."

A Spanish Plan Backfires

For the most part, these early buccaneers were content to live their lives hunting and trading, but occasionally during the rainy season, several buccaneers would commit small acts of piracy. In the dead of night, they would launch a small boat, or *pinnace*, and attack an anchored merchant ship. A pinnace was a small vessel, generally having two square-rigged masts. Pinnaces were small, fast, and maneuverable, and sometimes carried oars. They were frequently used as message boats within fleets and were also highly regarded by the buccaneers for scouting coastal waters. With a crew of ten to twenty sailors, a pinnace was perfect for sneak attacks on unsuspecting merchant ships that usually anchored close to shore at nightfall.

The buccaneers may have thought these small deeds went unnoticed, but the Spanish were very aware of the buccaneers and decided they needed to do something to stop them before their piratical practices accelerated. Knowing that the hunters depended on the wild-roaming livestock of Hispaniola, the Spanish sent out groups of soldiers to hunt down and kill all the cattle and hogs. This turned out to be a bad move on the part of the Spanish, as the buccaneers, who could no longer hunt and trade for their livelihood, turned to piracy full-time.

Pairing Up

A unique social element in the early lives of the buccaneers was that they lived in pairs, where personal belongings were held in common. The buccaneers developed tight bonds with their partners and were fiercely loyal to them and to each other. Some historians believe that many of these partnerships were homosexual in nature, but there is little factual evidence to support the contention. The stronger likelihood is that pairing off was a logical survival technique to deal with the physical hardships of living off the land, and for defending personal property from interlopers and the ever-present danger of Spanish military forces.

SHIVER ME TIMBERS

Despite a lack of hard evidence and no mention of homosexuality in ships' articles, some historians surmise that homosexual practices did exist in piratical society. The French term *matelotage* refers to the custom of two adult males or a man and a boy who coexist, share their possessions, and bear the right of inheritance of each others' property.

Burning Hatred

In an effort to maintain domestic control over its New World domains, the Spanish government forbade its merchants to do business with any trading ships other than those of Spain. This edict was generally ignored in the coastal port communities of the northern coast of Hispaniola as Dutch, English, and French merchantmen traded freely with the Spanish colonists and buccaneers for preserved meats and hides. In 1603, in a vain effort to curtail those trading operations, the Spanish governor in the southern port city of Santo Domingo implemented an order to clear all of the remaining Spanish settlers from the northern coast of the island. In their zeal to fulfill the order, the Spanish military forcibly removed the colonists from their homes and burned their settlements to the ground, further fueling the already well established hatred that most of the north coast residents had for Spanish authority. Soon after the military fleets departed, the buccaneers moved into the deserted settlements and rebuilt, and trade activities with passing ships continued unabated.

The Buccaneers of Tortuga

The small island of Tortuga is located only a few miles off the northwest corner of Hispaniola. Named by the Spanish for its relative shape of a sea turtle, Tortuga is about twenty miles long and only four miles wide. With a lack of any serious Spanish military presence on the north side of Hispaniola, French colonists established a settlement on Tortuga in 1625, where they lived unmolested for several years.

In 1629, the Spanish launched an expedition to force the French from the island, which succeeded only in driving the settlers across the channel and onto Hispaniola. In an effort to establish permanent control of Tortuga, the Spaniards built a fortress and left a small contingent of soldiers to defend the island. The fort was lightly built and weakly protected, and the French quickly and easily retook the island in a counterattack. They were also savvy enough to recognize the possibilities that the fort provided and set about improving its fortifications.

As a result of the French re-establishing Tortuga, the island would soon become a haven and base of operations for pirates and privateer activity against the Spanish. For a price, the governors of Tortuga would offer safe harbor to any ship that was not Spanish, and offered letters of marque to privateers.

Le Grand Victory

The first recorded pirate victory over the Spanish fleet occurred in 1635, when French buccaneer Pierre le Grand and a crew of twenty-eight captured the flagship of a Spanish vice-admiral. Le Grand and his buccaneers had been scouting for weeks with no luck when they came upon the Spanish fleet near dusk. Under the cover of darkness, they quietly rowed their small pinnace under the bow of the anchored galleon and silently slipped aboard. The Spanish captain and his officers were said to have been playing cards when the buccaneers burst into the cabin, taking the Spaniards completely by surprise. Le Grand scuttled their pinnace, delivered the Spanish crew to the shores of Hispaniola, and then sailed the captured galleon to Dieppe Bay in the French-held island of St. Kitts. With the wealth he'd stolen from under the Spaniard's noses, le Grand retired to a comfortable life, never setting sail again.

Spanish Retaliation

The Spanish response to the loss of one of their great treasure galleons was to launch the fiercest attack the buccaneers of Tortuga would ever witness. With several warships and a massive number of troops, the Spaniards overwhelmed the settlement and slaughtered everyone on the island. The few survivors who managed to avoid the onslaught fled once again to Hispaniola. Convinced that their victory was complete, the Spanish left Tortuga unguarded and deserted. The surviving buccaneers who had fled to Hispaniola returned, and within a few years, the island once again became a thriving French colony and a home to pirates and privateers (See Chapter 16).

Brethren of the Coast

The Tortuga buccaneers began referring to themselves as the *Brethren of the Coast* and swore allegiance to one another. They would choose their own captains and officers, and all would have an equal say regarding their missions. This attention to individual rights was unique in the world of seamanship, where captains and officers traditionally had the power of gods and lowly seamen were treated as servants. The buccaneers had learned to hate authority with a passion, and demanded respect for each of their members.

SHIVER ME TIMBERS

Buccaneers had an affinity for certain weapons, especially *flintlock* pistols and muskets. A flintlock describes the firing mechanism for the pistols and rifles that pirates used. The mechanism employs a small piece of flint that strikes a steel surface which then sends sparks into a gunpowder chamber, igniting the powder and firing a projectile.

As a result of their hunting and survivalist backgrounds, the buccaneers were invariably deadly shots with their flintlock muskets and exceptionally handy with knives and the short-bladed cutlass. The Brethren of the Coast would prove to be more than a match for the much-despised Spanish, both on the high seas and on land. Through many tactical and practical errors in judgment, the Spaniards had contributed greatly to the ferocity, cunning, and fighting skills of their own worst pirate enemy, and they would pay dearly in both lives and treasure.

Flail of the Spaniards

Born Jean David Nau in the French city of Les Sables d'Olone, Francois L'Ollonais developed a reputation as one of the cruelest pirates to sail out of Tortuga. There is little question that L'Ollonais hated the Spanish as much as any buccaneer alive, and would prove his opinion at every opportunity. Most of what is known about L'Ollonais was written by Alexandre Exquemelin in 1678 in his book *The Buccaneers of America*.

L'Ollonais came to the Caribbean in 1650 as an indentured servant, and worked for three years before being released, whereupon he took up with the buccaneers on Hispaniola. From those buccaneers, L'Ollonais learned the craft of piracy, and practiced his zeal for murdering prisoners. After a suitable and bloody buccaneering apprenticeship, L'Ollonais relocated to Tortuga. The French governor, Bertrand d'Ogeron, soon became aware of L'Ollonais and his exploits, and offered him the captaincy of a ship along with a letter of marque against the Spanish. L'Ollonais would use both with incredible audacity and inhuman cruelty.

Shipwrecks and Cunning

Early in his buccaneering career, L'Ollonais was shipwrecked near Campeche, Mexico. A company of Spanish soldiers attacked the surviving buccaneers as they made their way to shore, and killed them all except L'Ollonais, who covered himself in the blood of his shipmates and laid still among them. Left for dead, L'Ollonais made his way to the city of Campeche where French slaves aided in his escape and eventual return to Tortuga.

It is said that L'Ollonais typically hacked his prisoners to pieces bit by bit; first a piece of flesh, then a hand, then an arm, and a leg, then wrapping a cord around the neck and twisting it, "til his eye shoot out." On one occasion, L'Ollonais captured a Spanish company sent to hunt him down by the Spanish governor of Cuba. He beheaded all of the soldiers save one, whom he sent back to the governor with the message "I shall never henceforth give quarter to any Spaniard whatsoever." This behavior ultimately earned L'Ollonais the nickname "Flail of the Spaniards."

Sea Rover

The cruelty of Francois L'Ollonais is said to have known no bounds, and probably bordered on the psychopathic. The buccaneer surgeon and writer Alexandre Exquemelin wrote that L'Ollonais cut the still beating heart out of one of his prisoners and gnawed on it like a ravenous wolf. The act disgusted even his buccaneer compatriots, and many left his ship at the first opportunity.

The Sack of Maracaibo

Francois L'Ollonais was the first of the Tortugan buccaneers to lead successful land raids against the Spanish. In 1667, he sailed to the Spanish city Maracaibo in Venezuela with a crew of 600 buccaneers on eight fighting ships. Though the city was well defended by a fort with sixteen large cannons positioned to fire upon any seaward attacks, the landward entrance to the city was unprotected. L'Ollonais and his crew disembarked from their ships and took the city from the landward side with ease.

During the following months, L'Ollonais and his men pillaged Maracaibo, torturing the residents into revealing the location of their valuables. L'Ollonais then marched on the nearby Venezuelan port of Gibraltar, slaughtering the Spanish garrison there and holding the entire city for ransom. He was so successful and earned his crewmates so much wealth with these raids that buccaneers on Tortuga would clamor to go on his future expeditions. Though L'Ollonais was feared even by his own kind, he was greatly respected and greatly despised by the Spanish.

Exquemelin: The Buccaneer Chronicler

Alexandre Olivier Exquemelin is credited with transcribing an enormous amount of the historical information available about the buccaneers. Some historians have branded Exquemelin as an inveterate liar, and others as the victim of opportunistic publishers bent on stretching the truth for the sake of sales. The first accusation is possibly accurate; the second is undoubtedly true. What is known is that Exquemelin's accounts of buccaneering activity during the mid-1600s coincides with corresponding accounts from other sources. There is little question that Exquemelin witnessed many of his adventures firsthand, or at the very least was near enough in the vicinity to have accurate knowledge of them.

The Price of Freedom

Although little is known of his youth, Exquemelin was born in 1646 in the port city of Honfleur on the northern French coast. A Huguenot descendant, Exquemelin studied to be a surgeon for six years in Paris and Rouen, apparently to fulfill a lifelong ambition of becoming a naval surgeon. As part of his repressive actions toward the Protestant Huguenots, King Louis XIV decreed in 1666 that no Huguenot could practice medicine in France, an act that effectively dashed Exquemelin's dreams. That same year, he signed on as an indentured servant to a company sailing from Le Havre for Tortuga. Upon his arrival, Exquemelin's contract was sold, and he joined the buccaneers in order to buy his freedom. Of the many expeditions that Exquemelin would write about, he personally took part in two of them. The first was the sacking of Maracaibo in 1669 with Francois L'Ollonais and the second was a later raid in Panama with the infamous Captain Henry Morgan (see Chapter 8).

PIECES of EIGHT

In the second English edition of Exquemelin's *Buccaneers of America* accounts written by buccaneers Basil Ringrose and Bartholomew Sharp were added to the book. Both Sharp and Ringrose's adventures described buccaneering expeditions between 1680 and 1682.

Buccaneering Break

In 1672, Exquemelin left the buccaneering life and took passage on a Dutch ship bound for Europe. Between that year and 1686, Exquemelin returned to the Americas on three voyages. Dutch archives support knowledge of at least one of these, showing that Exquemelin enlisted with Admiral de Ruyter on a failed raiding expedition to the French Antilles. Exquemelin returned to Amsterdam and stayed long enough to be granted Dutch citizenship and to pass his surgeon's exams. In 1678, Exquemelin presented the Amsterdam publisher and printer Jan ten Hoorn a manuscript that would become *De Americaensche Zee-Roovers* (*The Buccaneers of America*). Jan ten Hoorn also published the work of Hendrik Smeeks, once thought to be a pseudonym of Exquemelin. The similarities between the styles of the two writers was eventually traced back to Jan ten Hoorn, who was known to have heavily edited the works of all of his authors.

Sea Dog to the End

Alexandre Exquemelin chronicled the lives and activities of buccaneers Francois L'Ollonais, Henry Morgan, Laurens de Graaf, and Sieur de Grammont, and sailed with most of them at one time or another. Even after his book was published and became a roaring bestseller, Exquemelin would return to the sea time and again, taking part in an incredible variety of privateering activities. Historians who have attempted to discredit Exquemelin's experiences have repeatedly been discredited themselves. As intriguing as Exquemelin's adventures were, he had one particular critic who actually went so far as to sue him for the way he was portrayed in the book. The plaintiff in this case was buccaneer Henry Morgan.

Chapter 8

Henry Morgan

Henry Morgan has been called a buccaneer, a privateer, and a pirate, and his story shows that he was at various times all three. A brilliant strategist, Morgan was, without a doubt, an intelligent, courageous, and resourceful man, capable of pulling off great military feats. Among his fellow buccaneers, he was known as the "greatest of the Brethren of the Coast," but he was also known for his cruelty, as his forces unmercifully tortured prisoners, both male and female.

Don't Call Him Pirate

Other than his birth in Wales in 1635, little else is known about Henry Morgan's early years, or about how he found his way to the Caribbean. In Alexandre Exquemelin's *The Buccaneers of America*, Morgan is portrayed as being born to a poor farmer and sold as an indentured servant in the West Indies. Morgan took exception to this and to Exquemelin calling him a "pirate," and he sued the book's English publisher for libel, winning £200 sterling. But despite winning his lawsuit, he never gave a more detailed description of his early life, so the question of how he came to the West Indies remains unanswered.

Whether he was an indentured servant, or whether he came across the ocean by working on a ship or serving in the navy, Morgan eventually ended up in Jamaica, which was a British settlement and an important base for the British Royal Navy and the privateers. Morgan spent his first few years in Jamaica taking part in raids on Spanish towns in Central America, and eventually married his first cousin, Elizabeth. In 1663, he led a raid on a Spanish settlement in Nicaragua, which showed him to be an important military leader. Four years later, he was appointed Admiral of the Brethren of the Coast, succeeding Edward Mansfield, who was killed during a raid on Havana, Cuba.

SCUTTLEBUTT

Was Henry Morgan a privateer or a pirate?
Morgan always had commissions that gave him permission to stop Spanish vessels. Spain and England came to a peace settlement during Morgan's time, but Caribbean governors chose to ignore the peace agreements and allowed privateers to continue plundering Spanish ships. Additionally, the commissions didn't give permission for Morgan to attack any Spanish settlements on land, so those were definite acts of piracy.

Portobello or Bust

Henry Morgan's first big raid as admiral took place in 1668, when he led a largely outnumbered troop of buccaneers against the Spanish treasure port of Portobello, Panama, which was at the time the third largest city in the New World. (As with many city names of the era, Portobello has many different spellings, including Porto Bello, Puerto Bella, and Puerto Bello.) The area of Portobello had a solid natural harbor for the Spanish galleons to enter, and a town composed of around 150 houses, two churches, a hospital, warehouses, and large stables.

Protected by three forts, each of which was always well-manned, the city was considered impregnable; attacking it would be a huge task for Morgan and his small force of approximately 450 men. Morgan told his men that although their "numbers were small," their "hearts were great," and that the smaller number of men meant that they would each receive a "better share of the spoils." His speech must have been inspirational, as the men put their unflinching faith in their leader and sailed into Panama. They landed miles up the coast from Portobello, deciding that an overland surprise attack would be the best strategy they could employ.

Man with a Plan

Morgan and his men left their ships in the charge of a small crew at the port of Boca del Toro in Panama. The rest of the men took canoes and rowed to Estera Longa Lemos, where they beached the canoes and hiked for three miles across land, arriving at Portobello's sentry outpost just before dawn on July 11, 1668. Morgan's men quickly overcame the sentries stationed there, but not before the sentries had fired their weapons in an attempt to warn the townsfolk of an impending attack. Moving onward, Morgan's men rushed forward and attacked a temporary fortification located outside of the town. The Spaniards stationed there put up a fight but were overcome, and the buccaneers blew up the enclosure with the Spaniards still inside. By the time the town residents awoke, they were under attack.

Some of the buccaneers raced through the town, taking the citizens prisoner and herding them into one of the churches. Others climbed a low hill and began shooting at the defenders in one of the forts. The buccaneers had control of Portobello, but not the forts defending the harbor where Morgan would have to anchor his ships in order to carry out the booty.

Ladder from Hell

There were three forts protecting Portobello, one of which was located on an island and was only half built. While the men inside refused to surrender at first, the sight of the approaching pirates was enough to make them change their minds. Within the city, Morgan and his men were having a much more difficult time taking the second fort, called Santiago Castle. The men inside were putting up a terrible fight, and for a time it looked as if they might withstand Morgan's onslaught. But Morgan ordered scaling ladders built, which were wide enough to accommodate four men climbing up at the same time. He then went to the church and ordered that monks, nuns, other women, and old men be brought to him. He forced the prisoners to carry the ladders and walk ahead of the pirates as they advanced on the fort. Though the soldiers in the castle fired at least once on the group, killing one of Morgan's men and injuring two of the prisoners, they reached the main gate, hoisted the ladders, and scaled the walls. A fierce battle ensued, and forty-five of the eighty soldiers inside were killed, but by the end of the day, the fort had fallen into Morgan's hands.

The buccaneers celebrated through the night, drinking and enjoying the company of women. In the morning, Morgan sent word to the commander of the third fort, Castle San de Phelipe, that he should surrender. The commander had almost fifty men, and although he had a good quantity of ammunition, he didn't have enough food to feed his men. The two sides fired shots back and forth for some time, then the pirates sneaked into the castle and the Spanish soldiers surrendered without further fight. Morgan had the British flag hoisted over the fort, and his ships, which had been waiting outside the harbor for the signal, sailed into the bay. Morgan and his small force had done what many would have considered impossible—they captured Portobello.

Ransoming the City

Morgan then sent word to the President of Panama, informing him that he would burn the city to the ground if the president did not pay Morgan a ransom of 350,000 pesos. The president refused at first, saying that the King of Spain does not "make treaties with inferior persons." Spain sent an army of 800 men to try and retake the city, but after enduring a march through the jungle in a downpour of rain, a lack of food and gunpowder, and being met by angry buccaneers upon their arrival, the Spaniards turned back. It took three weeks, but the president paid the ransom in the end, and Morgan and his men returned to Jamaica, where the pirates happily spent their share of the spoils on gambling, drinking, and whoring.

SCUTTLEBUTT

How much booty did Morgan and his men acquire?
The ransom paid for Portobello by Panama consisted of 4,000 gold coins, 40,000 silver coins, and over 40,000 pesos' worth of silver plate and bars. In total, the booty secured from both the raid and the subsequent ransom was a major coup for Morgan and his men. When it was finally added up, the loot was worth approximately 250,000 pesos.

The Demise of the Oxford

By October, the buccaneers had wasted most of their Portobello treasure on women and drink, and they were looking for another raid. Morgan subsequently set off for Isla de le Vaca, an island off the coast of Hispaniola, where he would careen his ships and set them up with provisions for their next voyage. After his last journey, Morgan had made quite a name for himself, and many buccaneers—both English and French—traveled to Isla de la Vaca to sign on with him. The governor sent the English warship the *Oxford*, which had recently arrived in Jamaica, to join Morgan. As the *Oxford* was a thirty-six-gun ship, this was quite a coup for Morgan, and he hastily began preparations for his next invasion.

Morgan had decided to use the *Oxford* as his flagship, but there was also a twenty-four-gun French ship that he wanted to enlist. However, the French sailors onboard refused, so Morgan invited the Frenchmen onto his ship to talk. Having little time for polite chatter, he of course immediately took them prisoner so he could make use of their ship. Once he had all his ships provisioned, Morgan called for a council of the captains of all the ships so that they could decide where they would begin their next raid. Once plans were made to begin with an attack on Cartagena, the pirates began to feast and drink. As they got drunker and drunker, they continued to toast each other's health, and began to fire off *salvos*, which are simultaneous discharges of two or more guns as a salute. Unfortunately, sparks from their guns landed in the gunpowder stores and the *Oxford* was blown to pieces. About 300 people, including the French prisoners, were onboard the ship at the time. Morgan was one of only ten survivors.

Undeterred by the minor setback of having his flagship blown to smithereens, Morgan decided to continue with his plans, making the French vessel his new flagship. He and his men spent a week fishing bodies from the *Oxford* out of the water, but not to bury them. Instead, they removed the corpses' clothing and took any jewelry they wore. Once they'd liberated the clothes and hacked off any fingers bearing rings, the bodies were tossed back into the water.

Pirate Central

The remaining ships and buccaneers set sail shortly afterward, planning to meet up on the island of Savona and make their decisions on where to attack from there. Several of the ships were delayed, and as provisions ran low and tempers ran high, Morgan decided to take the eight ships and 500 men he had and organize a raid on the Venezuelan port of Maracaibo. Upon their arrival, they found the Spaniards waiting for them in a fort defending the bay, but after a battle lasting less than a day, the Spaniards retreated. Morgan and his pirates tore down the fort and spiked the cannons by driving iron nails into the gunpowder touch hole, making it impossible to ignite the cannon, and thereby rendering it useless. After the destruction was over, they carried the fort's supply of gunpowder back to their ships.

The next morning, they set sail for Maracaibo, and found that once again the Spanish had fled, leaving the city mostly empty. The buccaneers searched the city to be sure no soldiers remained behind, then set up headquarters. Each day they sent out around 100 men whose job it was to round up prisoners and any treasure they could find. Any men they did imprison were tortured in an attempt to find out where the goods and other citizens were hidden. If a prisoner failed to reveal any pertinent information, he was put to death.

SHIVER ME TIMBERS

Woolding was a form of torture that was favored by Morgan and his men. A piece of cord would be tied around a prisoner's head and around a stick. The stick would be twisted until the victim's eyes would pop out of their sockets. This torture wasn't invented by the buccaneers, but was actually used by the Spanish during their Inquisition and in their secular courts.

Onward to Gibraltar

After about three weeks of capturing and torturing prisoners and collecting their riches, the pirates decided to move on to the Venezuelan port of Gibraltar. They loaded their ships with their booty and their prisoners, and then set sail. They sent an advance party to command the people of Gibraltar to surrender to Captain Morgan, telling them that no quarter would be offered to any individuals who resisted. The ships arrived to heavy gunfire from the fort, but when the buccaneers landed and made their way on foot to the village, they found it deserted.

Alexandre Exquemelin wrote that "only a simpleton was left behind in the village," further detailing how he was tortured and killed, as he could not give the pirates any specifics on where the city's wealth was hidden. Morgan and his men eventually captured a slave, and after promising him freedom, money, and a return to Jamaica, he led them to the Spaniards' hiding places. For several days they went where the slave led them, capturing prisoners and loading Spanish wealth on mules. When they had captured over 250 prisoners, they returned to the city.

Once back in Gibraltar, they interrogated and tortured the prisoners in order to find out where the citizens' wealth had been hidden. Once they'd gone through all their white prisoners, they questioned and tortured the slaves. One of the slaves promised to lead them to the hideout of the governor, and Morgan took 350 men and went in search of him. Bad weather and swollen rivers held them back, and although they returned to Gibraltar with many more prisoners, the governor was not among them. Another group, acting on the word of a different slave, did bring back a ship and four barques, complete with some, but not all, of the merchandise they'd originally carried. By this time, Morgan decided to leave Gibraltar and head back to Maracaibo with several prisoners who were to be ransomed back for 5,000 pesos. He and his men were anxious to get back to Jamaica, but in every port, there's a storm, and in this instance there was trouble ahead.

Fight or Flight

Upon returning to Maracaibo, Morgan learned that while he'd been in Gibraltar, the Spaniards had rebuilt and outfitted the fort at the mouth of the bay with artillery and soldiers, and that three Spanish warships had arrived and were blocking the only exit to the open seas. Morgan boldly sent men to the fort demanding ransom for the city of Maracaibo. The answer which came back from Admiral Don Alonzo de Campo y Espinosa was, "If you will surrender with humility all which you have taken, including all the slaves and other prisoners, I will have the clemency to let you pass and return to your own country." If Morgan would not agree, the admiral promised he would "destroy you utterly, and put every man to the sword."

With that threat, Morgan got busy. A captured Cuban merchant ship was disguised as a warship, and fitted with logs to simulate cannons. More logs were mounted on the deck, and painted and dressed to look like pirates. The ship was loaded with barrels of gunpowder that had been fitted with fuses. The merchant ship led Morgan's men on their attack, and it headed straight for the largest of the three Spanish warships. They sailed the vessel alongside it, fastened it to the warship with grappling hooks, and lit the fuses. The buccaneers onboard then escaped in small boats. The merchant ship quickly exploded and destroyed the Spanish warship. A second Spanish ship hurried away before it could catch fire, but hit a sandbank and ran aground. Amid the chaos, Morgan's ships captured the third Spanish vessel.

SEA ROVER

Alexandre Exquemelin reports that Morgan read the Admiral's letter in both English and French to all the buccaneers, then asked them if they would rather surrender their booty or fight for it. The buccaneers chose to fight, and so Morgan devised a plan.

At that point, only the heavily armored fort stood between Morgan's men and their freedom, and Morgan again used a brilliant ploy to trick the Spanish. This time, he sent boats loaded with men to the shore, to make the Spaniards believe a land attack was coming. However, they returned with the men still onboard, most hiding in the bottom of the boats. In the meantime, the Spanish moved their guns to cover the land approaches to the fort, and in the darkness of late night, Morgan's ships quietly rode the tide out of the harbor. They were not spotted by the Spanish until they were out of range, and Morgan once again returned home to Port Royal in triumph.

The Taking of Panama

When Morgan returned to Jamaica, he learned that the Jamaican Governor, Thomas Modyford, had just received word from England telling him that all hostilities against the Spanish must stop. As a result, Morgan used part of his booty to purchase over 800 acres of plantation land in Jamaica, and for a short time he retired from buccaneering. However, Spain was still authorizing raids against the English, and a few smaller settlements on Jamaica were attacked by the Spanish. With no time to contact England for instructions, Modyford gave Morgan a commission to "attack, seize and destroy all the enemy's vessels that come within his reach," as well as to take and destroy anything that would "tend to the preservation and quiet of this island."

Back in Business

With the receipt of this new commission, the buccaneers were back in business, and by the time Morgan sailed for his next conquest in December of 1670, he had thirty-eight ships and about 2,000 men with him. They had voted to head for Panama, the principal treasure port on the Pacific coast of Central America. Morgan first took the island of St. Catherine near Costa Rica to use as a base of operations. Next his men fought a battle against the Castle Chagres, which was at the mouth of the Chagres River in Panama. Morgan would need to control the river so that he could use it to transport troops and plunder in and out of Panama.

PIECES of EIGHT

The Castle Chagres battle was fierce and bloody, with both sides suffering heavy losses. The pirates might not have won except that the thatch roofs of buildings inside the fort caught fire. As the Spaniards fled, the buccaneers raced through the front gate and took the fort. With everything going as planned, Morgan and his men were now ready to begin their journey into Panama.

Morgan and 1,200 men took canoes up the Chagres River as far as they could, then they began to walk. But it was a terrible march. The Spaniards knew they were coming, and while they didn't dare fight the buccaneers, they did move ahead of them, killing all the animals, destroying all edible plants, and removing all food from the packs of fallen soldiers. Morgan and his men were quite literally starving. The overwhelming hunger was so bad, in fact, that many of the pirates took to eating their leather bags and leather shoes, hoping that the leather would ferment in their stomachs and give them some sustenance.

Last Stand

After about ten days of marching, Morgan and his men finally caught sight of the city of Panama, but the Spanish general, knowing they were coming, had stationed troops all across the road leading to the city. There were many more Spaniards than buccaneers, but the Spaniards were mostly new recruits, and they were no match for Morgan and his rovers. The pirates stood their ground and fired with deadly accuracy, and in no time more than 100 Spaniards were dead, and the rest were fleeing. Two herds of oxen were stampeded toward the buccaneers, but they simply shooed them back to the city, where they happily killed and ate them to help assuage their hunger.

The battle won, Morgan and his men took the city, only to find that much of its treasure had been moved out, and that gunpowder had been placed to blow up many buildings. The buccaneers raced through the city ahead of the burning buildings, searching desperately for gold and other valuables. Morgan's men searched the surrounding countryside, taking prisoners and torturing them to find out where the treasure was hidden. They succeeded in gathering a large plunder, but when they returned to St. Catherine's and divvied it up among everyone, it amounted to only about £15 apiece. Morgan insisted that he made a fair sharing of the plunder, that there wasn't that much taken, and that it was a smaller amount because it had to be shared among so many men. Many of the buccaneers were skeptical and felt that Morgan had cheated them by keeping the lion's share of the booty for himself. The truth of the matter is unknown, but Morgan felt it safest to let the buccaneers disperse, so he sailed back to Jamaica with just a few trusted friends.

A Drink Before Dying

While the Jamaicans were pleased with the results of the battle in Panama, the English government, anxiously trying to negotiate a peaceful trading settlement with Spain, was not. It was decided that Modyford did not have the authority to issue the commission that he did to Morgan, and as a result, Modyford was arrested and returned to London where he was imprisoned for two years in the Tower of London. Modyford's removal from office and his incarceration did not appease the Spanish, who wanted to see Morgan brought to justice for what he'd done. In April of 1672, Morgan was arrested and sent back to London, but because he'd been ill for months with a fever, he was received there with sympathy and was not confined in any jail. Instead, he spent two years in London, moving through society as he pleased.

SHIVER ME TIMBERS

The term *bigwig* is literally derived from one's hairpiece and the status that a large wig implies. During Morgan's time, wearing wigs was highly fashionable, and the length of the wig signified the relative importance of its wearer. Henry Morgan was known to have worn a full-length black wig.

During this time, the new governor of Jamaica, Thomas Lynch, was becoming worried because of the increasing attacks by pirates in the area, and because the French were going to attempt to capture Jamaica. In January of 1674, Lynch was replaced by Lord Vaughn, and Henry Morgan was appointed as the Lieutenant Governor. Before Morgan returned to Jamaica, he was knighted by King Charles II. Upon his arrival in Jamaica, he spent most of his time purchasing more land, and drinking and gambling in Port Royal taverns. He was called into service as Acting Governor for a time when Vaughn was recalled to England, and in the face of a threat from the French he declared martial law, ordered the building of two new forts in the harbor, and salvaged twenty-two cannons from sunken ships in the area to help fortify Port Royal. When the new governor finally arrived, he found Morgan a very sick man, suffering from too many years of drink. Morgan died in 1687 and was buried in Port Royal. In a final act, his bones were swept into the sea when the great earthquake and tidal wave struck and destroyed the port in 1692 (see Chapter 16).

The Hardship of Pirating

The rough-and-tumble lifestyle that eventually destroyed Henry Morgan's health was not unusual in the seagoing world of piracy. Every sailor faced daily threats of foul weather, cruel officers and shipmasters, and the ever-present dangers of handling the shipboard rigging and equipment that kept their wooden vessels afloat and seaworthy. In addition, they faced disease, starvation, and potentially life-threatening punishment incurred as a result of any infraction of a ship's code of conduct. In the next chapter, landlubbers will learn what life was like aboard a pirate ship, and all the hardship that being a pirate entailed.

Chapter 9

A Day in the Life

Popular culture, classic literature, and film have done much to sensationalize the life of a pirate, but in truth, a rogue's lifestyle and existence aboard a pirate ship was anything but glamorous. The image of a dashing captain dressed in flowing attire overseeing a crew of swashbuckling sailors belies the actuality of true piracy. Life aboard a pirate vessel was hard, and much like naval ships, pirates had codes they followed. When ashore, pirates were traditionally distracted by all manner of drunken debauchery, behavior that has become legendary in the chronicles of these seafaring rogues.

Smooth Sailing

The never-ending lure of the sea is one that many sailors have succumbed to over the millennia. After all, what could be more romantic than setting sail across a vast expanse of diamond-sparkling ocean in search of unknown treasure with the wind at one's back and a bright horizon ahead? Unfortunately, such piratical idealism is best left to romance novelists and cinematographers. Life aboard a pirate ship was no day at the beach, and while it did offer potential rogues an attractive package, and most definitely a few more liberties than the average naval seaman, it was an existence whose benefits had to be carefully weighed.

Men turned to piracy for many reasons—unemployment, poverty, starvation, or simply deciding to alter their profession from being a military or merchant seaman to upping the ante and giving piracy a try. For example, merchant seamen who became disenchanted with their superiors would often jump ship to become a sea dog. Others were forced into naval service by their country—or in the case of the British navy, given the option of joining in lieu of ending up in a debtor's prison for monies owed—and chose to join a pirate crew rather than adhere to brutal military standards aboard a warship.

Care to Pillage?

When pirates captured a vessel, they typically asked the raided vessel's crew if they'd like to join the pirate crew. For many individuals and especially those pressed into naval service, the thought of potential riches and the liberties piracy afforded such as drinking aboard ship, shore leave, and democratic codes were more attractive than defending queen and country. This also held true for captured vessels containing slaves, who, assuming they weren't treated as a commodity, could become active pirates and receive a share of booty for their service.

Individuals who appeared to be strong and able seamen or who possessed special skills such as carpentry or weaponry were highly prized. If they refused to join a pirate captain's crew, they were often taken against their will. This was especially true of *gunners* or their assistants, called *powder monkeys*, who were typically young boys. Their dangerous job was to carefully prepare cartridges and fill canisters with gunpowder, and transport and load them into weapons such as muskets and cannons. Dexterity and caution were traits necessary for these lads, and if they possessed these skills they were a valuable commodity to rogue raiders.

SHIVER ME TIMBERS

Mutiny also commonly turned able-bodied seamen into pirates. By definition, mutiny meant that men in the service of a particular captain turned against him and took over the ship. Being a serious liability, the captain was typically set adrift or killed if he protested, or simply became a regular crewmember. Mutineers who were captured by naval vessels were treated harshly as a result of their actions, with punishments ranging from flogging to hanging.

Many young boys and teenagers willingly joined pirate crews. In an effort to learn the trade of seamanship and perhaps also to avoid orphanages or being sold into slavery, they often served as cabin boys, servants, or apprentices to a ship's craftsmen. This type of recruitment afforded young men the opportunity to see in action what would be required to become a proficient seaman who could work his way up the ranks and someday possibly command a vessel of his own. The seduction of the sea was hardly as bad as the employment options left to a youngster on land, where the opportunities for becoming a skilled worker usually went as far as being a laborer or servant. Democracy on a pirate ship was such that everyone shared in the ship's booty—including boys—a practice that only sweetened the pot.

The bottom line for most seamen turned pirates was that service to a naval warship was often more cruel than allegiance to a pirate ship. When taking into consideration the conditions and low wages of military service weighed against the potential of robbing ships brimming with riches, the choice was tempting. But in truth, the enticement of wealth was in many respects a ruse. Throughout their entire criminal careers few pirates ended up with huge treasure chests overflowing with jewels and gold coins. The majority of the time, a pirate's booty primarily consisted of much needed food and medical supplies, slaves, munitions, trade goods, and, of course, bragging rights.

Debilitation and Disease

Unlike a modern-day Princess Cruise ship, a pirate vessel was terminally dank, insufferably damp, and rife with problems ranging from leaks to rotting food to rodents to disease as well as potentially explosive devastation due to a ship's gunpowder storage. Wooden ships didn't make for smooth sailing, given the constant deluge of water seeping in through their hulls. Regardless of fair weather or stormy seas, ships would have to be continually monitored for excess leakage. This was horrifyingly evident in the lowest deck of the ship, the *bilge*, where stagnant water that couldn't be pumped out became utterly toxic. To make matters worse, the bilge was often filled with rats, which only exacerbated the problem.

SCUTTLEBUTT

Why did pirate ships smell so bad?
Bilge water reeked, but that wasn't the only smell that permeated a pirate ship. Holds full of rotting meat, rodent urine, and the stench of pirates who lived, worked, and slept in the same set of clothes added to the mix. The *head*, or bathroom, was thankfully located at the bow of the ship where a plank with a hole in it was hung over the side of the ship.

Rodents, cockroaches, and other insects such as beetles overran pirate vessels. This naturally led to all types of disease including malaria, dysentery, yellow fever, and typhoid, to name but a few. Aboard a ship it was common for many crewmembers to die as a result of disease, and though decks were often scrubbed with salt water, vinegar, or alcohol, it did little to disinfect the inevitable petri dish that was a pirate ship. Added to that were the injuries sustained during raids or accidents that occurred during normal ship routines. The duties performed by sailors were inherently risky, given the logistics of sails and rigging, gunpowder, faulty firearms, munitions storage, and a host of other dangers.

Unfortunate pirates who incurred major injuries to limbs were often at the mercy of the ship's carpenter, who would perform amputations. Anesthetic and painkillers consisted of whatever alcohol was onboard, and cauterizing wounds would involve fire and hot tar. Without basic medicines, internal injuries would often prove fatal. If a pirate did happen to survive until the ship arrived at a port, he typically was taken ashore and removed from the crew. Given that pirates had a penchant for extreme drink and prostitutes, alcoholism and venereal diseases were also rampant.

Obtaining and maintaining fresh vegetables and especially fruit aboard a pirate ship was also a significant problem, one that caused many a rogue to suffer as a result of *scurvy*. The result of a lack of vitamin C, scurvy was quite common among sailors and was, in fact, a major killer. Bleeding from mucous membranes, sponge-like gums and inflammation, loss of teeth, horrible spotting and black and blue discoloration of the skin, anemia, joint pain, and limited mobility were all by-products of scurvy.

Without eventually ingesting some form of vitamin C, scurvy was fatal, and if a sailor went several months without fresh produce he was likely to develop the disease. Over the course of several centuries it was realized that lemons and limes could combat scurvy, and many ships made certain to keep them onboard whenever possible. The term *limey*, which is used to describe the British, came about as a result of England's Royal Navy providing sailors with lime juice in order to prevent scurvy.

Bon Appetit!

To say that pirates ate like kings would be a massive overstatement, although to some who turned to piracy as a result of starvation, it might arguably have been tolerable. For the most part, food and water were a constant concern on any pirate vessel where the modern-day conveniences of refrigeration and Tupperware were nonexistent. The inability to properly preserve any fresh food resulted in rotten, maggot- and worm-filled meat and fish, *hard tack*, or biscuits, infested with weevils and other critters, and fetid water spiked with rum or cinnamon and nutmeg in a vain attempt to make it more palatable. Beer and wine were also common thirst quenchers, which was good for drinking purposes but did nothing to reduce alcoholic propensities.

Some pirate ships had kitchens, while others did not. Food was typically stored in the ship's hold in casks or oak barrels and sometimes cooked in cauldrons far away from the ship's munitions and gunpowder storage, which was commonly on one of the lower decks of the ship. If a crew was lucky, their food supply would remain consistent, with the majority of meals containing salted meats, hard tack, and beer. Some ships even kept chickens, which were used for both egg and meat supplies. If pirate crews were unlucky, meat would consist of rats captured from the ship's bilge.

Any food supplies that could be stolen from captured vessels were a bonus for pirates. Staples such as sugar and spices helped make their precarious meals more palatable, and it was all the better if their conquests had holds full of fresh water, meats, fruits, or vegetables. Excess liquor was, of course, always a valuable treasure. Suffice to say that, by today's standards, pirate cuisine wouldn't be on any restaurant menu.

SHIVER ME TIMBERS

A pirate's breakfast often consisted of *burgoo*, a watery gruel flavored with sugar, salt, and butter. If a pirate was extremely lucky he could substantially feast on *salamagundy*, a mix-and-match meal which consisted of boiled onions and salt fish. To that could also be added any number of delectables including turtle meat, chicken, pork, duck, pigeon, anchovies, eggs, oil, wine, and various types of marinated shellfish.

Order in the Court

Serving on a pirate ship was in many ways similar to serving on most vessels of the era. On any given day, crewmembers would take care of regular maintenance, such as tending and repairing sails, ropes, and any leaks in the hull. If a ship did pull into an isolated harbor or cove, the crew might take the time to scrape barnacles off the ship's hull and keel. One of the common inevitabilities of serving on a pirate ship was that sometimes, as a result of taking on new crewmembers from captured ships, there would be more hands than were necessary to perform daily ship duties. This meant excess time, and to the average pirate that meant either drinking or boredom. It was common for ships to employ musicians who could provide a sense of both calm and levity during long voyages. Fiddlers, also called *catgut scrapers*, were often onboard. By and large, any escapades pirates chose to undertake in their free time were of course dictated by that ship's established code of conduct, but pirates who weren't busy rigging sails, swabbing decks, or performing various tasks kept themselves entertained by rolling dice, chewing tobacco, shooting guns, playing cards, or holding mock trials.

PIECES of EIGHT

These so-called mock trials provided much needed respite from long hours, days, and months at sea. Pretending they were the criminals on trial, crewmembers would assume various positions typical of a court including a judge, witnesses, jury, and victims. An elaborate trial would then be enacted, with everyone playing a part in the production.

Aye, Captain

Pirate ships usually carried the same complement of crewmen as the ships of navies and merchant traders. Every crewman knew his responsibilities in the mechanical function of sailing a ship, and knew what was expected in the heat of battle. One of the undeniable attributes that virtually all pirates possessed was that of able-bodied seamanship. Laziness or incompetence from any member created more work for others and also posed a threat of disaster for the rest of the crew during times of peace or battle. Such behavior was never tolerated.

The major variation between pirate crews and those of formal sailing vessels was the level of power and respect afforded the officers. Many pirates inherently despised the ruthless authority that they'd endured at the hands of naval commanders and the officers of merchant ships. As pirates, they learned to demand equality and respect. One of the key factors that created that equality and separated pirates from traditional seamen was simply that every pirate was armed to the teeth and capable of inflicting serious harm.

Leader of the Pack

Many pirate crews included an informal council to make important decisions by majority rule, and one of the most important of those decisions was to select a ship's captain. In running down prey at sea and in the actual heat of battle, every experienced sailor for thousands of years has known one inviolable rule: only one man can be in control of the ship, and that control must be absolute. On land, raiding bandits could afford a certain amount of autonomy. At sea, with nowhere to go but the deck beneath a sailor's feet, a single nonconformist acting individually could get an entire crew killed.

Elected captains on pirate ships were chosen for their leadership, their tactical knowledge for closing in on prey vessels, and their ability to orchestrate a successful boarding without destroying the target or harming the cargo. Pirate captains also needed to know trade routes and the locations of potential prizes. When in port, a good captain would intentionally cruise taverns, not so much to drink and make merry, but to gather every tidbit of information possible about incoming and departing ships, and the cargo they carried. For his efforts, the successful pirate captain received additional shares of plunder.

SEA ROVER

If a captain failed to produce potential prizes, or if he made tactical decisions that caused damage to the ship or cost lives, the crew would quickly depose him and install a new shipmate in his place. Usually accepting the majority decision of the crew, the deposed captain would simply assume other duties as a crewman.

Some pirate captains took control of their ships by intimidation and imposition rather than by democratic procedures. These captains, such as the infamous Blackbeard and buccaneer Henry Morgan, maintained their control by supplying their crews with repeated successes. Those that failed to do so faced mutiny, imprisonment, or even death.

Lieutenant and Ship's Master

A *lieutenant* was usually second in command to the captain. Acting as the captain's deputy, the lieutenant would help to carry out orders during a chase and in battle. He would also take command of captured vessels and help with the distribution of stolen cargo. The *ship's master* had oversight over the actual sailing of the ship. This individual had to understand how to coordinate every one of the many hundreds of functional parts of a sailing ship, and how to direct the ship with the greatest possible speed. On relatively small pirate vessels, the position and responsibilities of the master would often be assumed by the captain. In terms of seamanship, the ship's master would invariably be the most experienced and accomplished sailor onboard. If he was able, the ship's master would often assume the responsibilities for navigation.

Navigator

The *navigator* of any ship was ultimately responsible for getting the ship where it was going and circumventing potentially dangerous waterways. Early navigation was as much an art as a science, utilizing compass readings and the position of the sun and stars to determine the relative position of a tiny pirate vessel in a huge expanse of ocean. Navigators are probably the single most important member of any sailing crew and were often pressed into pirate service from captured merchant vessels. Without a good navigator, a pirate ship would quite literally be lost. A few captains had extensive navigational qualifications. Captain Bartholomew Roberts, for example, served as navigator of an English slave ship when he was taken prisoner and forced into piracy by rogue captain Howell Davis. As Black Bart, Roberts became one of the most prolific pirates in history.

Boatswain and Helmsman

The *boatswain*, pronounced "bos-un," was responsible for the ropes, lines, cables, and sails on the ship. Every functional piece of equipment was under the boatswain's domain, and he made certain that every seaman was handling his duties for the operation of the ship. The *helmsman* operated the large wheel that controlled the rudder of the ship, and worked in close cooperation with both the ship's master and the boatswain to coordinate the movements and direction of the ship.

Master Gunner

The *master gunner* was invariably a refugee from one of the formal navies, and was highly experienced with cannons and gunpowder. The gunner was responsible for taking charge of the cannon during attacks, and directing the crew in aiming, firing, and reloading the cannons. The master gunner would also ensure that gunpowder for the cannon was in good supply and, above all, dry.

SCUTTLEBUTT

What kind of ammunition was used in cannons?
Langrel was a type of cannon shot favored by privateers and pirates. Canvas bags of musket balls or bits of scrap iron and chain would be stuffed into the cannon muzzles in place of cannon balls and fired into the sails and rigging of fleeing vessels, effectively shredding all it touched. As one can imagine, langrel also had a devastating effect on flesh and bone.

Quartermaster

On a few pirate vessels, it seems that the quartermaster was second in ship's power only to the captain. On most ships, however, the quartermaster was responsible for keeping track of ship stores and inventory. Part of those duties involved keeping track of plunder and helping with its distribution among the crew. He would also serve as arbiter for disputes among crewmembers, and as the liaison between a ship's crew and its captain.

Carpenter

One of the busiest seamen onboard any early sailing vessel was a ship's carpenter. Wooden ships were, by their very nature, continually in need of repair from water damage, wear and tear on the many constantly moving parts, and damage resulting from combat. It's probable that most pirate ships were not given anywhere near the same attention that naval and merchant ships received in regard to carpentry. In the absence of a ship's surgeon and having skill with saws, the carpenter might also participate in amputating the limbs of fellow pirates who were seriously wounded in combat or shipboard accidents.

Honor among Thieves

The "pirate code" is the stuff of legend and lore, and has long been glorified into a sort of mythical ideology by novelists and filmmakers. In reality, regulating the personal conduct of pirates wasn't a social or ethical issue, it was a commonsense necessity for survival on the high seas. Sailing ships with cramped quarters and no place to go except over the side would be dangerous for the entire crew without rules and regulations, and each pirate crew usually defined its own terms. Punishments for infractions were swift and severe, and would range from slitting the nose and ears to marooning, lashing, or execution. Most pirates had served on naval ships or in the merchant marines and were accustomed to signing, or *making their mark*, on service documents that they probably could not even read. There's evidence that several pirate crews drew up similar sets of documents with *articles* defining shipboard regulations. These articles would be written by the few educated pirates, and then explained to the rest of the crew and new recruits as they came aboard. There's no doubt that most pirate crews were illiterate, and relied on memorized oral versions of rules and expectations particular to the ship they were currently sailing on.

Booty Share

All pirates were entitled to a share of any treasure from prizes they captured. The captain and officers were entitled to additional shares in order of their rank and responsibilities. The captain might receive two shares for his efforts and skill at directing the capture of a prize, and officers would receive one and one-quarter to one and one-half shares.

Life and Limb

Life aboard pirate ships was inherently rife with danger, and pirates generously compensated fellow crewmen who were crippled or sacrificed body parts in battle. The loss of the right arm was considered to be the most extreme injury. The loss of the left arm, right leg, and left leg would follow in importance. Interestingly, the loss of an eye was often regarded as no more serious than the loss of a finger.

SHIVER ME TIMBERS

The phrase *son of a gun* originated in the early days of the British Royal Navy. Wives and mistresses of sailors were permitted aboard ship for conjugal visits when ships were in port. Women occasionally gave birth aboard ship in the only clear space available—between the cannons on the gun deck. That is why a child born aboard ship was called a son of a gun.

The Articles of Bartholomew Roberts

The Articles of Bartholomew Roberts may be the best known and most commonly cited pirate document of service. His articles prohibited gambling, set forth punishments, explained procedures for the settlement of arguments, provided compensation for those injured aboard ship, and delineated the division of treasure among the crew and officers. What follows are his legendary articles:

ARTICLE I. *Every man shall have an equal vote in affairs of moment. He shall have an equal title to the fresh provisions or strong liquors at any time seized, and shall use them at pleasure unless a scarcity may make it necessary for the common good that a retrenchment may be voted.*

ARTICLE II. *Every man shall be called fairly in turn by the list on board of prizes, because over and above their proper share, they are allowed a shift of clothes. But if they defraud the company to the value of even one dollar in plate, jewels or money, they shall be marooned. If any man rob* *another he shall have his nose and ears slit, and be put ashore where he shall be sure to encounter hardships.*

ARTICLE III. *None shall game for money either with dice or cards.*

ARTICLE IV. *The lights and candles should be put out at eight at night, and if any of the crew desire to drink after that hour they shall sit upon the open deck without lights.*

ARTICLE V. *Each man shall keep his piece, cutlass and pistols at all times clean and ready for action.*

ARTICLE VI. *No boy or woman to be allowed amongst them. If any man shall be found seducing any of the latter sex and carrying her to sea in disguise he shall suffer death.*

ARTICLE VII. *He that shall desert the ship or his quarters in time of battle shall be punished by death or marooning.*

ARTICLE VIII. *None shall strike another on board the ship, but every man's quarrel shall be ended on shore by sword or pistol in this manner. At the word of command from the quartermaster, each man being previously placed back to back, shall turn and fire immediately. If any man do not, the quartermaster shall knock the piece out of his hand. If both miss their aim they shall take to their cutlasses, and he that draweth first blood shall be declared the victor.*

ARTICLE IX. *No man shall talk of breaking up their way of living till each has a share of £1,000. Every man who shall become a cripple or lose a limb in the service shall have 800 pieces of eight from the common stock and for lesser hurts proportionately.*

ARTICLE X. *The captain and the quartermaster shall each receive two shares of a prize, the master gunner and boatswain, one and one half shares, all other officers one and one quarter, and private gentlemen of fortune one share each.*

ARTICLE XI. *The musicians shall have rest on the Sabbath Day only by right. On all other days by favour only.*

The majority of pirates were experienced seamen, and even though they were by nature tough, rebellious, and ruthless, they understood the importance of regulations onboard a sailing ship. Whether a pirate signed a piece of paper or gave his word to abide by the rules of the ship, he was well aware that departure from those rules would result in serious repercussions and that no offense ever went unpunished.

SEA ROVER

According to the articles of the English pirate George Lowther, the first man to spot a ship to plunder was entitled to the finest pistol or small arm aboard the prize. Lowther was eventually marooned on a small island after fleeing his ship as it was under attack by an English warship. He was later found dead with an empty pistol in his hand and a bullet through his head.

Pirate Punishment

Every pirate ship's articles or codes of conduct addressed the issue of punishment. One of the points in Bartholomew Roberts' articles, for example, listed that "He that shall desert the ship or his quarters in time of battle shall be punished by death or marooning." A typical code, it clearly demonstrates that pirates weren't necessarily lawless, and how seriously they considered any perceptibly treasonous or cowardly acts among their own. A swift death for unmentionable acts by pirate standards was being kind to a rogue gone bad.

There were, in fact, far worse punishments that pirates were made to endure from their own kind including marooning, flogging, and a particularly nasty torture called keelhauling. In addition, pirates didn't even have much aversion to selling a disgraced pirate into slavery. With any punishment, it was usually a ship's quartermaster who saw to it that an offender's punishment was carried out to its fullest extent. When examining punishments, it must be said that walking the plank is arguably one of the greatest pirate myths. Few pirates ever used that type of punishment (see Chapter 17).

The majority of captured pirates the world over were hanged. Sometimes it was a small affair, other times it was a grand event witnessed by large audiences. For the most part, pirates were hung either by parties securing the noose and pulling them up off the ground or by having them stand atop a platform like a gallows, or even a cart situated below a crossbeam. The footing would then be removed so the pirate would swing above ground, his body twitching and convulsing violently. As a further show of punishment, hanged pirates would often remain on display, sometimes in chains or housed in a cage made of iron. Others would be decapitated or have various limbs cut off and skewered on iron spikes.

Marooning

A pirate crew with the ultimate punishment in mind would often maroon a disgraced comrade. The term "maroon" is derived from the Spanish *cimarron*, meaning a fugitive. The most popular case of marooning is, of course, Daniel Defoe's legendary *Robinson Crusoe*, allegedly based on the marooning of pirate Alexander Selkirk (see Chapter 18). The marooning of Robinson Crusoe, however, took place on a plush island with plenty of resources. Real-life marooning was a nasty business and one that all pirates took very seriously. For the most part, the practice involved putting any offending pirate ashore on an uninhabited island often void of natural resources. Unlucky victims would be left with no means to live, and on occasion not even the clothes on their backs. If a pirate was marooned on a tiny island or sandbar, he was virtually guaranteed a slow death as starvation and dehydration took over. He could also fall victim to the high tide or even sharks that could reach him.

Depending on a ship's captain and crew, marooned pirates would sometimes be given basic provisions or weapons, but little more than that. On occasion, all they'd receive is a musket or pistol with a single round with which they could commit suicide. The more fortunate maroon victims might be left on an island that at least had some measure of wildlife or sustenance. More often than not, marooning proved fatal to pirates, the punishment befitting the crime they committed against their former crewmates. Sometimes pirates who'd been marooned were picked up by a passing ship. If their rescuers didn't see fit to leave them on the island or kill them, they might have the good fortune to become part of a new crew of rogues. They might also be taken prisoner and end up in prison at that ship's next port of call.

Disgraced pirates, however, weren't the only seafarers who fell victim to marooning. Sometimes captured prisoners were simply dropped off on an island and left to fend for themselves. In 1821 near Cuba, Captain Barnabas Lincoln and eleven members of his crew were marooned by pirates who imprisoned them on an island only a few feet above water. Luckily, a few members of the marooned party were able to escape via a makeshift craft they built and could bring help.

SCUTTLEBUTT

What happened to marooners who weren't pirates?
One of the worst things about being marooned and subsequently rescued is that most crews who actually picked up marooners would automatically assume they were pirates—so victims who had the good fortune of surviving a marooning by pirates didn't always survive their rescue. Often they would be transported to the nearest port and turned over to authorities.

Keelhauling

The process of *keelhauling*, which reputedly was invented by the Dutch around the fifteenth or sixteenth century, was a particularly heinous act that no seaman—sailor or pirate—should be made to endure. Victims of keelhauling, often with lead weights secured to their legs, were tied to a rope hanging from the mast's yardarm. The rope and the ensnared victim were then subsequently tossed into the sea and dragged under the ship's keel on one side and then brought up on the other side to the corresponding yardarm. Aside from drowning torturously slowly, the victim was sure to be cut to bits by the inevitable scores of painfully sharp barnacles glued to the keel and hull of the ship. Keelhauling was a surprisingly standard punishment on British, French, and Dutch naval vessels, but by the mid-nineteenth century it was officially discontinued.

Flogging

Perhaps the most common punishment seafarers endured was *flogging*, or whipping. Typically accomplished by using a *cat o' nine tails*, flogging involved lashing offenders in various manners until they endured a certain length of time, number of beatings, or, in some cases, until they were dead. A cat o' nine tails was a short wooden stick or handle that had nine knotted ropes, each 18 inches long, secured to its end. Lashes inflicted in this manner were brutally painful, as skin was ripped by the hard knotted ropes. As the handle was drawn back, the ropes ranged over the victim's back, a process called *combing the cat*, so as to separate the bloody ropes from loose flesh stuck to them. To add additional misery, salt would sometimes be poured into the open wounds. Victims who suffered dozens of lashes died a horrible death, and the crew of the ship witnessed the punishment, which was usually held on the vessel's main deck.

The British navy, which began the practice around 1700, was fond of using flogging as punishment for disciplinary indiscretion, but they were by no means the only group, culture, or civilization to use the procedure. Indeed, the act of flogging has been used for centuries, from the ancient world to the time of Christ and modern-day slavery. For the most part, victims of flogging are tied to a stationary object or made to bend over something in order to provide the initiator full access to the area that is to be whipped.

PIECES of EIGHT

One particularly ghoulish punishment involved being nailed to a mast through one's earlobes and left to suffer until nightfall. This punishment was usually instituted when a sailor committed an infraction that wasn't serious enough for flogging. The threat "I'll nail you for that" is derived from this penalty.

Taking a Bow

A day in the life of a pirate was never an easy one, and a night's rest or a full meal were never guaranteed regardless of how successful a pirate and his crew were. The one consistent thing in a rogue's life was his ship, and in order to survive, pirates needed to know everything there was to know about how a ship was constructed, how it operated, the weapons it afforded, and above all, how to attack intended prey.

Chapter 10

Setting Sail

Many types of sailing ships were used by pirates over the centuries, and the vessels were as diverse as the pirates themselves. Upgrading to bigger and faster ships was a badge of honor in the pirate realm, and an ambition that most pirates took very seriously. Sailing under the Jolly Roger, pirate ships were generally fast, well-armed, and sturdy, and were capable of carrying large heavily armed crews. From faster boats to more firepower, successful pirates knew what they needed to carry out their attacks, and they weren't afraid to secure and use it.

Fast and Furious

Regardless of the type of vessel a pirate was sailing, there was a range of common characteristics that were necessary for any pirate ship. First of all, the ship had to be sturdy, and capable of holding together through high seas and raging storms. While this was important for any ship, it was vital for pirates, who didn't have the luxury of heading to the nearest port when a hurricane began battering their vessel. If a ship wasn't sailing near an isolated area of land, or a pirate haven such as New Providence, Port Royal, or Tortuga (see Chapter 16), it was destined to ride out fierce winds and overpowering waves.

Another important characteristic of pirate ships was that they had to be fast. A pirate crew's need for speed was twofold—the ship needed to be fast both in order to overtake prey and to provide escape when they were being preyed upon. Having a large ship would not be an advantage if the size of the ship slowed it down, and for that reason smaller was sometimes better. An extremely experienced crew could invariably coax more speed out of a larger, bulkier boat, but that required expending valuable energy. Often pirates had to make a decision on whether a larger boat, capable of carrying more weaponry and more crew, would be an advantage over a smaller boat that moved faster and could more easily be navigated in shallow waters.

While a speedy, well-armed, and sound ship was something all pirates aspired to owning, the truth is that pirates simply couldn't visit a local boatyard and purchase a ship any more than they could commission shipwrights to build one to their specifications. Most pirates started their rogue careers with whatever boat they could lay their hands on—sometimes as small as a canoe—and upgraded by capturing or stealing better ships and making modifications to better suit their needs.

Galleons and Warships

Galleons originally came to importance as the protectors of the Spanish treasure fleets. They were initially designed similarly to fifteenth century *carracks*, which were light, fast vessels that had three or four masts and high, rounded sterns. To the Spanish galleons were added high *forecastles* and large *sterncastles*, making them a more unwieldy vessel. The galleons were also designed to carry a large number of passengers as well as cargo, another upgrade destined to slow them down at sea. To make up for this, they were heavily armored and carried many soldiers, but ultimately their slow speed and difficult maneuverability made them an easier target than the Spanish would have preferred. Regardless of how shipwrights built the vessels, galleons invariably had to travel in fleets to assure their safety.

SHIVER ME TIMBERS

A *forecastle* is the portion of a ship located ahead of the tallest mast, or *mainmast*; it generally holds the sailors' quarters. A *sterncastle* (or *aftcastle*) is the upper portion of the sailing deck located behind a short mast, or *mizzenmast*. In pirate times, it was generally used for guns and as an onboard "fortress" from which pirates could defend the ship if necessary.

English Galleons

When the English privateers arrived on the pirate scene in the sixteenth century, they boasted their own style of galleon. Moving back toward the faster, lighter carracks, the English galleons were quicker and more maneuverable than their Spanish counterparts. They were designed to be sleeker, with lowered forecastles and a longer hull. The longer and lower hull made the vessel much more stable in the water, as did the squared-off stern on the ship. Each galleon had three to five masts, and they were powered entirely by sail. Unlike the carracks, which tended to weigh around 1,000 tons, these galleons were closer to 500 tons. They were designed to be heavily armed, often with cannons mounted on wheels for ease of aim, and became not only the favored ship of English privateers but the flagships of the Royal Navy as well.

Masts and Sails

A ship's masts are the poles that hold the sails, and they're named according to their position, moving from front to back, or *bow* to *stern*. Until the twentieth century, masts were made of *spars*, round poles constructed from straight tree trunks. For taller masts, two or three spars would be bound together. The *foremast* comes first, followed by the *mainmast*, which as the tallest mast was usually located near the center of the vessel. The *mizzen-mast* is typically the shortest mast, and in all but the largest sailing ships is the mast farthest from the bow. Each mast would be rigged with sails designed to catch the wind and move the ship.

Different types of *rigging*, or ropes and lashings, would be used for different purposes, and masts on the same ship could have different types of rigging. *Square-rigged* sails are rectangular sails draped from horizontal bars called *yards*, or *yardarms*, which are attached to the mast. If a vessel was *fore-and-aft rigged* it meant the sails were lined up with the hull, rather than being set at right angles to the hull as when they were square-rigged. When a ship was *lanteen-rigged*, it had triangular sails that were set on a yardarm at a forty-five-degree angle to the mast.

Merchant Vessels and Slavers

Most merchant ships in the 1600s and 1700s weighed somewhere between 100 and 200 tons, were manned by a very small crew, and contained very few guns onboard for defense. The same was true of the average *slaver*, or slave ship, of the time. The larger the crew, the more wages would have to be paid out, and the smaller the profits the shipping companies and merchants would receive. Both types of ship had large holds for carrying cargo or slaves, and generally had three masts. Because of their lack of manpower and armament, they were easy prey for pirates, even though pirate ships were generally smaller.

Anatomy of a Pirate Ship

When pirates captured a prize ship and claimed it as their own, they usually had to make some modifications to suit their needs. They would usually lower the decks and siderails as much as possible, and tear out any interior walls. Given that pirates lived communally onboard, it was typically only the captain who had separate quarters. Additionally, they would sometimes move extra guns below decks, and cut small square windows, or *portholes*, in the hull through which they could shoot the guns.

PIECES of EIGHT

In general, pirates were more likely to worry about how they could gain extra speed and maneuverability as well as extra armament on their vessels—comfort at sea was not something they cared much about. Because of this, there were certain types of ships that pirates favored, including pinnaces, sloops, brigantines, and square-riggers.

Pinnaces

Many pirates who prowled the Caribbean began their career with a pinnace, which in its original meaning refers to an oared longboat that belonged to a larger ship. It might have a single mast with a lanteen sail, and was usually used to move between two larger ships, or to put into shore when the water was too shallow for the larger ship to dock. About 40 feet long, the vessel could carry a cargo of fifteen tons. Buccaneers frequently used pinnaces, or other small boats like them (the Dutch *pingue*, and the Spanish *barca longa*), to raid larger craft or to attack settlements from water. These boats couldn't travel long distances from shore, so pirates would want to quickly trade up to a larger vessel.

Sloops and Brigantines

A common ship for many pirates during the 1700s was the *sloop*, which featured a single mast and usually a fore-and-aft rigged *mainsail* (the largest sail of a mainmast). The hull was usually between 35 and 60 feet long, and was commonly fitted with four to twelve guns. Almost half of the pirates cruising Caribbean and American waters during this time were sailing sloops. Stede Bonnet's *Revenge*, Blackbeard's *Adventure*, and William Kidd's *Adventure Galley* were all sloops.

Brigantines were larger vessels with two masts, and were usually rigged with a square-rigged *foresail* (the lowest sail on a mast) and a fore-and-aft rigged mainsail. They also often had a triangular sail called a *jib* that was attached to the bow of the ship. Cumbersome in size, brigantines were slow ships that were responsible for far fewer pirate attacks. Charles Vane's vessel was a brigantine named the *Ranger*.

SCUTTLEBUTT

What kind of ship is a schooner?
Schooners came about in the early 1700s, and generally had two masts with fore-and-aft rigging. They were never very popular as pirate ships, though pirate movies often use either schooners or the slightly larger square-rigged ships as the vessel for their fictional pirates. In reality, schooners didn't become popular until after the Golden Age of piracy had ended.

Square-riggers

When thinking of a pirate ship, many people today picture a large, square-rigged vessel. Both Bartholomew Roberts and Blackbeard captained square-riggers during their careers (see Chapters 11 and 12). Blackbeard's *Queen Anne's Revenge*, a former French slaver he captured, was between 200 and 300 tons. His primary modification was refitting it with over forty guns. Roberts' *Royal Fortune* was a former French warship, but as a pirate ship it carried a crew of over 200 men and forty-two guns. Both vessels had three masts, with square-rigging and jib sails. *Queen Anne's Revenge* was lost when she ran aground in the shallow waters off North Carolina in 1718. The *Royal Fortune* took a broadside shot from a British warship and was captured in 1722. Because these larger ships were less wieldy, and because they required a more experienced crew, few other pirates dared sail them.

Tools of the Trade

There were certain items that all sailors—whether merchant, pirate, privateer, or Naval officer—could not sail without. These were the tools that were needed in order to navigate across the world's oceans. One of the most important was the *sextant*. Used to measure the angle of the sun or stars above the horizon, the sextant helped captains and navigators determine their latitude. Another important tool was the *compass*, which helped guide them in the direction they were headed. Without these tools, it would have been easy to miss land and sail completely off course, which could be devastating on a ship with limited stores of supplies.

Pirates also followed *charts*, which were maps drawn by cartographers or other individuals who'd sailed the same routes. The charts depicted specific areas of water and the coastal regions surrounding it, pointing out hazards and landmarks that could be used to assist in navigation. Given the complexity of high seas transport, it's little wonder that the navigator ranked as one of the most important crewmembers on a ship.

The Jolly Roger

The words "Jolly Roger" generally bring to mind a black flag, emblazoned with a grinning skull menacingly hovering over a pair of crossed bones. While this is traditional, pirate flags have gone through many incarnations. The name Jolly Roger came from the French phrase, *Jolie Rouge*, which means "pretty red." The French buccaneers were among the first to fly pirate flags.

PIECES of EIGHT

The earliest known pirate flags were made of a plain red or black sheet, and meant to strike terror into the sailors who would see it. In antiquity, red denoted battle and black meant death, so both were good choices for a flag meant to instill fear.

As time passed, the red flag came to have a more specific and ominous meaning. When the red flag was being flown no quarter would be given, meaning that once a battle began, pirates would take no prisoners, instead fighting to the death. In many cases, flags became identified with certain pirates. For example, if a ship saw Blackbeard's flag, with its devil-horned skeleton wielding a spear aimed at a bright red heart, it was an immediate indicator that a surrender was in order lest a gruesome battle ensue.

Skull and Crossbones

The stereotypical skull and crossbones had been around for centuries prior to its use by pirates. The "death's head" over the crossed bones was used in cemeteries in Medieval times, and had been worn as a badge on the caps of soldiers in Europe during the sixteenth century. Adding it to the plain pirate flag was a way of ensuring that the pirate mantra of "Surrender or Die" was clearly understood. In the early 1700s, many pirates began putting their own personal touches on their flags, hoping their reputations might further terrorize their victims. A number of pirates added an hourglass to their pennant, symbolizing the limited time victims had to surrender before an attack would begin.

Thomas Tew chose a black flag with an arm brandishing a saber for his flag. Edward Low used a black flag with an entire bright red skeleton painted on it. Christopher Moody preferred a red flag which sported an hourglass next to an arm with a knife, followed by a skull in front of crossed bones, symbolizing that time was flying before certain attack and death. For Henry Every, the traditional skull and crossbones on the black flag was enough, but he changed it slightly by showing the skull in profile wearing a bandanna on its head. Calico Jack Rackham cleverly mocked the skull and crossbones—he used a grinning skull over crossed swords instead.

𝔓IECES of 𝔈IGHT

Most of the pirates who sailed during the Golden Age adapted the flag in some way in order to make it their own. For many, this served to quickly identify them to potential prey. Shortly after the Golden Age ended, flag creativity ceased and the traditional skull and crossbones on a black background became the standard flag for all pirates.

Flags of Deception

In addition to the Jolly Roger, many pirates would sail under the flag of a particular nation. Those who were sailing with a letter of marque would use the flag of the country authorizing their commission. Crafty pirates who preferred a more sinister ruse would collect flags of many nations, and approach a merchant ship they wanted to attack while flying a flag the captain of their future prize would welcome as "friendly." Only when the pirates were close enough to attack and prepared to fire their first volley would they hoist their pirate flag and reveal their true identity. It may seem strange that they would take the time to change flags and lose the element of surprise, but in reality most pirates preferred to win by intimidation. They would far rather have the enemy surrender without a fight than risk losing potential booty, and most sailors would surrender quietly when they knew the alternative was death.

It's interesting to note that sailing under the flag of another country was not just a pirate practice. During the days of the privateers, many merchant ships carried a variety of flags and would hoist the enemy's flag when sailing in waters where they expected to meet up with them. While this certainly made more sense than flying a flag that singled them out as an enemy, it by no means ensured a ship's safety. The privateers, pirates, and military were all well aware of the practice of using the "wrong" flag. The best defense for any vessel was simply to sail quickly in the opposite direction of any unknown ship.

The Element of Surprise

Throughout history, pirates would frequent shipping lanes waiting for unsuspecting merchant or slave ships to cross their paths. When necessary, pirates would carry their deception even further than sailing under a false flag. If a confrontation required extreme deception, pirate crews would dress in the clothing of the country they were pretending to be from, sometimes even using a crewmember or prisoner who spoke their language to further envelop their prey in a false sense of security. Many pirates attacked at night, when they had the advantage of being able to quietly approach their prey when most of them were asleep and the ship was lightly guarded.

If pirates could exploit the element of surprise they always would, as they preferred to avoid heavy gunfire that could potentially damage their booty. Whether they were seen by their victims or not, they would typically move in close to the other ship at the first opportunity, and when near enough would toss grappling hooks to fasten their vessel to the other. They would then pull the vessels close, swarm over the side of the boat, and engage the enemy in combat. Since pirate ships generally had crews over ten times the size of the average merchant ship crew, raids were usually over in a hurry. Either the crew surrendered, if the pirates were allowing it, or they were quickly killed.

SCUTTLEBUTT

What does "shiver me timbers" mean?
The expression shiver me timbers originated from the shock or surprise that resulted from the vibrations of the wooden masts or timbers of a sailing vessel when it was struck by a cannonball or if the vessel suddenly struck an unseen object.

Once a battle was over, pirates would search the captured vessel looking for whatever cargo they could use or sell, and would then transfer it to their own holds. When they could find nothing else of any use, they would occasionally let the ship and her captured crew go free or set them adrift, but more often than not, they would load the prisoners onto their own ship, then burn or scuttle the victim's ship to sink it. Many pirate captains offered prisoners the option of joining their ship or alternately force them to sign the articles and be drafted. Sometimes the pirates would lock the prisoners in a hold before they burned the ship and then leave them there to die, or simply maroon them on the nearest island.

Fire Power

While pirates preferred not to fire their weapons at all, they were well-prepared to use them on the fly. Their *cannons*, or guns as they were called, were frequently mounted on wheeled carriages, which allowed them to be moved around the deck as needed. It usually took four to six pirates to man a gun, so if ten guns were being fired in a broadside, forty to sixty pirates would be required to man the weapons. Most cannons were manufactured by the French or British and were initially made of bronze and later cast iron. They were usually about 4 feet long, and weighed around 700 to 900 pounds apiece.

When a pirate ship was close enough to its prey, it was common for the rogues to unleash weapons such as *granado* (or *granada*) *shells* and *stinkpots* onto their prey. Granado shells, or powder flasks, were a primitive type of grenade made of hollow balls of iron, glass, clay, or wood, which weighed about two pounds and could be filled with gunpowder and set with a fuse. During battle, pirates would light the fuse and toss the shells onto the vessel being attacked, causing major chaos as well as injury and death.

$\mathfrak{S}$HIVER ME $\mathfrak{T}$IMBERS

As one would expect, a *stinkpot* was a container filled with any vile smelling item pirates could find. Often, they contained rotted meat among other items, and they would frequently be lit when tossed so that the smoke would spread the smell. Stinkpots were particularly effective if victims were hiding in a hold or cabin, as the odor was sure to send them rushing out to face waiting pirates.

Once pirates had boarded their prey, they would quickly finish the fight with their pistols, knives, and swords. Pistols of the time contained only one shot each before having to be reloaded, so it was not uncommon for a pirate to load several pistols before a battle and string them from ribbons around his neck so he could quickly grab a loaded gun. These hand-to-hand fights were vicious and bloody, the very opposite of the romantic vision of pirates that has been elevated over the centuries. The pirates who sailed during the Golden Age of piracy, like those before and after them, were often bloodthirsty and cruel, not dashing swashbucklers as they are frequently portrayed. This was never more evident than during piracy's heyday, when pirates of the Caribbean struck fear into the hearts of entire nations.

Chapter 11

Pirates of the Caribbean

The Caribbean and West Indies attracted pirates like moths to a flame. Many legendary pirates performed their greatest exploits in these areas and along the eastern coast of America. These are the pirates whose names are most familiar, the individuals who come to mind when the word "pirate" is mentioned. Blackbeard, Charles Vane, Black Bart, and Samuel Bellamy are among those who terrorized and pillaged the area with a vengeance. It was the Golden Age of piracy, and rogues sailed with the single-minded goal of gaining power and securing treasure.

The Golden Age

One might think that the Golden Age of piracy lasted for hundreds of years. In truth, it lasted only a relatively short time. Most historians place the Golden Age as running somewhere between thirty and fifty years, from around 1680 to 1730 with its heyday from 1714 to 1722. By 1730, piracy had nearly disappeared from the Caribbean, but from the last decade of the seventeenth century through the first few decades of the eighteenth century, many factors came together to cause a resurgence in piracy that was as brutal and unpredictable as it had ever been throughout history. During the Golden Age, pirates weren't looking for treasure ships filled with gold and silver—though they certainly wouldn't turn them down if they came upon them—but were instead preying upon regular merchant ships carrying goods from Europe to the Americas and back, or slave ships carrying slaves from Africa to the Caribbean and returning with cargoes of rum and sugar. Fictional pirates in film and literature present us with a romantic and exotic view of pirates, and while those stereotypes were rarely true, there were plenty of fascinating pirates operating during this "golden" era.

Back with a Vengeance

Many factors contributed to the rise of piracy during the Golden Age. First of all, the buccaneering era was coming to an end in the Caribbean. Secondly, by 1687, the Jamaican government passed anti-piracy acts, and the remaining buccaneers and pirates were forced to move outward and expand their target area. War between various European countries was another reason piracy flourished, as privateers acting under letters of marque performed legalized versions of piracy (see Chapter 6).

PIECES of EIGHT

This privateering era would continue until 1714, when peace between England and Spain effectively brought an end to privateers. Suddenly unemployed, these once highly revered sailors were left with choosing between low-paying jobs on merchant ships or becoming pirates. Many saw piracy as the more attractive option.

As slavery increased on Caribbean plantations and in colonial America, the ability to take a slave ship and sell slaves for profit was a huge incentive for men to become pirates. Functioning slaves commanded high prices, and when they could be taken from a slave ship at no cost, the entire price of the cargo would be pure profit once they were sold. Another factor that contributed to the rise in slave trading was that colonial governments were not well regulated, and illicit trade between pirates and colonists was relatively easy, and often welcomed—especially when pirate ships arrived bearing contraband. All of these forces came together and caused the explosion of piracy during the Golden Age.

Destitution or Doubloons

Treasure was not the main commodity that most Golden Age pirates were searching for when they captured a ship. Typically, the first thing that a pirate captain searched for when he claimed a prize was food and medicine for his own men. Blackbeard himself lay siege to the entire port of Charleston, South Carolina so that he could obtain medicine. For the most part, pirates were poor and basic necessities aboard ship were scarce. They would often spend weeks or months at sea, and their food and water stores would quickly be used up or spoil. Stores of medicines would be filled prior to a voyage if possible, but often wouldn't last long given the amount of disease and injury that crews often incurred. In addition, a pirate captain would always be on the lookout for men with certain abilities, and would force those men to join his crew.

Doctors and carpenters were two of the most sought after sailors. Their expertise could come in handy on a pirate ship, and for the most part, they were considered as valuable as food and medicine. After the basics were out of the way, raiding pirates would take cargo, looking for what they could easily sell. They would then either take the captured ship as their own, return the ship to the original crew and let them go, or burn the ship after murdering crewmembers who refused to become pirates. Pirates would deal with captured ships in different ways. Many Golden Age pirates were cruel, and torture and murder were common occurrences.

Once pirates had sold their booty, they would split their share of the profits and head to a safe pirate haven, where they would quickly drink, gamble, and womanize their way through their profits. When their wealth was depleted, they would look to their captain to lead them on another voyage. Pirate life was a vicious circle, and very few were able to save their money and retire from piracy. A closer look at some of the real pirates of the Caribbean shows how at times some of them could be considered fair individuals, but as a group, most were extremely brutal. On occasion, a pirate would retire and live to old age like "Red Legs" Greaves, but most died young and violently like Black Bart.

Sea Rover

Benjamin Hornigold was best known as being mentor to Blackbeard and Samuel Bellamy. Hornigold served as a privateer during the War of Spanish Succession, but when peace was declared in 1713 he moved to pirating. In 1718, he accepted a pardon from Bahamian governor Woodes Rogers, and was later commissioned as a pirate hunter by Rogers, capturing ten pirates and bringing them to justice.

Black Sam Bellamy

Born in Devonshire, England, in 1689, Samuel "Black Sam" Bellamy traveled to America and for a time settled in Massachusetts. Various legends tell of him falling in love with a young girl by the name of Maria Hallett. In 1715, Bellamy heard of a Spanish treasure ship that had sunk off the coast of Florida, and he and a friend decided to salvage the ship. They sailed for Florida, but were unsuccessful in their salvage efforts. Not wanting to return to Maria without some form of riches, Bellamy joined a pirate crew on a ship called the *Mary Anne*, captained by Benjamin Hornigold. When the crew of the *Mary Anne* voted to attack ships of all nations, which was contrary to Hornigold's beliefs, he was summarily deposed and Bellamy became captain. Within a year, Samuel Bellamy had established a base at Trellis Bay on Beef Island in the British Virgin Islands, and had plundered more than fifty ships in the Caribbean and the Atlantic Ocean. Bellamy was additionally referred to by the descriptive nicknames "Black" Bellamy or "Black Sam," because he grew his black hair long and tied it back with a black ribbon.

In late 1716, the British navy sent ships to the Caribbean to capture Bellamy and Blackbeard. Both men evaded capture, and Blackbeard drove the navy out of the area, but Bellamy decided that perhaps it would be wiser to leave the area altogether. As he was departing from the Caribbean, heading back to New England and his love, Maria, he spied an English slave ship called the *Whydah Gally*. The *Whydah* had already taken her cargo of slaves from Africa and traded them in the Caribbean for goods including sugar, indigo, ivory, coins, and weapons. Bellamy and his crew captured the slave ship and took all its booty as their own, then continued to sail north along the Atlantic coast.

In late April of 1717, the *Whydah* struck a sandbar along the coast of Cape Cod during a violent storm. The ship sank, and Bellamy and most of his crew of approximately 140 pirates were killed. The few who survived were captured and tried in Boston, where 7 were hanged and 2 were released after it was decided that they'd not been willing participants in Bellamy's piracy. In 1984, the *Whydah* became the first known pirate ship in United States waters to be salvaged (see Chapter 19).

Charles Vane

Little is known of the early life of Captain Charles Vane, who was an active pirate from 1716 to 1720. He was born in England sometime around the year 1680, and began his pirate ways by joining the crew of Henry Jennings, who at the time was working to salvage a Spanish treasure fleet that had gone down in a storm in 1715. Vane stayed with Jennings for three years, but by early 1718 was sailing as the captain of his own ship, basing himself out of New Providence in the Bahamas. He quickly made a name for himself as a cruel pirate, and by May of that year he'd been reported to the governor of Bermuda by the captains of the two different ships he'd plundered. Both captains were reeling from the torture and murder Vane inflicted upon members of their crews.

By August, governor Woodes Rogers (see Chapter 16) arrived in New Providence with a large contingent of British naval officers, offering pardons to all pirates who were willing to give up pirating. Vane was the only pirate in the town who did not accept his offer.

Charles Vane was entirely against abandoning his piratical career. Pirates who refused to accept Roger's pardon would be tried and executed, and Vane would have nothing of the sort. Instead, he set one of his own ships on fire, steered it directly toward the governor's ship—which was docked in the bay—and fired his cannons. Amid the resulting smoke and turmoil, Vane made a hasty escape.

Terror in the Carolinas

Deciding that the Caribbean was not the safest place for themselves at the time, Vane and his closest and most trusted mate—a pirate by the name of Yeats—set sail for the Carolina coast. Almost immediately after their arrival, they captured four ships. Adding them to their fleet, they began attacking other ships that sailed into or exited the port of Charleston. Angered by pirate attacks, especially those of Vane, the governor of South Carolina commissioned Colonel William Rhett to take two armed sloops and attempt to capture Vane. Around the same time Rhett was pursuing Vane and his fleet, Yeats became enraged that Vane was still considering him a subordinate, and not an equal. Yeats took a ship, fifteen crewmembers, and a hold full of slaves they had recently captured, and left Vane's ship in the dead of night. He sailed into Charleston harbor, turned himself in, and accepted a pardon from the governor.

Vane, in the meantime, sailed off and spent some time at Ocracoke Island, North Carolina, where he met and caroused with Blackbeard. After they went their separate ways, Vane continued to plunder ships bound to or from Charleston, but he was careful to make sure that the crews of the plundered ships overheard his pirates talking about where they were heading. Of course that information would always be incorrect. Unfortunately for

Colonel Rhett, he followed this misinformation, and completely lost track of Vane.

Accusations of Cowardice

Leaving the Carolina area in the latter part of 1718, Vane headed north toward New York. He plundered another two ships off the coast of Long Island, and then saw a third ship that he chose to attack. This proved to be Vane's undoing, as the third ship turned out to be a French warship. Vane decided to retreat, and his men obeyed him, given that their pirate code stated that in a time of battle the captain's word is always the final one, but they weren't happy that Vane turned tail and ran. The next day, Vane's crew, led by his quartermaster Calico Jack Rackham, declared that Vane was a coward. They immediately voted to remove him as captain, and replace him with Calico Jack (see Chapter 15). Vane and the few men who had remained loyal to him were given a small ship and set adrift.

SCUTTLEBUTT

What is a cay?
A cay (pronounced "key") is a small, low island composed mostly of coral or sand. A cay's size is entirely dependent on the weather because they are formed when tides and wind deposit coral and sand onto flat reefs. They can be quickly destroyed as a result of a hurricane.

Vane was down, but not out, and in the next few months he and his remaining crew plundered several ships. For a short time, he regained some of his notoriety, but in February of 1719 Vane's ship met a fierce storm and he was shipwrecked on an uninhabited island in the Bay of Honduras. He and one crewmember were the only ones to survive the shipwreck, and they lived for months on the island by eating fish and turtles. Finally, they were rescued by a passing ship, but Vane's string of bad luck was far from over. While aboard his rescuer's ship, the crew encountered another pirate ship captained by a former buccaneer named Holford. Holford saw Vane working on the ship, and informed the ship's captain who he was rescuing. Holford then put Vane and his surviving crewmember in chains and sailed them to Port Royal, where they were hanged as pirates in March of 1720, following a quick trial. Vane's body was then hung in chains at the entrance to Gun Cay as a warning to other pirates of what would befall them if they were convicted of piracy.

Stede Bonnet

As far as pirates go, Stede Bonnet was one of the more unusual rogues. An established plantation owner on the island of Barbados, Stede was educated, relatively wealthy, and living a comfortable life among upper-class society when he suddenly, and for no known reason, left his plantation owner's life to become a pirate. Since most pirates of the Golden Age were lower-class, uneducated, poor working men, this set Bonnet apart from the majority of his contemporaries, especially in regard to his ship and crew.

When Bonnet decided to become a pirate he purchased his own ship, rather than stealing or capturing one as most pirates did. His ten-gun sloop was called the *Revenge*, for reasons Bonnet shared with no one. Going against normal pirate convention, Bonnet did not have his men sign ship's articles, instead paying them with his own money. He found his crew of about seventy men by going into the taverns in Bridgeport, Barbados, and offering out-of-work seamen jobs as pirates. He told his family and friends that he'd purchased the ship and hired a crew in order to trade between local islands. He then departed in the middle of the night, headed not for other islands, but for the Virginia Capes, the New York coastline, and finally the coast of the Carolinas, where he and his crew plundered several ships, captured a few for Bonnet's own use, and burned the remainder.

In the fall of 1717, Bonnet met up with Blackbeard, who took the *Revenge* for his own fleet and kept the gentleman pirate onboard his ship, the *Queen Anne's Revenge*. Eventually Blackbeard returned to Ocracoke Island, where he allowed Bonnet to take his own ship and leave. Bonnet subsequently went to the governor of North Carolina and secured a pardon and a letter of marque authorizing him to attack Spanish ships. Whether Bonnet intended to "go straight" as a privateer or not, he became sidetracked off Ocracoke Island where he was hunting for Blackbeard, whom he was still angry with over the taking of his ship and his share of loot. He didn't find Blackbeard, but he did decide to revert to piracy, capturing another nine vessels off the Virginia and Carolina coasts, before heading into the Cape Fear River to careen his ship's hull. This pit stop would prove costly, as Colonel Rhett, who was following the false leads Charles Vane had left for his pursuer, found not Vane but Bonnet and his crew. With their ship run aground the pirates were unable to leave, and after a fight that lasted a few hours they surrendered. Rhett took Bonnet and his crew prisoner and moved them to Charleston, where they were imprisoned awaiting trial. Bonnet escaped, but was recaptured; in November of 1718, he and thirty of his crewmembers were hanged.

SHIVER ME TIMBERS

The term *careening* refers to a process where a wooden ship is taken to a shallow area, the masts pulled to the ground, and the ship placed on its side so that it can be repaired and cleaned of seaweed and barnacles that make it awkward to steer. This had to be done every two or three months, and was the most dangerous time for a pirate crew as they were extremely vulnerable to attack.

The Trickster

Howell Davis was a Welsh pirate whose career lasted less than a year in total but was highly intriguing. In 1718, Davis was serving as chief mate on the *Cadogan*, a slave ship that was captured by pirate Edward England off the African coast. It is said that Davis was a very likable man, and England offered him the *Cadogan* as his own. Davis sailed the ship to Barbados, but unfortunately ended up being jailed for three months on suspicion of piracy. Upon his release, he sailed for the West Indies on a ship called *The Buck*, and convinced the crew of the ship to return to piracy and elect him as their captain.

Davis was known for his ability to trick his way through more than a few dicey situations. On one occasion he captured a ship that was larger than his own, which was rare for a pirate, who usually preferred vessels more easily apprehended. Shortly thereafter, he came across an even larger

French ship that he wanted, so he forced the prisoners on the first captured ship to pretend to be pirates, and the French, believing they were about to be attacked by two ships full of pirates, surrendered without a fight. A short time later, Davis even tricked a Portuguese governor into giving him supplies by convincing him that he was an English privateer.

Unfortunately for Davis, his luck sadly ran out in 1719, when he was unable to repeat the privateer ruse on a different local governor in Principe, an island off the coast of Guinea. During his ploy, he was killed by Portuguese soldiers, who determined that his real plan was to hold the governor for ransom.

PIECES of EIGHT

After his death, Davis' crew elected a man by the name of Bartholomew Roberts as their new captain, and his first act as their leader was an attack on Principe to avenge his former captain's murder. This act set the stage for one of the most prolific and brutal pirates on record.

Terror of Black Bart

Bartholomew Roberts was born in Wales and began his career at sea by working as a mate on a slave ship. In June 1719, the slave ship was captured by Howell Davis, and Roberts joined his crew. Now a captain, Roberts' life of piracy would last for less than three years, but it would be one of the most prolific and successful pirate careers in history. After avenging Davis' death, Roberts sailed for Brazil, where he captured booty from several ships, but after the successful plunders, a few of his crew stole the *Rover*, one of the ships in his fleet. Not one to let rebellious thievery stop him, Roberts sailed off in another of his fleet's sloops and continued to capture ships, which he then sailed to New England. Once there, he sold the ships and their cargo and continued his pirating ways in the waters off Newfoundland, where he captured approximately 170 vessels. In late 1719, after commandeering a French ship with twenty-eight guns, he sailed south, capturing more prizes along the coast of colonial America and eventually ending up in the Caribbean.

Rampage in the Caribbean

By now, Roberts had earned the nickname "Black Bart," reportedly because he was very tall, dark, and handsome. He was alternately called the "Great Pirate Roberts," which most likely referred to his immense success as a pirate. In the pirate realm, Roberts was unlike most pirates on several accounts. He didn't drink alcohol, preferring tea instead, and he was known as a flamboyant dresser who liked to wear crimson coats and pants, a red feather in his hat, and a diamond cross on a gold chain around his neck. He was highly respected by his crew, but greatly feared by others, as he was equally known for his brutal and bloodthirsty methods of torture. Roberts' arrival in the Caribbean in 1720 was a continuation of the rampage he'd begun farther north, and in approximately nine months' time he had captured another hundred ships.

Near the end of his time in the Caribbean, Roberts captured a fifty-two-gun warship. Unfortunately for the governor of Martinique, he was present on the ship when Roberts captured it. Roberts hanged the governor from the yardarm of his own ship, then proceeded to torture and murder the rest of the crew. He renamed the ship *Royal Fortune*, and made her his flagship. It was aboard the *Royal Fortune* in 1721, leading his convoy of pirate ships, that Roberts sailed off on what would be his last voyage across the Atlantic.

⚓CUTTLEBUTT

Why did Roberts' flag show two skulls with the initials "A.M.H." and "A.B.H." written on them?

Roberts had a special hatred for the people of Martinique and Barbados. He designed his black flag to show a picture of himself—holding a flaming sword in one hand and a dagger in the other—standing on two human skulls. The skulls were marked with the initials to show that they represented "A Martinican's Head" and "A Barbadian's Head."

West African End

Bartholomew Roberts arrived in West Africa in the summer of 1721, and immediately announced his presence by capturing several slaving vessels. Among other atrocities, Roberts had a history of commandeering slave ships and their human cargo, then forcing the ship's owners to pay a ransom to retrieve their property. During his African voyage, the owner of one of the ships Roberts captured refused to pay the ransom, so Roberts had the ship burned—with the cargo of slaves still onboard. It was at this point that authorities had finally had enough. In February of 1722, the British navy tracked Roberts and his ships and captured the *Great Ranger*, one of his fleet. The following day a British warship caught up with the rest of Roberts' fleet. As the warship passed alongside the *Royal Fortune*, it fired on Roberts and his flagship, and Roberts was struck and instantly killed.

Bartholomew Roberts had always said that he didn't want to be hung out as an example to other pirates, so his crew quickly threw his body overboard so that it couldn't be taken by the British. They continued to fight, but after about three hours they surrendered. The British then liberated three of Roberts' ships, and a large haul of gold and other booty. The remaining members of Roberts' crew were returned to Cape Coast Castle in West Africa, where a mass trial was held. Fifty-four pirates were hanged, thirty-seven were sentenced to life in prison, and seventy African pirates were sold into slavery. The trial and hangings marked the end of the era of Black Bart, who had captured over 400 ships during his brief career as a pirate.

Red Legs Greaves

Many pirates of the Golden Age were known for their inexplicable cruelty, but not all of them were entirely ruthless. One exception to the rule was "Red Legs" Greaves, who was active during the 1670s and 1680s. Greaves was a pirate who was well-respected by his crew, and later, when he lived on his plantation in the Caribbean, was known for his good deeds and charity. From slave to pirate to respected landowner who died of old age, Greaves lived a life that was a direct contradiction to most pirates of the era.

SHIVER ME TIMBERS

The term *red legs* was a common nickname for Scottish sailors of the day. Scottish men were known to wear kilts year round, with nothing to protect their legs from the harsh elements. The Caribbean heat and sun often caused the men to have red legs, especially those who, like Greaves and other Scots, were of fair complexion.

The Stowaway Pirate

Red Legs Greaves was born to Scottish parents who had been sold into slavery after Oliver Cromwell became Lord Protector of Great Britain in 1657. Greaves' parents were tried and found guilty of treason as a result of civil war, and they were sentenced to a life of slavery in Barbados. Shortly after their arrival, their son was born, and as was the custom, the child of slaves became a slave himself. At first Greaves' life was not too terrible, as his parents were lucky enough to have a kindly master, but his fortune changed when both his parents and master died and he was sold to a new master who took pleasure in beating him. One night Greaves decided that escape was his only chance for survival, so he swam across Carlisle Bay and hid aboard a docked ship. His plan was to stow away on the ship when it sailed and remain on it until he reached a distant port where he could feel safe. Unfortunately for Greaves, he picked the wrong ship.

The vessel Greaves had chosen to stow away on was in fact a pirate ship, owned by Captain John Hawkins (not to be confused with the English sea dog of the same name). Hawkins was known as an extremely cruel pirate, who ruled his men by fear, delighted in torturing then murdering his prisoners, and enjoyed mistreating every woman he could lay his hands on. When Hawkins discovered young Greaves hiding on the ship, he forced the boy to sign the ship's articles and become a member of his crew. Ironically, Greaves quickly became a very proficient pirate and earned the respect of his fellow crewmen, but he had no respect for Hawkins and his murderous ways.

A Kinder, Gentler Captain

At some point during their association, Greaves and Hawkins had a falling out. Some stories say that Greaves challenged Hawkins to a duel, while others relate that Hawkins attacked Greaves when Greaves refused to follow his orders. However it came about, when the fight was over, Hawkins was dead. The crew, who were grateful that Greaves had rescued them from the tyranny of serving under Hawkins, immediately elected Greaves as their new captain.

Life aboard ship under Captain Greaves' command was very different for the crew, all of whom signed new articles that included severe penalties for any man who mistreated a prisoner or a woman. Cruelty was no longer tolerated on their ship, and while the pirates continued to capture and plunder vessels, they treated prisoners with respect. As a result of these policies, Greaves soon had a reputation for kindness and morality, as well as being a very successful pirate captain.

PIECES of EIGHT

Red Legs Greaves' greatest success came when he carried out a huge raid on a Spanish pearling fleet (one that transported harvested pearls) off the island of Margarita. After taking the fleet, he also captured the forts located on the island, where he and his crew secured a huge booty of gold and pearls.

Social Security

Throughout history there have been few pirates who legitimately retired and died in peace. Most pirates would squander their earnings and continue pillaging, and amid that vicious circle, most would die violent deaths at a young age. Greaves, however, once again proved that he was not a typical pirate. His share of plunder from the Margarita raid was more than enough for him to live on for the rest of his life, so he headed to the Caribbean island of Nevis, where he purchased a plantation and set about living life as a free man—or so he thought.

Greaves' pirate past came back to haunt him when he was recognized by a former victim, who immediately turned him in to authorities. Like all pirates, he had a bounty on his head, and the victim wanted to collect it. Despite the fact that Greaves hadn't committed the atrocities other pirates had, he was found guilty of piracy and sentenced to die by hanging. While awaiting his execution in Port Royal, Jamaica, the great earthquake of 1692 struck the town and most of the residents were drowned (see Chapter 16). But once again, luck was with Greaves, and he was one of the few survivors of the devastation. After the disaster, he was rescued by a whaling ship and joined their crew for a short period of time. Later he became a pirate hunter, and earned a pardon for his piracy, which allowed him to return to his plantation home on Nevis, where he lived out his life doing good deeds.

Black-hearted Demons

Many pirates of the Golden Age exhibited a single-minded ferocity that only thieves and murderers would likely understand. A handful of these rogues stand out above the rest, either because of their mindless atrocities or their successful pillaging. There is no doubt that a pirate the caliber of Black Bart was feared by any man, woman, or child who sailed across an ocean and, given his reputation for brutality, there was ample reason to be frightened. But Black Bart wasn't the only loathsome creature making waves across the Caribbean. There was indeed another pirate wreaking havoc on innocent mariners, one so feared that he was said to be the devil incarnate.

Chapter 12

Blackbeard

Few people would immediately recognize the name Edward Teach, but it's likely that everyone would recognize his alter ego—Blackbeard. Though his career as a pirate was short, his exploits and legendary rule-by-fear tactics left an indelible mark on maritime history. For a single man to strike such fear in people speaks highly of his remarkable piratical abilities. The light that shines twice as bright, burns half as long, and Blackbeard's light would blaze across oceans and nations, whose residents would embellish his legend for centuries to come.

Fear and Loathing on the High Seas

The stories of renowned pirates are riddled with questionable "facts," sketchy personal descriptions, and tales of unbelievable depravity, all obscured by a mist of lore and legend. This is perhaps most true of Edward Teach, who in 1717 was described as "a tall spare man with a very black beard which he wore very long."

In searching for facts about Teach's formative years, confusion begins with his surname, which is variously given as Thatch, Tach, Tache, Tash, Teach, and even Drummond. His true name will likely never be known with certainty. But that matters little in the scheme of things, given the fame and fortune that Mr. Teach enjoyed as a result of his piratical career. Blackbeard was by no means the most prolific pirate, but he was without a doubt the most famous.

The Privateering of Edward Teach

When piracy was at its height during the Golden Age, the public was in awe of the adventurous audacity of pirates, and Edward Teach was one of the most audacious pirates to command a crew. Teach is thought to have been born around 1680 in the British seaport of Bristol. Unlike most pirates, Teach could read and write, which suggests he was educated at some point in his youth. Many accounts of his early years suggest that he set his sights on becoming a merchant seaman, which seems plausible given the talent he later exhibited under his captain, Benjamin Hornigold.

There's little information about Teach until he signed on to become a privateer primarily focused on attacking the French. Some reports have it that he landed in Jamaica and became a privateer for the English sometime during the War of Spanish Succession, also known as Queen Anne's War, which lasted from 1702 to 1713.

PIECES of EIGHT

Soon after Queen Anne's War, it is said that Edward Teach allegedly migrated to the Bahamas and ended up in the pirate haven of New Providence. It was there that he met renowned privateer Benjamin Hornigold and signed on to his crew.

Queen Anne's Revenge

During the war, Benjamin Hornigold, like many other privateers, was enjoying great success in capturing and plundering both Spanish and French vessels. The ending of that war and the subsequent peace agreements left privateers in a precarious position. Many were unable or unwilling to abandon the lifestyle that such freedom afforded them. As a result, Hornigold and many of his contemporaries turned to piracy as full-time employment. Teach proved to be a highly capable seaman when serving under Hornigold, a successful and well-respected privateer who had one fatal flaw. Being an Englishman, he refused to allow his pirate crew to attack British or Dutch vessels.

As is the case with most historical records of piracy, accounts vary as to what transpired next on Hornigold's ship. Some say that Hornigold's crew became angry about his loyalty to the British and they removed him as captain in favor of Samuel Bellamy. The more common version of the story has it that Hornigold maintained his captaincy despite his refusal to attack the British. Whether under Hornigold or Bellamy, it's known that the pirates captured a French slave ship named *La Concorde* in late 1717, and that it was given to the command of Edward Teach.

Sea Rover

One of Blackbeard's trusted compatriots was an escaped African slave called Caesar. It's said that Caesar was an African chieftain prior to his being captured by slavers. Bad weather enabled him to escape his captors and eventually serve under Blackbeard. Caesar was aboard *Queen Anne's Revenge* when she was taken in 1718. He was later hanged as a result of his loyalty and piracy.

Teach renamed the ship *Queen Anne's Revenge*, likely in reference to the English war against France in which he'd first taken part as a privateer. Teach outfitted the vessel with an additional twenty cannons, bringing the total to forty, which turned *Queen Anne's Revenge* into a formidable warship by any standard of the day. With his powerful flagship, Teach began nurturing his image and what would become his legacy as Blackbeard.

Murder and Mayhem

Blackbeard sailed throughout the Caribbean and as far as the coast of Africa, taking English, French, Spanish, and Portuguese prizes. He was a tall and physically imposing man, and was known to braid his long beard into plaits tied with ribbon. Before storming captured ships, he would arrange slow-burning cannon matches under his hat and set them smoldering to increase his fearful appearance. The wisping smoke that curled around his face and head gave people cause to wonder if he was Satan.

As a pirate, Blackbeard made a point of terrifying his victims as much as was humanly possible, and very likely took a certain amount of professional pride in doing so. The tactic of frightening his prey served a practical purpose as his legend spread like wind across the high seas. Those who quickly surrendered and turned over their treasure loads to Blackbeard were usually spared. Those who resisted were punished, and the greater the resistance, the worse the punishment would be. One of his most famous exploits took place in May of 1718, when he brought the city and port of Charleston, South Carolina, to its knees by holding one of its citizens for ransom. He and his flotilla lay in wait at the harbor's entrance and captured all ships that dared leave or enter the port. Tempers flared as several days passed, and the siege escalated until Blackbeard's requests were finally addressed. What one might find particularly interesting about this encounter is that Blackbeard's impetus for threatening the town was his dire need for medicines for his crew. When at last he received the medicines, after a week-long negotiation, he promptly left the area.

A Gentlemanly Friendship

While sailing off the coast of the Carolinas in America, Blackbeard came across "gentleman pirate" Stede Bonnet. While Bonnet was a completely inept seaman, Blackbeard took a liking to him and invited him aboard the *Queen Anne's Revenge* as a guest, at the same time taking Bonnet's ship into his own fleet. While it's probable that Bonnet was a virtual prisoner aboard Blackbeard's ship, the arrangement seemed to suit them both. Bonnet was relieved of any real decision-making, and Blackbeard's fondness for Bonnet seemed genuine. The two would eventually part ways when Blackbeard swindled Bonnet out of his shares of stolen loot and left him ashore. Blackbeard then found a safe refuge on Ocracoke Island off the coast of North Carolina. The island was surrounded by shallow inlets and bays that provided a good deal of security for Blackbeard's ships and crews. Fully manned British warships found the area around the island virtually impossible to navigate, so Blackbeard moved about with impunity.

Downsizing

With a fleet of three ships—*Queen Anne's Revenge*, the sloop *Adventure*, and another unrecorded sloop—and a crew of about 400, Blackbeard attempted to sail into Beaufort Inlet in North Carolina in 1718. While doing so, the heavy *Queen Anne's Revenge* was firmly grounded in the shallows. Despite attempts to free her, the ship was stuck fast, so Blackbeard transferred her cargo to the lighter sloops and left her stranded, along with most of his crew. Blackbeard would never return for his crewmates—he left them to their own devices for survival. In one fell swoop, Blackbeard reduced the unwieldy size of his crew from 400 to about 40. Some historians maintain that the grounding of the flagship was an unintentional accident. Given Blackbeard's propensity for lying and deceit, especially among those who trusted him, the argument for his having planned the incident to rid himself of too many crewmembers is difficult to ignore.

ₚIECES of ℰIGHT

One of the enduring legends about Blackbeard's excesses relates that during a drinking bout with his crew in the cabin of the *Queen Anne's Revenge*, Blackbeard cocked both of his pistols and fired them indiscriminately. One of the musket balls tore through the kneecap of Blackbeard's first mate, Israel Hand, crippling him. Legend has it that Blackbeard's only comment was, "If I don't kill one of them now and then, they'll forget who I am."

Begging Your Pardon

Shortly after grounding the *Queen Anne's Revenge*, Blackbeard requested a meeting with the governor of North Carolina, Charles Eden, and arranged for a King's Pardon. It's likely that a bit of bribery was part of the arrangement; Blackbeard and twenty of his crewmen were indeed granted pardons. With stolen documents, Blackbeard managed to legally register the sloop *Adventure*, and keep her anchored close to home. Blackbeard also bought a fine home in the town of Bath, and married sixteen-year-old Mary Ormond, the daughter of a North Carolina planter. While it appeared that Blackbeard was changing his ways and aspiring to a life of respectability, the realities of his life were far different. For starters, Blackbeard's new wife was not his first—but was said to be his thirteenth.

While on the surface Blackbeard was playing the part of a country squire, he continued to sneak out to sea with his crew, plundering small coastal ships. Even while he socialized with many of the local aristocracy, including the governor, Blackbeard's thieving ways were hardly behind him. From most accounts, it appears that to the North Carolina gentry, Blackbeard was a bit of a roguish celebrity, and while piracy was perhaps a bit shady, it was hardly despicable.

SCUTTLEBUTT

Where did the expression "scuttlebutt" come from?
Gossip was always virulent aboard a pirate ship. Scuttlebutt is the naval equivalent to the modern-day practice of gossiping "around the water cooler." The "butt" was a barrel of fresh drinking water, and the "scuttle" a hole in the barrel through which sailors would draw water. Sailors would go to the butt for a drink and linger to chat with others.

In 1718, Blackbeard went to sea with his crew and sailed to the Bahamas where they captured two French ships, one of which was laden with sugar and cocoa. Blackbeard sailed the loaded ship back to Ocracoke Island and met with Tobias Knight, the chief justice of North Carolina. Blackbeard told Knight that the French ship had simply been "discovered," apparently abandoned. During court proceedings, the ridiculous story that Blackbeard had concocted about the French vessel was found to be the truth, and he was permitted to keep everything he'd "found," after delivering sixty barrels of sugar to Governor Eden and twenty barrels of sugar to Tobias Knight.

Blow the Man Down

While the governor of North Carolina turned a blind eye to Blackbeard's acts of piracy and openly accepted what could only be described as outright bribes, the governor of Virginia, Alexander Spotswood, had precisely the opposite reaction. Although the North Carolina coast was undoubtedly far outside of Spotswood's jurisdiction, the governor was unflinching in his resolve to rid the Americas of piracy. Blackbeard and his legendary seafaring atrocities were too notorious to ignore. Spotswood was also aware that one of Blackbeard's former crewmembers, William Howard, was being held for trial for his association with piracy, and particularly with Blackbeard. In an effort to save his own neck, Howard gladly gave the details of Blackbeard's hideout on Ocracoke Island.

Calm Before the Storm

At the behest of Governor Spotswood, Lieutenant Robert Maynard of the Royal Navy was put in command of fifty-five sailors and marines to track down Blackbeard and his gang of pirates. Spotswood sweetened the expedition by putting a £100 bounty on Blackbeard's head. Maynard knew that a British man-of-war ship couldn't possibly sail into the shallows of Ocracoke Island, so he commissioned two small sloops, the *Jane* and the *Ranger*, to attack the pirate lair. Records indicate that Blackbeard was aware that he was being hunted, although there's no explanation as to why he would choose to stay and fight.

Damnation for Quarter

On the morning of November 22, 1718, Maynard sailed his sloops into the inlet where Blackbeard lay at anchor in his own sloop, the *Adventure*. Blackbeard's crew cut the anchor ropes of *Adventure* as Maynard and the

Jane drew within shouting distance. It's said that Blackbeard yelled out, "Damnation seize my soul if I give you quarter or take any from you." Then the pirates fired a broadside of grapeshot across the bow of the *Jane*, killing or injuring nearly half of her crew. Maynard immediately ordered his remaining men below decks and into the hold where they were to remain utterly still and at the ready.

As the two ships came closer together, Blackbeard saw that there was no one left alive on the decks of the *Jane*, and ordered his pirates to board her, thinking that all of the British had been killed in the first volley. As soon as the pirates boarded, Maynard called his remaining troops out of hiding, and a bloody hand-to-hand battle instantly ensued. It was reported that Maynard broke his sword blade against the cartridge box Blackbeard was wearing and then stepped backward, fully expecting to be killed on the spot by the huge pirate. Instead, Blackbeard was cut down by the sword of a Scotsman who was one of Maynard's crew. When Blackbeard finally perished, it seemed a miracle. It's said that he continued fighting despite taking a half dozen or so shots and over twenty cuts to his body. Upon his death, the remaining pirates immediately gave up the fight and were taken into custody.

PIECES of EIGHT

Lieutenant Maynard lopped off Blackbeard's head with a cutlass and threw the corpse overboard, where according to legend, the headless body swam around the ships three times before sinking out of sight. Blackbeard's head was tied to the bow of the *Jane* as a trophy and proof of the famed pirate's demise.

Immortalization of a Raging Rogue

Blackbeard's death at the hand of Lieutenant Maynard and his crew marked the end of a rampage that had literally held siege over maritime industry. As a man, Edward Teach was an intelligent and highly capable seaman. As a pirate, Blackbeard was a seemingly soulless demon whose hellish appearance is perhaps unrivaled among history's most vile criminals. One must ask, what is it about Blackbeard that generations of people, including historians and scholars, have found so fascinating? Was it his allegedly Satanic appearance? Or his brilliant strategies and rule-by-fear tactics? Perhaps it was his lust for achieving that which most pirates could only dream of. Whatever the reason, it is remarkable that Blackbeard's short stint as a pirate should have given him such long-lived fame.

Head's Up

One can argue that Blackbeard's end was a fitting one for a pirate of his stature. After all, any rogue worth his salt wouldn't dare go down without a fight, any more than he'd lay claim to the virtue of shooting fish in a barrel. Blackbeard had a heroic death, the stuff legends are made of, and it was befitting for a pirate who fought so hard to make a name for himself. That said, one might find it intriguing to know that the minor complication of Blackbeard's decapitation failed to end his worldly presence—or so it's alleged.

SCUTTLEBUTT

Did Blackbeard really bury his treasure?
No one knows for certain if Blackbeard's alleged buried treasure even exists, and to date nothing has been recovered aside from his prized flagship, *Queen Anne's Revenge*, which is currently being excavated. Toward the end of his life, Blackbeard is said to have emphatically stated "Nobody but me and the Devil knows where my money is buried and the one what lives longest will get it all!"

Almost fifty years ago, author Robert I. Nesmith wrote about his friend and colleague Edward Rowe Snow in a collection of tales entitled *Dig for Pirate Treasure*. In it, he relates a night that Snow, himself a prolific writer of New England pirate lore, summoned him to his home in Cape Cod on a dark and stormy night to see something very exciting that he'd acquired. What Snow revealed to Nesmith was a box that contained what Snow believed to be the "silver-coated" skull of Edward Teach. According to Snow, the skull was retrieved by a man in Bath, where Blackbeard's head ended up on display after it was removed from the *Jane*. After being covered in silver, it began a journey of ownership from a college fraternity through several generations of a tavern owner's family where it made occasional appearances in the tavern—as a drinking cup. As a matter of chance, Snow learned of its existence and purchased it for himself. Nesmith was skeptical, but Snow, an entirely sober individual, insisted it was Blackbeard himself—especially given the fact that it spoke to him. The skull was donated to the Peabody Essex Museum in Salem, Massachusetts, when Edward Snow passed away in the 1980s. To this day, many individuals remain hopeful that it will one day be authenticated.

Notorious Pirates

13

A handful of pirates became more renowned than others because of their larger-than-life adventures or their singular accomplishments or failures. A few pirates, such as William Dampier, would become known in scientific and seafaring circles for their observations and navigational skills. Others entered piracy and privateering after long and reputable careers as naval officers and shipping merchants. Still others, such as Woodes Rogers, would find themselves appointed to powerful political positions. Pirates and privateers came from all walks of life, and some established reputations that would be recorded in history and legend.

The World According to Dampier

William Dampier was a buccaneer of questionable ability and a navigator of considerable skill who circumnavigated the world three times. Although he was known by his shipmates as a poor leader in battle, for his use of foul language, and for his unabashed conceit, he was also a gifted and exceptionally curious explorer who wrote detailed accounts of the places that he visited and the flora and fauna that grew there. Dampier began his life as the son of a cobbler in Somerset, England, in 1651, and in his youth was apprenticed to a shipmaster. Records indicate that Dampier sailed to the East Indies and took part in naval engagements during the Anglo-Dutch War in 1673. After falling ill, he was put ashore in Jamaica, where in 1674 he found work as an under-manager on a sugar plantation. It appears that Dampier soon returned to the sea, engaging in trading along the coast of Jamaica and nearby islands, eventually drifting to Central America.

Becoming a Buccaneer

Dampier spent some time in Central America, working with log cutters—who, when they weren't cutting logs, would join passing pirates to assist in raids on villages or merchant ships. Eventually Dampier joined a pirate group that traveled up and down the coast of Central America, raiding settlements along the way. By 1679, he was back in Jamaica, where he spent the next several years as a pirate, sailing with various buccaneer crews. When he wrote about his travels during this time, he referred to himself as a privateer, and though the captains he served under usually did have some type of privateering commission, they certainly didn't limit their attacks to vessels they had permission to raid. Dampier sailed under such captains as Richard Dawkins and Bartholomew Sharp, and participated in attacks on Portobello, Panama, and Arica, Peru, as well as numerous smaller towns in the Caribbean and along the Central American coast.

The First Step

Dampier joined John Cook on a journey around South America to ports on the Pacific side of the continent. They captured a few ships, but had limited success in taking rich prizes. He eventually left the group to join with

Captain Charles Swan, who was sailing to the Orient. On this voyage, Dampier had the distinction of becoming the first Englishman to set foot on the Australian continent.

By the time he arrived back in England, Dampier had made his first "round the world" trip, and used his journals written during the adventure to write and, in 1697, publish his first book, *A New Voyage Round the World*. The book was well received by the admiralty of England, and he was subsequently given command of the *HMS Roebuck* and sent to explore the South Seas. The 1699 trip was a disaster, as Dampier made no new discoveries and the *Roebuck* sank after developing a serious leak. In addition, Dampier was court-martialed and condemned for his treatment of an officer while asea, and was declared unfit to command any of Her Majesty's ships.

Dampier spent the remainder of his sailing years serving as navigator on various voyages, including sailing under privateer Captain Woodes Rogers. He wrote two more books detailing his travels and the lands he visited—*Voyages and Descriptions*, published in 1699, and *A Voyage to New Holland*, published in 1703. During his life Dampier crossed three oceans and visited four continents, leaving behind a very well-written and descriptive tale of the places he traveled. He died in London in 1715.

PIECES of EIGHT

Two hundred years before William Dampier's time, Ferdinand Magellan had named the Pacific Ocean from the Latin *Mare Pacificum*, or "peaceful sea." Dampier found the vast ocean anything but peaceful, and drew maps of his own that labeled only the waters just off western South America as the "Pacific Sea." He stubbornly insisted on renaming the rest of the ocean "The Great South Sea."

Christopher Myngs

A distinguished naval officer and war hero in England, Christopher Myngs was also a buccaneer and mentor to Henry Morgan. Born in 1625, Myngs joined the Royal Navy at a young age; by 1656, when he first arrived in Jamaica, he had worked his way up to the rank of captain. A year later, he became the commander of the Jamaican squadron of naval ships and began leading raids on Spanish vessels and settlements. At first, profits were small, as Spanish port inhabitants would learn in advance that the English were coming and would take their treasure and flee inland. Myngs countered this by making surprise attacks with small fleets. He orchestrated attacks on the ports of Cumana and Coro in Venezuela, and Puerto Caballos in Honduras, with several small forces at the same time. The raids yielded more than £250 million. Myngs divided the treasure among his troops without saving shares for the governor or for the English treasury, and he was ordered back to England to be tried on charges of embezzlement.

Fortunately for Myngs, his arrival in England coincided with King Charles II's return to the throne, and amid political upheaval, charges were never pursued. Myngs returned to Jamaica in 1662, serving as the captain of the *HMS Centurion*. With Spain and England now at peace, Myngs was not supposed to raid Spanish settlements, but he ignored his orders and led an attack on Santiago, Cuba, and a subsequent raid on the port of San Francisco on the coast of Mexico. Spain complained to England about the attacks, and Charles II recalled Myngs to England. Instead of meting out punishment, Charles promoted him to vice-admiral. Myngs died in a battle against the Dutch in 1666 after being struck by a cannonball.

Woodes Rogers: Beginning of the End

Born in England in 1679, Woodes Rogers began his career as a privateer preying on French vessels sailing in English waters. When French prizes became scarce, Rogers headed for the Pacific Ocean, with the intent of becoming a buccaneer. Because he'd never sailed the Pacific, he hired William Dampier to be his navigator, and in 1709 they rounded South America's Cape Horn and began attacking Spanish vessels along the South American coast. They continued raiding the coastline, traveling as far north as California before returning to England in 1711. In 1717, Rogers was appointed governor of the Bahama Islands, a pirate haven that was in need of moral renovation. Upon his arrival at the islands in 1718, he offered the King's pardon to any pirates who would give up piracy. Most of those present did so—at least for a short time, and Rogers even hired some of them as pirate hunters. Rogers' efforts signaled the end of the Golden Age of piracy. He died in New Providence in 1732.

George Lowther

Little is known of George Lowther's life until he became first mate on the English slave ship *Gambia Castle* in 1721. The vessel was docked for months off the coast of Gambia, Africa, waiting for a cargo of slaves, a delay that didn't help the crew, who were suffering from dysentery, malaria, and scurvy. Lowther and his crewmates grew weary of waiting and dealing with illness, so they decided to sail away with the *Gambia Castle* while the captain was ashore. Once that was accomplished, the crew elected Lowther as their new captain and decided to go on the account.

SHIVER ME TIMBERS

Going *on the account* refers to making a voyage as pirates. As such, the crew were aware that they might perform illegal acts, and that each of them would have to account for their own actions with the law if necessary. The pirates would also sign articles under the stipulation of "no prey, no pay," meaning that they were working for free if they didn't take any prizes.

While sailing for the Grand Cayman Islands, Lowther and his crew came across the English naval ship *HMS Greyhound*, which was captained by Benjamin Edwards. Lowther surprised the *Greyhound* at anchor, beat the crew, then set the ship afire and sailed away. Following that incident, Lowther sailed with pirates Charles Harris and Edward Low, and took a few prizes with them, but they parted company after a short time. In 1722, Lowther and his men put up at a small cay known as Blanquilla, north of Venezuela, to repair his ship. The crew had almost completed the job when a Royal sloop, the *HMS Eagle* captained by Walter Moore, spotted them and attacked. The pirates attempted to run, but only about a dozen—including Lowther—escaped through a cabin window of the ship and hid on the island. Moore's men set off to find the escapees with plans to bring them to justice. They captured most of them, but when they found Lowther he was dead, with a pistol in his hand and a bullet in his head. Lowther, it seemed, preferred taking his own life to facing a trial and the hangman's noose.

The Tale of William Kidd

Captain Kidd is often assumed to be one of the more successful pirate figures in history. Although William Kidd was certainly an adequate sea captain who saw his share of successes, his final legacy was as a hunted pirate and political dupe. Born in 1645 in Scotland, William Kidd went to sea as a young man and achieved some successes against the French as a privateer for England. In 1691, he settled in New York City and married a wealthy twenty-year-old widow with whom he fathered two daughters. Kidd's wealth by marriage put him in the company of New York elite, and he became a respected merchant captain and businessman.

A Questionable Deal

In 1695, Kidd entered into a contract with the governor of New York and several other wealthy businessmen to assemble a privateering vessel and crew for the purpose of raiding French interests in the East Indies (present-day Southeast Asia). The details of the contract forced Kidd to invest thousands of dollars of his own money, and to guarantee the success of the privateering venture with his own capital. The financial risks he accepted as part of this endeavor were highly unusual for the time, and it appears that Kidd was coerced into the arrangement by political pressures and threats to his personal business interests.

The ship Kidd was to take into this venture was supposed to have been a privateering vessel built expressly for the purpose and manned by the most experienced and capable hands that he could assemble. The ship, the *Adventure Galley*, turned out to be a leaky and untrustworthy refitted merchant ship past its prime, and the crew of handpicked expert sailors was conscripted and pressed into service by the English Navy almost as soon as the *Adventure Galley* left port. Kidd was left with an ill-suited and untrustworthy crew of malcontents who would contribute greatly to his eventual undoing. During his cruise to the East Indies, he ran low on provisions and lost dozens of his crew to scurvy and cholera. The *Adventure Galley*'s few run-ins with potentially lucrative vessels proved disastrous, and as a result, Kidd quarreled with his gunner, William Moore, who accused Kidd of cowardice in the face of conflict. In a rage, Kidd struck Moore in the head and killed him with the closest and unlikeliest weapon at hand—an iron-hooped wooden bucket.

The Privateer Turns Pirate

The only substantial prize Kidd and his crew took on their journey was a heavily laden Armenian ship commanded by an English captain. When news of the capture of this vessel reached British authorities, Kidd and his crew were branded as pirates. Upon his return to America, Kidd attempted to negotiate with the governor of New York, his original financial business investor, and agreed to come into the city of his own free will. Much to Kidd's dismay, he was immediately clapped into irons and sent to England in 1700 to stand trial for piracy and the murder of William Moore. Kidd was found guilty and hanged at Execution Dock in London on May 23, 1701. His body was displayed for two years as a warning to would-be pirates.

PIECES of EIGHT

William Kidd's body was encased in a *gibbet* hanging from a bridge over the River Thames in England. A gibbet is an iron cage designed specifically to display the bodies of executed criminals. A popular display for curious gawkers, it would often remain in place for years.

Edward England's Fancy

Little is known about the early life of Edward England, except that he was born Edward Seeger somewhere in Ireland. His birth year is unknown, but by the mid-1700s he was working as an officer on a Jamaican trading sloop that was captured in 1717 by pirate Christopher Winter. Seeger joined Winter's crew, and for unknown reasons changed his surname to England. He remained with Winter until 1718, when he stole a sloop in New Providence and set sail with his own crew. They soon captured a larger ship, which they named the *Royal James*, and began plundering their way along the coast of Africa, capturing a dozen ships in the next year.

By 1720, England and his first mate, John Taylor, were sailing in the Indian Ocean. England subsequently captured a thirty-four gun Dutch ship, which he named *Fancy* and made his new flagship. In August of that year, the *Fancy* took on an English ship called the *Cassandra*. A long and bloody battle ensued, during which both ships were badly damaged and both crews suffered major losses. England lost ninety of his crewmembers. In the end, the captain of the *Cassandra* gathered his surviving men and escaped to an island near Madagascar, leaving England's crew to liberate the *Cassandra*'s booty, which amounted to a hefty £75,000.

SCUTTLEBUTT

What is a round robin?

Anglicized from the French term *rond roubon*, a round robin was a petition submitted by seamen to ship's officers requesting changes aboard ship. The document would be encircled and secured by a ribbon that was signed by crewmembers. This practice prevented the officers from identifying a single individual as the instigator.

After about a week, the *Cassandra*'s captain and his men, who were on the verge of starvation, emerged from the woods of the island and surrendered to England. Taylor and most of the other pirates wanted to kill them, but England insisted they be set free, even giving them the damaged *Fancy* to make their escape. In an absolute rage over England's generosity, Taylor led a mutiny against his captain and marooned him on the island where *Cassandra*'s crew had hidden. England eventually made his way to Madagascar, where he was reduced to begging for food. A victim of his own humane nature, he died shortly thereafter.

The Life and Times of Henry Every

Henry Every (or Avery) was born in Plymouth, England, sometime in the mid-1650s. Accounts of his early years place him as a sailor in the Royal

Navy and an illegal slave trader. By 1694, Every was operating as a privateer for Spain with a license against the French. He reportedly stole the ship he was serving on while his drunken captain was passed out, and in doing so he and the crew sailed into a life of piracy. They subsequently captured one French and three British vessels before taking the ultimate prize that would make him a celebrity in his own time—and the subject of a stage play entitled *The Successful Pyrate.*

In 1695, Every's forty-six gun flagship, also called the *Fancy,* joined up with five other pirate vessels off the Arabian coast. There they captured two Indian treasure ships carrying 500 passengers and crew. During the assault, they raped the female passengers, and then took the larger of the two ships and returned to the Bahamas where Every bribed the governor in exchange for protection. As it turned out, he needed it. The ships Every and his crew plundered were owned by the Great Moghul of India, who was so angered by the attack that he offered an astonishing reward of £500 per crewman for their capture. Because of the publicity, Every reportedly purchased a small sloop and sailed to Ireland, where he is thought to have changed his name to Benjamin Bridgeman and lived in obscurity for the rest of his life, even while his piratical tale was being showcased on the stages of London.

Jean Lafitte: The King of Barataria

The swamps and bayous of southern Louisiana in the early 1800s were home to one of the most famous and colorful privateering characters in American history. Jean Lafitte was born in unclear circumstances around 1781 to parents of possibly French and Spanish heritage. Little is known of his early life until he came into prominence as a pirate and businessman who dealt primarily in contraband goods around New Orleans. It's thought that Lafitte was the eldest of three brothers who were born in France and made their way to South America as privateers.

Smuggling and Contraband

In 1807, the United States placed embargoes on foreign trade goods coming into New Orleans, and the Lafittes relocated to Louisiana to take advantage of the possibilities that were offered by the resulting black market of smuggled goods. The region around the island of Grand Terre, near New Orleans, became a center for smuggling operations and was dubbed Barataria by the pirates and smugglers who brought their contraband into the country to avoid the trade embargo. Jean Lafitte spearheaded the operations of his family, organizing the disposal of smuggled goods through legitimate merchants and distributors in New Orleans. Eventually, the flamboyant activities of Lafitte and his fellow smugglers caught the attention of the governor of Louisiana, who in 1814 ordered the pirates to disperse and offered a bounty for the arrest of the Lafittes.

$\mathbb{P}$IECES of $\mathbb{E}$IGHT

In an effort to bring order to the smuggling and piracy activities in Barataria, Louisiana governor William Clairborne offered a $500 bounty for the arrest of Jean Lafitte. Lafitte responded by doubling the dollar figure and offering a bounty on the head of the governor himself!

Lafitte at War

During this same period, the United States had declared war with England (called the War of 1812), and the Lafittes in Barataria had been approached by the British with an offer to join English forces. Lafitte requested a few weeks to consider the suggestion, and immediately made a proposition of his own to the Louisiana governor in which he offered his services to the United States in return for clemency. The governor wisely accepted Lafitte's proposal, and Lafitte's band of pirates, probably numbering over 1,000, went on to play a deciding role in the American victory at the Battle of New Orleans on January 8, 1815. Unbeknownst to either the American or English forces, a peace treaty had been signed two weeks earlier, and this battle would be the last violent act of war between the two countries. Despite Lafitte's heroic support of the United States government, his smuggling operations were effectively squelched by the Louisiana authorities. Lafitte then moved his base of operations to Texas and eventually returned to piracy and privateering in Central America. His final days are unrecorded, but he continues to be one of the most romantic and revered characters in American pirate lore.

A Walk on the Wild Side

Piracy was a path designed to attract fascinating, desperate, and in many cases, inherently unstable adventurers and rebels who were destined to experience life completely outside any normal boundaries. The next chapter continues to explore the deeds and misdeeds, lives, and inevitable demises of famous and not-so-famous pirates of the high seas. Fame, fortune, and fatality were the keys to every pirate's existence, and skill and luck were the only things that kept most pirates alive.

Chapter 14

Fame, Fortune, and Fatality

In the pirate realm there were thousands of men who set sail with the hope of finding a better life. For some, this meant attaining great riches and the status that comes with retiring as a successful pirate. Others chose their path early in life and continued because pirating was all they knew. Many of these pirates stayed the course, while others took a path riddled with madness and unspeakable acts of torture. A lucky few achieved true fame and fortune, but the vast majority were fatally expelled to Davy Jones' Locker.

14

From Rags to Riches

Most pirates lived from voyage to voyage, plundering a ship before heading back to port to spend their share of the booty on booze, gambling, and wenches. There were a few, however, who either saved and invested their shares or made a huge haul or two and then retired to live off their wealth. While those who used piracy to go from rags to riches are the exceptions to the rule, they did exist and some of them lived out their lives in the lap of luxury. Buccaneer Henry Morgan and Red Legs Greaves are two of the more famous pirate success stories, but other pirates including Robert Surcouf, Henry Jennings, and Nathaniel North also found prosperity in their piratical careers.

Robert Surcouf

Robert Surcouf was a French privateer operating in the late 1700s and early 1800s. After beginning his career as captain of a French slave ship, he moved on to piracy, capturing several ships in the West Indies but losing his share of booty to the government because he didn't have a letter of marque. After securing one from France, Surcouf continued disrupting British shipping in the Indian Ocean. He captured nearly fifty vessels during his career, and later acted as advisor to Napoleon Bonaparte on matters of naval strategy. Surcouf died wealthy and well-respected among his peers, and was even escorted to his burial at sea by a flotilla of fifty sailboats.

PIECES of EIGHT

Captain Sir Francis Verney was a British corsair during the 1600s. A restless soul, he was unwilling to wait for his family inheritance, so he turned to piracy. One historian states that Verney had an odd manner of dress, favoring turbans and shoes that curled at the toes, but that didn't help his success as a pirate. He died in a pauper's hospital in 1611.

Henry Jennings

Henry Jennings spent two years, from 1715 to 1717, as a British privateer operating under a license from the Jamaican government. In July 1715, Jennings led 300 men and three ships in a raid against a salvage crew working the wreckage of a Spanish treasure fleet that went down during a hurricane. Jennings and his crew defeated the salvagers and liberated the 350,000 pesos' worth of treasure recovered from the wreck. On their way back to Jamaica, they attacked and captured another Spanish ship and its cargo, which was worth another 60,000 pesos. Jennings continued to capture rich prizes for another two years, then accepted a pardon from the British government in 1717 and comfortably lived out his life in Bermuda.

Nathaniel North

In contrast to Henry Jennings, Nathaniel North was a seaman who spent his pirate years working on other captains' ships. His ability to swim (which was unusual at the time—even for pirates) saved his life on more than one occasion. North earned enough wealth during his years on the sea to retire to Madagascar, where he acquired an estate and "several wives and children," staying there until he was killed while trying to settle a dispute among native tribesmen.

Others who made their fortune from piracy include:

John (James) Plantain: A Jamaican-born pirate who sailed the Indian Sea in the 1720s, then built a fortress at Ranter Bay, Madagascar. Plantain declared himself the "King of Ranter Bay" and lived a lavish life.

John Taylor: After beginning his piratical career sailing with Edward England, Taylor went on to captain the *Victory* and capture the *Virgim de Cabo* and her treasure, which was worth over £100 million plus enough small diamonds for each crewmember to receive his share of forty-two stones.

Rene Duguay-Trouin: A French corsair who sailed in the early 1700s, Duguay-Trouin captured over 300 British ships during his career, and was made an admiral in the French navy after capturing and ransoming the governor of Rio de Janeiro for an amount that doubled all of his investors' money.

Thomas Dover: After sailing as ship's surgeon with Woodes Rogers, Dover was given command of the *Bachelor* in 1709. A year later he attacked the *Acapulco* and captured a prize worth £1 million. He retired to London and spent the next thirty years creating and selling medical powders.

Thomas Pound: In Boston in 1689, Pound began his pirating career with a small fishing boat. He went on to capture larger and larger ships, and by the time he retired to a life as a gentleman in London in 1699, he was worth over £200,000.

Career Pirates

Not unlike workers in any other career, some pirates spent only a few years on the sea before retiring or moving on to another way of life. Piracy was a challenging endeavor at best, and for some men it proved to be too difficult and entirely too dangerous. Many others, however, learned to love the lifestyle, either because they enjoyed their share of the wealth or because they knew no other way to make a living. For some pirates, the thrill of battle and the opportunity for cruelty were also a strong pull to piracy. But regardless of the reason, thousands of men spent their entire adult life as pirates, often dying as a pirate either in battle or by hanging.

Staying the Course

While some pirates had careers that lasted for only a few years, others made piracy their vocation. John Coxon, a buccaneer who began plundering in 1669, spent almost thirty years sailing the seas, attacking ships and going ashore to prey upon Spanish settlements. In the 1670s, he spent time journeying with Bartholomew Sharp and John Hawkins. In time, the men joined up with William Dampier, and together they led an army of buccaneers in an attack on Santa Maria, Panama. Afterward, the captains went their separate ways and Coxon continued his life as a pirate, often carrying a letter of marque. Despite being arrested and either escaping or being pardoned several times, he sailed until the late 1690s.

Another pirate who enjoyed a long and steady career was Captain Laurens Cornelis de Graaf, who was born in the Netherlands and served in the Spanish navy before deserting and becoming a buccaneer. De Graaf began his time as a pirate in 1667, and over the years steadily captured larger and larger ships. By 1669, he was captaining a twenty-eight-gun vessel, the *Tigre*, which he'd captured from the Spanish. By the 1680s, de Graaf had a reputation that caused Henry Morgan, who was then the governor of Jamaica, to call him a "great and mischievous pirate."

By 1683, he joined forces with Nicholas Van Hoorn and Sieur de Grammont, and they made plans to capture the city of Veracruz, Mexico, and its 6,000 inhabitants. The pirates discovered that the Spanish in Veracruz were expecting the arrival of two Spanish ships, so they loaded two of their own ships with pirates, hoisted the Spanish flag on them, and sailed boldly into the harbor. Their ploy worked. They easily took the town, and ransomed it for a handsome bounty. De Graaf retired from the sea shortly afterward, but continued to lead attacks on land against Spanish settlements for another ten years.

SEA ROVER

Shap 'Ng Tsai was a Chinese pirate who commanded one of the largest pirate fleets ever known. During a battle on the Tonkin River in 1848, 1,700 of his fellow pirates were killed while another 1,000 rogues managed to elude capture. Shap 'Ng Tsai had luck on his side and was among those who survived.

Captain Simon Danziger (also spelled Danseker or Dansker) was another Dutch pirate who enjoyed a lengthy career. He began as a French privateer in the early seventeenth century, but later sailed against France as a commander with the Barbary Corsairs. Although he captured many Christian ships for the Muslims, he refused to convert to Islam. Despite that refusal, he became known among the corsairs as *Dali Rais*, which means "Captain Devil." Danziger wanted to go back to France to be with his wife and children, but for a time was unable to negotiate a pardon from French King

Henry IV—not until he captured a Spanish galleon and took it to France as a present for His Royal Highness. While this secured Danziger his pardon, it did nothing to endear him to the Dey of Tunis (the leader of Tunis on the Barbary Coast), under whom he'd been sailing, and when Danziger made the mistake of returning to Tunis in 1611 in an attempt to negotiate the release of several captured French ships, he was taken prisoner and summarily hanged.

There were many other rogues who lived the life of a pirate from the time they went on account until they retired, became ill, were hanged, or died in battle. These men include:

John Bowen: During the early 1700s, Bowen was captaining a merchant ship in the West Indies that was attacked by French pirates. Marooned for eighteen months with other survivors of his crew, he became a successful pirate in his own right after his rescue, and enjoyed prosperity until he died of an intestinal illness a few years later.

John Callice: (Also spelled Callis or Calles) A Welsh pirate in the late 1570s, Callice was a navy man who became a notorious pirate. He was sentenced to hang on more than one occasion, but always managed to escape or be pardoned. He continued to plunder until his death in the Mediterranean Sea in the late 1580s.

John Eaton: An English pirate during the 1680s, Eaton took several Spanish vessels on his own, then joined with John Cook, Charles Swan, and Peter Harris to attack several large Spanish towns and vessels. In time they were joined by more pirates, and bought blank commissions from the Governor of San Dominque to become privateers. Eaton's fate is unknown.

John Halsey: A Boston privateer in the early 1700s, Halsey turned to piracy and was originally branded a coward. Later he proved his bravery by attacking and taking a pair of larger British ships.

Olivier Le Vasseur: Also known as "The Buzzard," Le Vasseur was a French pirate in the early eighteenth century who at the time of his capture was thought to possess the Fiery Cross of Goa, a gold cross covered with rubies, diamonds, and emeralds. He refused to disclose the whereabouts of the treasure, and was hanged in 1730 while challenging the crowd to find it.

Thomas Moone: Originally a carpenter, Moone began his piratical career in 1572 while sailing with Sir Francis Drake. He joined Drake on his around-the-world voyage, commanding various ships in Drake's fleet and participating in the attack on Valparaiso. He sailed with Drake again on his second voyage, but was killed during an attack on Cartagena.

Off Course

During their careers, some pirates steered a bit off course. Either some form of insanity led to their demise or they met their maker in an unconventional manner. William Lewis was unusual for a pirate in that he could speak several languages, which, given his international crew, proved to be both helpful and dangerous. Active in the early 1700s, Lewis captured everything from small vessels to man-of-war ships. He was captured by the Spanish, escaped, and continued his career until 1727.

Legend has it that Lewis attempted to capture a prize ship off the Carolina coastline. In the ensuing battle, Lewis' ship, *The Morning Star*, was hit and severely damaged by cannonfire. Lewis allegedly climbed to the top of the mainmast, screaming and pulling his hair out by the roots, offering it as a sacrifice to the devil in return for victory. The tide of battle suddenly shifted, and the prize was taken. Some say that this unexpected victory made Lewis' superstitious crew fearful about the pact he'd made with the devil, and a crewmember was selected to murder Lewis in his sleep.

Another version of Lewis' death claims that international tensions among his crew reached a murderous peak, and the French faction of the crew revolted and killed him. Either way, it appears that Lewis died at the hands of his own band of pirates.

Thomas Green and his crew met their end in 1704 when they were convicted of piracy and sentenced to hang. This was not an unusual occurrence, except that Green and his crew weren't pirates, and their hanging almost caused a war between England and Scotland. Green was the captain of a trading ship that had been blown off course during a storm and came into port at Leith, Scotland. The crew was questioned about whether they knew the whereabouts of a local ship that had not returned to port, and although they said they didn't, they were arrested and charged with piracy of the local vessel. After they were found guilty and sentenced to die, two of Green's crew offered to give evidence against the others if they would be pardoned. The details they offered were ridiculous, but the death sentences were not overturned. The arrival of two members of the crew of the missing boat should have delayed the execution, but under pressure from the Scottish public the hangings went on as scheduled. Years later it was proved that the missing boat was actually taken by Captain John Bowen—far too late to be of any help to Green and his men.

PIECES of EIGHT

Sometimes a ship's name turned out to be very appropriate. Captain William Death, a British privateer, met his end when his ship, the *Terrible*, was engaged by a French vessel, the *Vengeance*. Death, all of his officers, and 150 of his crew were lost in the battle.

John Massey began his career as a captain in the British army. Sent to the African country of Gambia in 1721, he found that the governor was sick and being taken advantage of by the natives. Worried about the governor's safety, Massey joined up with George Lowther, and together they planned to rescue the governor and return him to England. As it turned out, the governor refused to leave with them, so Massey and Lowther set sail and left him behind. No longer following military orders, Massey and Lowther had become pirates. After parting ways with Lowther soon after, Massey sailed to Jamaica, where he requested and received a pardon for his piracy as well as passage to London. Had he been using his head, he would have picked up where his earlier lifestyle ended and let sleeping dogs lie. Instead, he wrote a full confession of his piracy and sent it to the Governor and to the Directors of the Royal African Company. He also checked with the Lord Chief Justice to inquire if he was a wanted man. Learning that he was free apparently didn't suit him, so Massey dutifully left his address should a future arrest warrant be issued for him. The Lord Chief Justice obliged Massey a short time later, and he was arrested, tried, and hanged at Execution Dock, an apparent victim of his own guilty conscious.

Other pirates who went off the beaten path include:

Chui-Apoo: Chui-Apoo was a Chinese rogue who led a huge band of pirates off the Chinese coast in the 1850s. A British warship, the *HMS Columbine*, and a British sloop, the *HMS Fury*, battled Chui-Apoo and his band of thugs, sinking twenty-seven pirate junks then taking the pirates' village, where they discovered an enormous store of ships and munitions.

David Williams: A British pirate in the late 1600s, Williams had very bad luck. He lost his ship while in Madagascar and was made a servant by a local prince, then was traded to another prince, and to yet another before he finally escaped and joined a pirate crew. Unpopular among pirates, he moved from crew to crew until, back on shore in Madagascar, he was captured, tortured, and killed by Arabs.

Gustav Rau: A German pirate active in the early 1900s, Rau made the unusual move of successfully leading a mutiny aboard a ship he promptly sank.

Henry Johnson: An Irish pirate active in the 1730s, Johnson was nicknamed Henriques the Englishman. As a pirate, he was a walking contradiction. A black-hearted sea devil feared by all who knew of his torturous acts, he was also vehemently opposed to violence against women and prevented his crew from raping captured females.

Kuo-Hsing Yeh: A Chinese pirate in the mid 1600s, Yeh was extremely successful at raiding and plundering along the coast of China. In an attempt to stop Yeh and his fellow pirates, the Emperor ordered eighty sea towns to move inland, but Yeh continued his raiding, eventually taking Formosa and helping to make it a part of China. In an odd twist for a pirate, Yeh was officially canonized after he died.

Peter Heaman: In 1821, French sailor Heaman murdered his ship's captain and conspired with the ship's cook to attempt to kill the rest of the crew. Heaman was eventually captured when a former cabin boy reported him and the cook, who were summarily hanged and their bodies donated to science.

Thomas Howard: A British pirate active during the early 1700s, Howard stole and lost plenty of treasure, was marooned, rescued, and eventually settled in India with his fortune. It is said that his moroseness and "ill nature" resulted in his Indian wife's relatives murdering him.

Vincent Benavides: A former South American soldier who feigned death during an execution in Chile, Benavides went on to become a resourceful pirate. When he was eventually hanged, his hands were cut off and put on display so as to point in the direction of the crimes he'd committed.

Cruel and Unusual

More than a few pirates took great pleasure in inflicting various tortures on their unfortunate captives as well as each other. While there are exceptions, by their very nature pirates seem to have had an inherent propensity toward cruelty; there are several rogues whose sadistic methods and behavior are horrific by any standard.

Perhaps at the top of the rogues' gallery is Jean David Nau, otherwise known as Francois L'Ollonais, whose behavior was over-the-top psychotic even among pirate ranks (see Chapter 7). Known as the Flail of the Spaniards, L'Ollonais committed unspeakable acts of torture during the late 1600s, but while his actions were despicable, he wasn't the only depraved pirate to make the history books.

Lowdown Dirty Rogue

Edward Low (also known as Ned Lowe or Loe) terrorized parts of the Caribbean, the Azores, and the North American coastline during the 1720s. He was born in Westminster, London, and it's often surmised that his tumultuous childhood as a pickpocket and thief launched his career as one of the most sadistic pirates on record. Like most pirates, there are various accounts of Low's early years. Wholly lacking in education, Low is said to have ended up in Boston with his brother, possibly escaping his homeland after having murdered his father.

SEA ROVER

Edward Low, Pedro Gilbert, and Benito de Soto were a few madmen who exceeded the boundaries of common torture. In many cases, the viciousness and actions a pirate crew inflicted upon their victims often had much to do with the particular situation, a crew's temperament, and, ultimately, a pirate ship's captain. This was definitely the case for Edward Low.

While in Boston, Low acquired work as a ship rigger, but he eventually fell out with his employer and ended up joining a crew headed for the Gulf of Honduras with a cargo of logwood. It wasn't long before Low made a failed attempt at murdering the ship's captain. He and several other men were either set adrift or escaped, after which they quickly captured another vessel and began their piratical careers. Low was highly prolific, seizing many vessels in waters from the Azores to the New England coast. In less than two years, he captured an impressive 140 vessels, and with each capture his minions grew, whether by force or desertion from his plundered ships. The *Fancy* was one of the many ships Low captured, and it ultimately became his flagship.

With a Vengeance

Low's maniacal behavior and his lust for torture were disturbing not only to his unfortunate victims, but even to his crews, who bore witness to his cruel practices. It's said that Low inflicted all manner of torture on captured prisoners. In many instances, a prisoner's flesh was cut off and he was made to eat it. On another occasion, the captain of a captured vessel had his ears cut off, sprinkled with salt, and then fed to him. During a particularly violent skirmish, a captured Portuguese ship's captain tossed his booty overboard to prevent Low from liberating it. As a result the poor soul endured the most inhuman of acts—Low cut off the man's lips and forced him to watch as they were cooked. Adding to his sadistic reputation was Low's appearance. It is said that he was horribly scarred around the mouth as a result of a wound that was badly stitched up.

At times during his career, Low sailed with Captain Charles Harris and his ship, the *Ranger*. In the Caribbean in 1723, Low and Harris crossed paths with what turned out to be the *HMS Greyhound*, a British man-of-war ship. Low quickly abandoned Harris and fled, leaving the *Ranger* to its own fate. Not long after, an alleged fight between Low and his crew over Low's supposed murdering of his own quartermaster resulted in the sadistic pirate being set adrift. Low was soon rescued by a French ship, but despite all efforts he was recognized and taken to Martinique for trial and a date with the hangman's noose.

Where did the phrase *dead men tell no tales* come from?
Charles Gibbs was an American-born privateer turned pirate who by his own admission was said to have murdered close to 400 individuals. When he was hanged in 1831 in New York, it is alleged that his final dastardly statement was: "No mercy did we ever show, for dead men tell no tales."

SCUTTLEBUTT

Two Peas in a Pod

Not unlike modern-day murderers, pirates had a flair for the dramatic. The only difference is that they often performed their horrific crimes in front of an audience. Don Pedro Gilbert (or Gibert) was such a man. An American pirate active in the 1830s, Gilbert is often listed as the last pirate to commit acts of piracy in the Atlantic. Aboard his ship *Panda* in 1832, Gilbert and his crew captured the *Mexican*, an American brig loaded with silver worth $20,000. When Gilbert's crew asked what should be done to the captured crew, he allegedly said "Dead cats don't mew. You know what to do." With the prisoners locked below decks, the ship was plundered and set afire, the crew left to burn alive. Fortunately they escaped to tell their tale, and Gilbert and his crew were eventually apprehended, tried, and hanged several years later.

Benito (or Bonito) de Soto was yet another unconscionable rogue who took pride in his murderous endeavors. A Portuguese pirate, de Soto devised and carried out a brutal mutiny on the *Defense de Pedro* while en route to Africa in 1827. Both crew and captain of the vessel were cast adrift. Loaded with slaves, de Soto christened his new ship the *Black Joke* and, after selling his cargo, set out terrorizing the Caribbean, particularly Spanish ships, where he murdered, pillaged, and sunk everything that had the misfortune to cross his path. By 1832, the feared pirate blasted then captured the *Morning Star*, a British barque carrying trade goods. De Soto then murdered the captain with his cutlass and set his crew loose to rape any women and kill the *Morning Star*'s passengers and crew.

Once de Soto's crew were done with their prey, the victims were locked in the hold and the ship left to sink. It's said that the survivors were able to escape and ultimately repair the ship, but de Soto was long gone. He continued his murderous rampage until the *Black Joke* became incapacitated near Cadiz, Spain, forcing her crew to make their way ashore. As if by fate, the rescued crew of the *Morning Star* pulled into port at the same time de Soto and his men entered Gibraltar. The rogues were identified, tried, and hanged in 1833. As warning to anyone thinking of becoming a pirate, de Soto was decapitated and his head decoratively displayed atop a spike.

Outrageous Behavior

In one form or another, pirates were known for their outrageous behavior, be it their anti-social ways or their cruelty toward their unfortunate victims. Some were also known by their unusual antics or induction into the pirate realm. According to one expert, one of Black Bart's crewmen, pirate John Mansfield, allegedly joined piracy "for drink rather than gold." It would seem that Mansfield spoke the truth, because when he was captured he was entirely inebriated and hadn't a clue what had happened to him. Pirate Robert Hains, one of Edward Low's crewmembers, didn't care much for his captain or his own piratical lifestyle. During a particular capture, Hains escaped with the victims Low was setting ashore in the Azores. But once safe in the prisoner's boat, Hains realized he'd neglected to take his prized silver tankard, so he quickly retrieved it before returning to the prisoner's boat and liberating himself from Low's terrible reign.

SEA ROVER

William Coward was a pirate whose career was short-lived. In spite of his name, or perhaps because of it, Coward and three cohorts are said to have boarded a vessel in the dead of night in 1689 in the hope of capturing it. As it turned out, the assault was simple, given that the entire crew of the vessel was inflicted with smallpox. Coward and his cohorts were easily captured and hanged the following year.

The Party Pirate

Danish pirate Gustav Wilmerding was an oddity on several accounts, the first being that he survived his pirate career and retired to a comfortable life in the Virgin Islands. Allegedly nicknamed "Ding-Dong" Wilmerding, he was known to have hosted memorable parties both on land and at sea, where he often fought battles while onboard musicians provided appropriate background music. Apparently mesmerized by his legendary partying skills, the British Virgin Islands continues to honor the pirate by holding the annual Gustav Wilmerding Memorial Challenge Regatta.

Bone Breaker Francis Spriggs

During the 1720s, Francis Spriggs sailed for a time under Edward Low before departing on bad terms in a ship ironically called *Delight*. Spriggs' personal delight was plunder and torture. During one particular capture in 1724, Spriggs and his crew took pleasure in torturing their captives by tying them, pulling them up toward the sails, and then letting go of the ropes so the poor men would break all their bones when landing on deck. Never one to pass up an opportunity, Spriggs liberated a cargo of horses during another plunderous foray; his crew galloped around the decks, allegedly upset that they lacked the attire and accouterments that gentlemen of the era would have possessed.

Method and Madness

One thing a pirate was not often accused of was being sane. Some pirates, however, have shown themselves to be more daft than others, whether by circumstance, strategy, or just plain fate. One might surmise that the simple act of hanging or dying in poverty or as a result of disease is just payback for a pirate's atrocities. For many rogues that was certainly the case, but for others, the path to nirvana was not that simple.

The endgame of Dutch sailor turned pirate Hiram Breakes, for example, was not that of a traditional pirate. In 1764, at age nineteen, he was a young legitimate sailor and son of a prominent councilor. After quickly being elevated to ship's commander, he became besotted with a married woman called Mrs. Snyde. In a turn of events, Mr. Snyde was murdered, allegedly by the adulterous couple, who were tried and acquitted. Breakes then swiped a vessel he later named *Adventurer*, abandoned his legitimate career, and turned to piracy. Intent on terrorizing unsuspecting vessels, Breakes had the good fortune to capture the *Acapulco*, whose cargo provided him with a pile of gold, some of which he used to entice the Venezuelan Governor of Gibraltar into awarding him a letter of marque.

Now a "legal" pirate, Breakes set out to pillage the Mediterranean, where he eventually invaded a Balearic Island nunnery. One can only imagine the insanity Breakes mustered when he kidnapped the nuns so that his crew could each have one as a "wife." In time, Breakes returned home to Holland to learn of tragic news. During his absence his infant son had been murdered by Mrs. Snyde, who was hung for her atrocity. Instead of retiring a wealthy pirate, Breakes chose to commit suicide by jumping into a canal.

What Comes Around Goes Around

More than a few pirates suffered as a result of bad karma. Early in his career, Scottish pirate Andrew Robertson once flogged a Spanish officer. Years later, Robertson was tossed overboard by a crew with whom he had fought. In an act of pure destiny, a Spanish ship rescued him from certain death—that is, until he was recognized by the ship's captain as the man who had once tortured him. With turnaround being fair play, Robertson was summarily flogged by his previous captive.

PIECES of EIGHT

The same karmic payback was bestowed upon Englishman Walter Kennedy, a pirate who crewed with notorious rogues Black Bart and Howell Davis. After a plunderous career, Kennedy escaped to England to become a proud brothel owner. In this case, luck was no lady, as a member of his wenchery had him arrested for robbery and eventually piracy, for which he was hanged in 1721.

Ruthless murderer and pirate Joseph Thwaites received equal payback. Thwaites spent the 1760s robbing everyone and making enough to support both his English family and a trio of Armenian wives. He retired from piracy long enough to live in a newly built mansion, but ironically succumbed to the bite of a rattlesnake. Kennedy's demise was atypical for a pirate. Most were generally hanged, an execution that knew no sexual boundaries. What many individuals realize is that more than a few female pirates joined their contemporaries both during their wild adventures and at the gallows.

Chapter 15

The Pirate Queens

A career in piracy wasn't just for men. Over the centuries dozens of adventurous women took to the high seas, and in some cases proved more ruthless than their male counterparts. Firing their pistols and waving their swords, they joined their male crews in overcoming prize ships, taking prisoners, and sharing in plunder. From the Viking Princess Alvilda to Grace O'Malley to Anne Bonny and Mary Read, these women not only lived the life of a pirate—they embraced it.

Women on the High Seas

Life for a woman at sea, whether as a pirate or on another type of vessel, was not an easy one. With few exceptions, most women who took to a life of sailing donned male clothing, lowered their voices, and pretended they were men. It was a hard life, filled with long hours of physically demanding and dangerous work, and most men refused to believe that women were capable of doing it. The vast majority of pirates didn't want women aboard their ship; many articles (see Chapter 9) expressly stated that no women would be allowed onboard and that any man found hiding one would be shot. Many captains felt that a woman would be a distraction, one that would most certainly cause fights among the crew. Women who masqueraded as men aboard a pirate ship faced the inherent danger of being discovered and subsequently raped, tortured, or even murdered.

PIECES of EIGHT

Some captains took the precaution of hiring unmarried men for their crews, and on occasion even freed prisoners who were married. Unwed captives were typically made to sign a ship's articles and join their crew. Few captains wanted men thinking about their loved ones, or considering leaving the crew to return home to wives and children.

Motivation for Mayhem

Why a woman would choose to become a pirate is a difficult question to answer. For many who did, it was out of necessity. Throughout the millennia, it was never easy for a woman to find a job to support herself. Pirating offered a chance to share in the loot and perhaps earn additional wealth that could never be achieved on land. Some women, of course, may have been following a man when he signed on to a pirate crew. Love has always been a strong motivator, and no doubt there was a woman or two who fell for a pirate, and became one herself to be near him. For most of these rogue women, piracy offered a chance to live a life of adventure. Many of the known female pirates were rebellious individuals who enjoyed getting drunk and gambling, things they couldn't acceptably do in their hometowns. These women were not afraid to fight—or die. For them, pirating would offer a chance to live a life they otherwise could only have dreamed of.

Rough Waters

Life aboard a pirate ship was extremely precarious for female pirates, especially in regard to personal issues. Sleeping quarters were always cramped, and a woman would have to be careful not to undress where she could be seen. The same held true for bathroom facilities, which were primitive and out in the open at the bow of a ship. For the duration of their piratical service, these women would also have to engage in the same work as their male counterparts, and they would have to do it equally well. They would need to be strong and willing and able to fight. In addition, they'd have to be able to survive on little food and water for long periods of time, tolerate the foul odors of rotting food, and overcome the rough language of pirates. Yet regardless of the perils, women did choose to live this life and many died living it.

Royal Rogues

Many of the earliest female pirates were members of royalty. There's not much detail about the lives of these seafaring women, but they included Queen Teuta of Illyria in the 200s B.C., Princess Rusla and Princess Sela, both Norwegian Vikings in the 400s A.D. One of the more prominent female pirates in antiquity was said to have been Alvilda, a Danish princess who lived in what is now Sweden sometime around the ninth century A.D. She was to marry Prince Alf of Denmark, but rejected his proposal and left her father's home with a group of women. At some point they encountered a band of pirates whose captain had recently died. Amazingly, the pirates were so charmed by Alvilda that they made her their new captain.

Led by a woman, this pirate crew became a threat to ships sailing along the Danish coast, an action that ironically forced Prince Alf to attack their ship. After a fierce battle, his men furiously rushed onboard and began killing the pirates. Captain Alvilda was taken prisoner and brought before Prince Alf. He of course recognized her immediately, and impressed with her bravery and skills, he once again proposed marriage to her. This time she accepted, and after quitting piracy, they were married and she became the Queen of Denmark. As engaging as Alvilda's story is, it's reputed to be false. No definite time frame exists for her or her alleged pirating career, and as a result, it remains debatable as to whether or not she ever really existed.

Amazing Grace

During the 1500s, an Irish legend was born. Becoming the inspiration for stories, songs, novels, and plays, the life of Grace O'Malley was one of piracy, trials, tribulations, and triumphs that included Irish rebellions against England. Called "The Mother of All Rebellions," Grace was born in 1530 in County Mayo, Ireland, the daughter of Owen and Margaret O'Malley. The O'Malleys were a wealthy seafaring family who combined a legitimate trading business with piracy and were successful at both. In a show of sheer determination, Grace endeavored to follow in her father's footsteps and become a sea captain, and she was not about to let the fact that she was a female hold her back.

According to legend, at a young age she asked to accompany her father on a trip to Spain. When he refused to take her, Grace hurried off to her room where she cut off her hair and donned boy's clothes in an attempt to prove that she could handle the journey. Her father and brother promptly nicknamed her *Grainne Mhoal*, which means "Bald Grace." The incident impressed her father enough that she was allowed to join him on voyages (and the nickname unfortunately stuck with her).

SEA ROVER

It is said that on one journey, the O'Malleys' ship came under attack. Grace was ordered below decks, but instead climbed the rigging. Seeing an attacker approach her father from behind, she swung down and landed on the attacker's back, kicking and screaming. The diversion saved her father's life, and allowed the Irish to gain the upper hand and win the fight.

Pirate Mother

At age sixteen, in 1546, Grace married her first husband, Donal O'Flaherty, and despite the fact that they had three children, she continued her life at sea. Legend has it that one of her sons was born aboard ship, and that the next day, when the ship was attacked by Turkish pirates, Grace rose from her bed and fought alongside the men of the ship, helping overcome the Turks. As time passed, Ireland was slowly falling to English reign, and it was becoming very difficult for Irish traders to make an honest living. Grace turned more and more to piracy, waylaying merchant ships and forcing them to pay her protection money; if they refused her offer, her men would loot their ships. When Donal was killed in a battle, Grace returned to the O'Malley homestead on Clare Island to regroup and plan her next invasive maneuver.

The Family Business

Grace's next plan quickly came to fruition, as she gathered about 200 men. Using the fleet of O'Malley ships, she began setting up a pirate empire with the intent of waging a private war against the English. It was during this time that she married her second husband, Richard Burke, allegedly as part of a deal struck between them to combine their family clans and resist British invasion. She and Burke had one son, and she continued her pirate ways, attacking ships for money or their precious cargo.

As a result of her actions, merchants appealed to the British government for assistance, and were appeased when her home, Rockfleet Castle, was attacked in 1574. At sea, however, Grace's pirates were able to overcome the English siege, and they continued their piracy as before. In 1577, Grace was captured during a raid, and she spent a year and a half in a jail in Limerick, Ireland, which at the time was known as Dublin Castle. Most prisoners held there died in the castle, but Grace managed somehow to arrange for her release and return home.

In 1583 her husband Richard died, and in 1586 the new governor of the area, Sir Richard Bingham, and his men captured Grace and a small band of her followers. He promptly took possession of all their property and arranged for their execution, but just before she was to be hanged, Grace's son-in-law offered himself as a hostage for her freedom, and

Bingham released her. He didn't return her property, so Grace was free but found herself living in poverty.

Audience with the Queen

Believing that she had been wronged, Grace wrote to Queen Elizabeth I in 1593 and asked for help in retrieving her land and wealth, but before she'd received an answer, Governor Bingham arrested her sons and her brother. In true piratical fashion, Grace decided to act, so she traveled to England with plans to meet the Queen face-to-face. Why Elizabeth I agreed to the meeting is not known, but in September of 1593, Grace was received by the Queen and several of her court members. Grace told Queen Elizabeth that her acts were not against Britain, but were self-defense against the governor, and his desire to destroy her and all of Ireland. She offered to use her fleet and her pirates to assist Elizabeth against her enemies, if she would command the governor to release her family members and return her possessions. Elizabeth agreed, and the Governor did release Grace's family, but he didn't return her lands. Within two years, he was replaced as governor, and the O'Malley fleet was soon sailing again. They continued their pirate ways, but without Grace, who at age sixty-five had grown too old for life at sea. The fiery pirate queen died in 1603 and was buried in the O'Malley plot on Clare Island.

What was the most difficult problem Grace and Elizabeth had to overcome during their meeting?
When the Queen met with Grace, they had a major language barrier. Grace did not speak English, and the Queen was unable to speak Gaelic. Fortunately, they were both fluent in Latin, so their entire meeting was conducted in that language.

SCUTTLEBUTT

Calico Jack's Legendary Women

Captain John Rackham, often called Calico Jack because he loved to wear clothes made of calico, is probably best known not for his own pirating but for two members of his crew. During the Golden Age of piracy, when the few women who were sailing the seas were doing everything within their power to hide their sex, Calico Jack had not one but two female pirates in his crew—and everyone knew it. Anne Bonny and Mary Read are two of the most notorious female pirates in history, and their stories are the stuff legends are made of.

A Bonny Lass

Anne Bonny was born in Kinsale, County Cork, Ireland, in 1698, the illegitimate daughter of lawyer William Cormac and his mistress, Mary Brennan. Mary was employed as a maid for William's wife, who discovered her husband's affair with Mary and left him. What happened next is uncertain. One account states that William, who deeply loved the maid and their daughter, actually brought Anne into his household after his wife's departure. To avoid questions of impropriety (and losing the stipend his estranged wife was still granting him), he dressed Anne as a boy and told people that he'd taken the lad in and was raising him to be his clerk. Eventually his wife discovered the true identity of the child and ceased William's financing. William then moved Mary and Anne to the colonies, the three of them settling in South Carolina. Other accounts suggest that William's wife had both William and Mary arrested for adultery and fornication, and that when Mary was sentenced to take her child and move to the colonies, William traveled with her.

The couple and their daughter settled in Charleston, South Carolina, and William became a very successful planter, raising Anne in privilege as the daughter of a plantation owner. When she was thirteen, her mother died and she took over the management of the plantation. Things went well until, at age twenty, she married a fisherman named James Bonny. William was furious, as he'd planned on betrothing Mary to someone with a higher social status, and as a result, he removed her from his will. The newlywed couple left for the Bahamas in 1718, and it was there, in the pirate haven of New Providence, that Anne would meet Calico Jack. So charmed was she by the dandy pirate that she deserted James Bonny to run off and lead a pirate's life.

The Double Life of Mark Read

Like Anne Bonny, Englishwoman Mary Read also began life as an illegitimate child. Her mother, whose husband had disappeared or died at sea shortly after the birth of their son, found herself pregnant by another man, so she moved away from her husband's family, lest they discover her scandalous pregnancy. Soon after Mary's birth, which is said to have occurred sometime around 1699, her older brother died, and after a short while Mary's mother found herself in financial trouble. In order to continue receiving payments from her mother-in-law to support her child, she moved back and dressed Mary in boy's clothing, pretending that she was her brother. This worked for awhile, but the grandmother eventually uncovered the truth and stopped giving her money. Mary, in the meantime, continued to dress as a male, and was subsequently hired out to work as a footboy in order to help support her mother.

In her early teens, Mary—still dressing as a boy and using the name Mark Read—found work on a British warship as a cabin boy. At some point she left the navy and joined the army instead, and there she met a handsome Flemish soldier and fell in love. Obviously, she was faced with a serious sexual dilemma and was forced to inform the object of her affection that she was really a woman. Apparently delighted with Mary's revelation, the man married her and they both left the army. For awhile they ran a tavern, catering to soldiers and making a good living, but then Mary's husband died, and peace brought a shortage of soldiers to their tavern. Finding herself in poverty once again, Mary returned to her cross-dressing ways, and around 1717 secured a job on a Dutch ship that was sailing for the West Indies.

SEA ROVER

When the Dutch ship was captured by pirates, Mark Read decided to make a lifestyle change; "he" signed the pirate ship's articles and joined her crew. It is thought, but not known for sure, that the pirate ship was captained by Charles Vane. If true, Mary would have met Calico Jack, who was Vane's quartermaster at the time.

Under her assumed name, Mary sailed as a pirate for about a year, then was granted and accepted a pardon from King George I while she was in the Bahamas. She subsequently delved into privateering against Spain, and was sailing on a Dutch ship when she decided to join Calico Jack and Anne Bonny's crew. The three began a journey that would eventually end in doom.

A Tale of Two Women

When Anne Bonny took up sailing with Jack, the other men in Jack's crew were apparently aware that Anne was a woman. It wasn't long after she joined the crew that she realized she was pregnant, either by Jack or by her husband. After delivering the child in Cuba, she quickly rejoined Jack on his ship. There's no record of what happened to the child, but it's assumed that Anne gave the baby away or it died. Some stories say that Mary joined their crew as Mark Read, and that it was only when Anne became enamored with "Mark" and Jack became jealous of him that Mary revealed her true sex. Regardless of how it came about, Mary and Anne became close friends. Both were comfortable dressing as women during average days on the ship, but during battles they dressed as men.

As pirates, Anne and Mary proved that they were excellent fighters who were highly skilled at handling weapons. As such, they were accepted as equals by the men of the crew, and drank, swore, and gambled with them. In battle they were utterly fearless, and as a result, tales of Calico Jack and his wild women soon spread back to the Bahamas where Governor Woodes Rogers issued a proclamation for their arrest. The mere fact that Jack had not one but two wanted women onboard was nothing short of extraordinary.

During the summer and fall of 1720, Jack's crew plundered their way through the Caribbean, boarding and raiding many ships and sharing a wealth of booty. On October 22, 1720, the crew was down in the hold of the ship, drinking and playing cards. Mary and Anne went up on the deck and noticed a governor's ship drawing alongside them. They yelled for the men to come on deck, but the majority were too drunk. Captain Jonathan Barnett asked the pirates to surrender peacefully, and at first Jack refused. A few cannon shots were then exchanged, and when Jack's ship was disabled, he surrendered and joined his men below deck. Mary and Anne did not. Instead they fought the governor's men as they boarded. Both women fired their pistols and swung their swords, but were finally overpowered and taken to jail with the rest of the crew to await their trials.

Trying Times

On November 16, 1720, the trial of Calico Jack Rackham and his men began. In the end, they were all charged with piracy, and the very next day were found guilty and sentenced to hang. Rackham himself was hung on November 18, but before he was executed he asked if he could see Anne. His request was granted, but being the wily wench that she was, she didn't have much sympathy for him. Legend has it that she looked him in the eye and curtly stated that "If he had fought like a Man, he need not have been hang'd like a Dog."

SHIVER ME TIMBERS

Pirates referred to their hanged companions as having been *swung off*, probably in reference to the way in which the body of a hanged man tended to swing back and forth when suspended by a rope. A body that was left hanging as a warning to other pirates was referred to as being *sun dried*.

Ten days later, the two women were tried on the same charges as Calico Jack. Both pleaded not guilty despite witness after witness taking the stand to testify how the women were willing participants in the pirate way of life and the violence of battle. Anne and Mary were subsequently found guilty and sentenced to be hanged like the rest of their fallen comrades. After their sentencing, both women immediately claimed to be with child, however, and after examinations proved they were indeed pregnant, the courts temporarily suspended their execution.

Questionable Ends

Details of what actually became of Anne Bonny and Mary Read are still in dispute. Mary Read allegedly died in prison, and some stories say that she died of fever. The date of her death, April 28, 1721, corresponds to the end of her pregnancy. This, coupled with the fact that she was given a proper burial despite being a condemned woman, makes it seem more likely that she died in childbirth. What happened to Anne and her child is less clear.

After delivering her child, it appears that Anne received several stays of execution and was eventually pardoned and allowed to return to the colonies. The most common story is that Anne's father, upon hearing of his daughter's plight, used his connections or a bribe to secure her release. Other stories allude to pirate Captain Bartholomew Roberts threatening to "release his wrath on all the Bahamas" if she wasn't released. It does appear that Anne somehow escaped to America, as her father's records showed her marrying a Virginia man in December of 1721. If that is to be believed, she apparently lived out her life in anonymity and without causing any further problems.

Dragon Ladies

In Chinese culture it has long been common for entire communities of floating villages to exist along the shores of rivers, with women and children typically joining men in living and working on sailing *junks*, or boats. Women worked and toiled alongside the men and were comfortable at sea, even commanding their own junks and sailing them into battle. Growing up in this culture, it was not unusual for a woman to become the leader of a pirate community and such was the case with Cheng I Sao, who became a notorious and extremely clever pirate queen.

Mrs. Cheng

In 1801, a pirate commander named Cheng I married a former prostitute from the Canton province of China. That prostitute was Cheng I Sao, or Mrs. Cheng, and because of her marriage she suddenly found herself second in command of a community that at its pinnacle included about 50,000 pirates. A formidable force of rogues, the couple and their fleet attacked any unprotected boat along the southern coast of China, and subsequently lived off their plunder by ransoming boats as well as running a protection racket. When Cheng I died in 1807, his wife assumed command of their pirates with the support of her husband's relatives, including his adopted son Chang Pao. One thing led to another, and Chang Pao, who was highly regarded among Chinese pirates, wed Mrs. Cheng several years later. Together they proved to be a relentless duo, their loyal pirates staving off government attempts to end their empire. Their attacks proved highly successful and difficult to avoid, as they had the advantage of sheer numbers in terms of ships and pirates.

In 1810, with the aid of Portuguese and British warships, the government planned a massive assault on the pirates, but before launching an attack offered them amnesty. Much to everyone's surprise, Mrs. Cheng cleverly arrived at the Governor General's residence with a group of unarmed women and children. She negotiated a surrender that allowed the pirates to keep their plunder and included the offer of a place in the Chinese army to any former pirate who desired it.

PIECES of EIGHT

Mrs. Cheng's brilliant negotiations were well received. Two days later, over 17,000 pirates formally surrendered and turned over more than 240 junks to the Chinese government. Only 126 of Mrs. Cheng's former pirates were executed, and fewer than 400 received any punishment at all. Until her death in 1844, she operated a gambling establishment.

Lai Choi San

Known as Queen of the Macao Pirates, Lai Choi San (also Loi Chai San) commanded a group of twelve junks and the pirates who manned them in the waters surrounding Hong Kong during the 1920s. A vicious woman, she often took captives when raiding boats, and would attempt to ransom them. If the relatives didn't pay the ransom, she would give them a warning by cutting off her captive's finger or ear and sending it to them as proof of her sincerity in murdering their loved one. If they still didn't pay, she would kill the captive. Despite her brutality, or perhaps because of it, Lai Choi San disappeared in the 1930s and no one is sure what happened to her.

Wily Wenches and Private Ladies

While Grace O'Malley, Anne Bonny, Mary Read, and Mrs. Cheng are probably the most famous of the female pirates, other women pirates are known, and there are probably many more who lived as men and were never discovered to be women. A host of female marauders are mentioned in pirate history, but few details are known about their lives or the extent of their high seas exploits. Despite having served as pirates during different eras and throughout various cultures, all female swashbucklers had one thing in common: they seemed to share an enjoyment of violence and were willing participants in their piratical deeds.

Lady Mary Killigrew

During the 1500s in England, piracy was allowed, provided it was done with authority, quietly, and with little bloodshed. John Killigrew was the Vice-Admiral of Cornwall, and his wife, Lady Mary, was reported to have led several authorized pirate raids along the English coast. In the winter of 1583, storms forced a ship into the harbor at Falmouth in Northern England. Some reports say the ship was Spanish, others say it was German. Regardless, Lady Mary led her pirates out to the ship, boarded it, massacred the crew, then plundered the ship's cargo of jewels, silver, and coins. When Queen Elizabeth I heard about the attack she was understandably very angry, and her ire led to Lady Mary's immediate capture. She was then tried and found guilty of piracy and was sentenced to be hanged, but in an interesting twist of fate, the Queen eventually pardoned her.

Why did the Queen pardon Lady Mary Killigrew?
No one knows for sure, but because the monarchy quietly authorized some piracy, and because Lady Mary had done a good job pirating for Queen Elizabeth in the past, it is suspected that the monarch thought she might have need of her services sometime in the future.

SCUTTLEBUTT

Cutlass Liz

Elizabeth Shirland was born in 1577 in Devonshire, England. As a young woman she disguised herself as a man and served under British privateer and sea dog Sir Francis Drake. In 1595 she returned to England and married, but was soon bored as a housewife and returned to sea. In time, she became captain of her own ship, and eventually informed her unsuspecting crew of the truth about her sex. Liz was a fiery female pirate, and in a perhaps apt twist of piracy, she used the men of her ship for her own personal pleasure. In this case, forewarned and forearmed should have been the crew's mantra, because if she was angry with them, she would slit their throats with her cutlass, a maneuver that earned her the nickname "Cutlass Liz."

As a pirate, Liz was not very successful, taking only one major prize in 1604—a Spanish merchant ship from which she stole gold and silk before setting the vessel on fire. A few weeks later, she was betrayed by two of her crewmembers who secretly allowed several Spanish soldiers to board her ship while she was busy being pleasured by a third conspirator. The invading Spaniards dragged her off the ship, but not before she killed her traitorous lover with a hidden dagger. Choosing not to wait for a trial and hanging, the Spanish soldiers acted on their impatience and killed her immediately.

Rachel Wall

Rachel Schmidt was born in 1760 in Carlisle, Pennsylvania, and was likely the first true American female pirate. At age sixteen, while in Harrisburg, Pennsylvania, she met George Wall, and they soon left town and were married. Afterward, the couple moved to Boston, where George was a fisherman and Rachel worked as a maid. Not long after their move, George and a few of his friends decided to take up piracy and asked Rachel to join them. When she agreed, the group borrowed a boat from another friend, to whom they promised a share of their plunder, and headed out to sea.

Rachel and George's piratical tactics in luring prey were highly deceptive. Typically, they would fish until a storm rolled in and would then put out a distress signal. When another ship responded, they would kill the crew, transfer the cargo to their ship, and then sink the aiding vessel to make it appear that it had simply gone down in the storm. In 1782, their ship really was caught in a bad storm during which George and at least one other man were thrown overboard and drowned. Rachel, however, was rescued and went back to Boston where she continued to steal from boats harbored at the docks, until she was finally apprehended and convicted of murdering a sailor.

PIECES of EIGHT

Sentenced to die for the sailor's murder, Rachel denied to the end that she was guilty of that particular incident, though she did confess to her crimes of piracy. When her execution was carried out in October of 1789, she became the last woman to be hanged in the state of Massachusetts.

Dens of Iniquity

Pirate queens were in many cases just as brutal and conniving as their male colleagues. As such, they took advantage of the same devious career paths that any good pirate followed. Any individual involved in a criminal act requires the use of a lair. Pirates were no exception to this rule. Whether by chance or by design, several major areas became ideal hideouts for pirates. Most of these havens, including Port Royal, Tortuga, and New Providence, were boom towns that recognized the value of piracy and the riches pirates were willing to waste on sinful delights.

Chapter 16

Kingdoms of Piracy

When a pirate wasn't at sea, he was typically planning his next exploit. Many port towns such as Tortuga and Port Royal welcomed pirates, not because they were dangerous criminals but because they had money to spend and were good for a port's economy. Since the dawn of piracy there have been safe havens that pirates, privateers, and buccaneers frequented, each area earning notoriety as a result of the corruption, whoring, and debauchery that inevitably ensued when pirates arrived. Wine, wenches, and wild behavior are but a few attractions these historic pirate kingdoms showcased.

Devilment and Debauchery

Every self-respecting criminal needs a hideout, and pirates are no exception. Often pirate captains would make use of private coves, inlets, or remote islands and cays where a crew could careen their ship, make repairs, and replenish food and water stores if an opportunity arose. These forays, however, weren't necessarily fun and games. When a ship was careened, pirate crews were extremely vulnerable to attack by any passing ship, so pit stops such as these were a risky endeavor. Where then did pirates go when they needed to cut loose after months at sea?

Any good captain worth his salt knew that going ashore was not only beneficial to his crew's morale but could provide him useful information about potential victims and the riches their ships would be carrying. This meant paying a visit to a pirate-friendly port or town where pirates could abandon all semblance of morality and engage in whoring, gambling, and drunken debauchery.

Since the time of the ancient mariners there have been many ports that pirates frequented, but some of the more contemporary hideouts were more famous than others. Port Royal, Madagascar, Tortuga, Havana, Bermuda, and New Providence are just a few of the pirate havens that attracted the likes of even the most notorious pirates such as Blackbeard, Henry Morgan, and Black Bart. These areas served as safe harbors for black-hearted rogues, who were more than willing to partake of any luxury, cuisine, recreation, and wenching they could afford.

Turtle Island

Tortuga Island, often called Turtle Island for its sea turtle-like shape, is located off the shore of what is now modern-day Haiti. When the French bucaneers were forced from their home on the island of Hispaniola, they migrated to Tortuga, which had a solid port, a harbor with a clear, sandy bottom, timber, and an abundance of herbs and plants, tobacco, fruits, and vegetables. In time, the bucaneers were joined on the island by others, the majority of whom were criminals evading capture, runaway slaves, and displaced Europeans who as punishment for various crimes were sentenced to relocate to Spanish Main areas and serve as indentured servants. These varied characters were all bound together by a hatred of the Spanish (see Chapter 7).

Tortuga continued to be ruled by the French throughout most of the 1600s, and all of the French governors who were assigned there would offer safe harbor to any non-Spanish ship. They would also offer letters of marque to privateers to attack Spanish ships, as long as they shared the booty they stole from the Spanish with Tortugan governors. The buccaneers eventually became known as the Brethren of the Coast, and Tortuga became their home.

Sea Rover

Henry Morgan, Jean L'Ollonais, Jean le Vasseur, Pierre Le Grand, John Davis, and Roche Braziliano were just a few buccaneers and pirates who spent time in Tortuga. These and other lesser-known rogues made their way around the island, hiding from the Spanish when necessary, and attacking them whenever the opportunity arose.

By the 1680s, the changing political atmosphere would alter the lives of the buccaneers of Tortuga. When Spanish treasure ships sailed past the island less frequently, the buccaneers angered the British by attacking Jamaican plantations and English merchant ships. The French attempted to control the buccaneers, but their attempts proved unsuccessful. As a result, the buccaneers were becoming full-fledged pirates, attacking not only Spanish ships but any passing vessel that didn't belong to the French. With the signing of the Treaty of Ratisbone, the French and the Spanish ended decades of hostility, and letters of marque were officially withdrawn. This meant that there were no longer any privateers and the buccaneers were officially practicing piracy. Many were quickly caught and hanged, while others would make their new home base on the exotic isle of Jamaica.

The Wickedest City in the World

Throughout the centuries many cities have been known for their dubious activities. Pirates found respite in a number of ports, but only one was charged with the daunting title of the "richest and wickedest city in the world." The Jamaican city of Port Royal was as renowned for its taverns, brothels, and illicit dealings as it was for the earthquake that utterly destroyed it in true biblical fashion in 1692. The migration of Tortugan buccaneers fueled by their newfound lust for piracy would make Port Royal the ideal stomping grounds.

Target Practice

Jamaica became a British colony in 1655 when the British successfully took the area from the Spanish, who'd first laid claim to the island in the early 1500s. Sheltering Kingston Harbor from the Caribbean Sea was the ten-mile long Palisadoes sand spit located at the southern coast of Jamaica. A natural harbor, the area was named Port Royal, and it proved to be the perfect location for pirates and buccaneers who sought refuge, valuable information, recreation, sale of their contraband, and the ideal base for targeting Spanish ships and ports. Located south of Cuba, Port Royal was surrounded by Spanish and Portuguese territories as well as major shipping lanes for vessels going to and from Panama and Spain. This made it easy for buccaneers and pirates to attack the Spanish Main and to sack ports such as Portobello, located in what is now Panama, and Cartagena (modern-day Colombia).

The Buccaneers of Sin City

Insecure with their defense of Jamaica, the British actually encouraged buccaneers fleeing Tortuga to come to Port Royal. By making the harbor a so-called safe haven, they assured that the city would continue to grow and be defended. Four years after the island was conquered by the British, the fort at Port Royal had over 200 shops, warehouses, and homes surrounding it. A true boomtown, the port became a safe harbor to privateers, buccaneers, and pirates, all of whom were more than happy to peddle and spend their wares at any of the town's many shops, inns, taverns, gambling dens, and brothels.

In 1660, Britain and Spain finally made peace, but that didn't stop the attacking of Spanish vessels. Privateers and buccaneers who held letters of marque had little trouble securing allies when they set out to plunder

Spanish ships (see Chapter 6). For the next decade or so it is said that Port Royal's fifty-one acres of land had an estimated population of over 5,000, with its harbor eventually accommodating up to 500 ships. Their bustling economy of stolen goods included gold, silver, jewels, and just about anything a pirate could steal and sell—including slaves.

PIECES of EIGHT

In 1661, new licenses were issued to forty taverns in Port Royal. In addition to its growing population of pirates, thieves, and strumpets, the community had a number of merchants, goldsmiths, tavern owners, and artists. Though it seems unlikely given the antics of a pirate haven, the town is also said to have had several churches of different religions.

Sodom of the New World

It's no secret that rampant drinking and prostitution gave Port Royal its wicked reputation. It has been said that there was one tavern for every ten residents of the town, and if that's true, it's no wonder that so much drunken debauchery and whoring ensued. The majority of Port Royal's food was imported and expensive, but that mattered little to pirates whose goal it was to spend all of their booty on wenches and anything from inexpensive home-brewed alcohol to lethal rum concoctions.

The illicit practices of Port Royal may not have shocked the majority of its population, but it certainly did give many individuals cause for concern. One minister who arrived at Port Royal with the intention of staying quickly left, but not before famously calling the port the "Sodom of the New World" and stating, "Since the majority of its population consists of pirates, cutthroats, whores and some of the vilest persons in the whole of the world, I felt my permanence there was of no use."

The Day the Earth Shook

British buccaneer Sir Henry Morgan is intrinsically linked to Port Royal, as he became a privateer for Jamaica in 1668 and later served as lieutenant governor of Port Royal (see Chapter 8). The town continued to prosper, but by 1687 the tide was changing and anti-piracy laws were enacted. As a result, one of the town's newest and busiest establishments became Gallows Point, where dozens of pirates were hanged, including infamous rogues such as Calico Jack and Charles Vane. As piracy was being suppressed, slavery became Port Royal's next vice, but by 1692 the town's wicked ways would finally catch up with it.

On the seventh of June, 1692, Port Royal fell victim to a series of disasters beginning with a devastating earthquake. Given the unstable nature of the sandy Palisadoes spit on which the town was built, this resulted in the ground shifting to such an extent that all of its western side simply disappeared into the ocean, taking all structures and humanity with it. As the earthquake subsided, the area was then struck by an enormous tidal wave that further decimated the town and its residents. In the end over 2,000 individuals died, with some historians speculating that the number was as high as 5,000. In the aftermath, chaos and devastation reigned over the world's wickedest city, which was now nothing more than a wrecked patch of sand separated from mainland Jamaica.

Port Royal would never recover from the revenge brought upon it by Mother Nature. Most survivors migrated to Jamaica's capital city of Kingston after the catastrophe, choosing to relegate their sins to a watery grave. At the time, it was a commonly held belief that the earthquake and subsequent destruction of Port Royal was an act of God—retribution for the inordinate sins committed by all its residents. The town has since been resurrected and enjoys a small population of around 1,400 residents. Though it's no longer the den of iniquity it once was, Port Royal continues to attract treasure hunters, and efforts are being made to rehabilitate the area as a tourist attraction (see Chapter 19).

Notorious Hideaways

Florida, the Bahamas, and Bermuda were three areas from which pirates could easily maneuver around the Caribbean basin and easily hide when a warship or privateer was in hot pursuit. Florida's location made it a strategically important area, even though it was not a treasure port itself. The Spanish often used Florida as an area for various treasure ships to convene and prepare to convoy back to Spain. In 1564, the French Huguenot pirates established a settlement near present-day Saint Augustine, Florida, with the intent of using it to attack the Spanish treasure fleet. In an effort to defend themselves, the Spanish quickly sent Pedro Menendez to set up a colony in Florida and rid the Spanish of French pirates, as well as any future pirates who would establish subsequent settlements. Menendez was successful in driving the French out, and there were no further pirate havens set up in Florida, but the same cannot be said about the Bahamas and Bermuda, where pirate hangouts flourished during the Golden Age.

Why was Cuba a popular pirate haven?

Spanish presence on the island of Cuba prevented pirates from setting up colonies, so instead they spent time in the saloons and whorehouses of Havana, listening for tips on when the Spanish fleet would be arriving. The citizens of Havana would gladly give such information, as it would result in either pirates having money they could spend in Havana or a pirate's hanging, which was a popular form of entertainment.

SCUTTLEBUTT

A Heavenly Haven

New Providence, an island in the Bahamas, was one of the last Caribbean pirate havens to come to prominence. It was founded by the British in 1656, but after repeated attacks by the French and Spanish, the British abandoned the island. It remained mostly unsettled and ignored until 1714, when privateer Henry Jennings attacked and robbed several Spanish divers who were attempting to salvage the cargo of a Spanish treasure ship that had sunk during a hurricane and scattered atop reefs in Florida. Jennings needed a nearby base, so he quickly settled on New Providence.

The island proved to be an ideal base for pirates. The harbor between New Providence City (present-day Nassau) and Hog Island (now Paradise Island) allowed two ways in and out, but neither was deep enough for a warship to enter. It was also in close proximity to the American colonies and Cuba, which made it an easy place to sell and trade plundered goods while also ensuring that resident pirates had an abundance of ships to attack. The island provided adequate food, fresh water, timber, and other provisions, as well as secluded beaches where pirate ships could be careened and repaired. Pirates readily enjoyed themselves in New Providence, and it was often said, "When a pirate slept, he didn't dream that he'd died and gone to heaven, he dreamed that he had once again returned to New Providence."

Besides Henry Jennings, New Providence enjoyed a famous clientele including Blackbeard, Benjamin Hornigold, Charles Vane, Calico Jack Rackham and his female pirates Anne Bonny and Mary Read, and Samuel Bellamy. For about four years, New Providence was truly a haven to the pirates of the Caribbean, a fact that didn't sit well with the British government, who owned the island. In 1718, King George I sent Woodes Rogers to New Providence as the new governor, with orders to "clean up the pirate mess."

Rogers had spent several years as a very successful privateer (see Chapter 13) and he knew pirates and their habits. He arrived in the harbor at New Providence in September of 1718, bearing royal pardons for any pirates who would accept them, and promising to defeat any pirates who would not. Of all the resident pirates, only Charles Vane offered resistance before escaping from the harbor. The rest accepted pardons, at least temporarily. Rogers then sent a handful of pardoned sailors in pursuit of other pirates, and he subsequently hung those who were caught. By 1721, Rogers had rid the island of pirates, cleaned up New Providence, and rebuilt the fort the pirates had previously destroyed. With the downfall of New Providence, the Golden Age of piracy had reached its end.

ℙIECES of 𝔈IGHT

Execution Dock was a place no pirate wanted to visit. Located in the Wapping district of London along the Thames, the dock served as gallows for many pirates, including Captain Kidd. After pirates were hanged, incoming tides would rise over bodies, which by the third tide would wash the victims away. As an example to others, some pirates were hanged, covered in tar, and suspended in irons at Graves Point.

The Devil's Triangle

Unlike the Bahama Islands, Bermuda wasn't situated on the primary trade routes for most Spanish ships, but it did serve as a refuge for slave traders sailing to North America. A British colony since 1609, Bermuda is around 600 nautical miles east of the United States and is a collection of several main islands and over 130 smaller islands. This, of course, provided ideal hiding places for pirates and smugglers who sought a safe haven that was somewhat off the beaten path. The British saw the potential that Bermuda offered and eventually established the islands as its Royal Navy headquarters.

Unlike many of the other pirate havens, the primary target of piracy in the Bermuda area was slavery. Many ships carrying slaves from Africa stopped in Bermuda en route to America or other destinations. On occasion, the indigenous population would fall victim to pirate attacks, but for the most part there was not as much violence as on the other pirate havens. In the end, it was the increased presence of British military that eventually turned Bermuda into an anti-haven for pirates who were engaged in anything other than smuggling.

One pirate who made Bermuda his base of operations was American Thomas Tew, who left his home in Rhode Island in the early 1690s to become a privateer. Once established in Bermuda, Tew set about securing financing, and with the eventual help of a consortium purchased an eight-gun sloop that was named *Amity*. A letter of marque from Bermuda's governor gave Tew the power to target French vessels, and he began his first captaincy by sailing for the coast of West Africa in order to conduct a raid on a slaving station. It is said that en route to his destination, Tew's ship was caught in a violent storm and he was separated from the other ship he was sailing with. At that point, Tew convinced his crew that more riches were to be gained through piracy than by working for the government. With that pivotal move, his career as a pirate began.

The first timber on the hull of a wooden vessel was called "the devil" because it was difficult to work on during ship repairs. Typically the longest seam of the ship, it required caulking with pitch or *pay*. All seamen hated performing the repair. Subsequently, the action became known as *paying the devil* and was synonomous with unpleasant situations.

Madagascar and Libertalia

Located approximately 250 miles off the eastern coast of Africa is the island of Madagascar. Situated between the Indian Ocean and the Red Sea, Madagascar was an ideal location for a pirate hideout, given that both seas were popular routes for merchant ships bearing rich cargoes. In addition, the island featured many harbors that were not easily accessible by any authorities. No European country had any power over Madagascar, which meant that while on land pirates weren't hindered by any particular laws, nor did any religion with its attendant morals hold sway.

King and Castle

In many ways Madagascar was the perfect tropical utopia. Its natural harbors and beaches were ideal for careening pirate ships; there was an abundant supply of fresh fruit, beef, chicken and eggs, and fresh drinking water was plentiful. All of these resources and advantages provided pirates the ideal area to rest, rendezvous with other pirates, make repairs, and stock up on provisions.

Madagascar's native population was sparse, primarily comprised of small tribes of indigenous peoples. The tribes were separated by the mountains and forests of the inland section of the island, and they generally fought with each other most of the time. Pirates would befriend various tribes and assist them in their primitive battles, and in return the tribes would welcome them and even offer them prisoners who would serve as their personal slaves.

By 1691, various pirate groups had established their own territories on Madagascar, each band headed by a self-proclaimed "king." These small kingships were located at Ranter Bay, Reunion Island, Johanna Island, Fort Dauphin, Saint Augustine's Bay, and Ile Sainte Marie. By the end of the seventeenth century, there were approximately 1,500 pirates living in Ile Sainte Marie alone, and Europeans in general were becoming very concerned about Madagascar piracy and its effect on commerce.

SEA ROVER

Ile Sainte Marie, also known as St. Mary's Island, was headed by Adam Baldridge, a Jamaican-born buccaneer who left Jamaica after killing a man and fled to Madagascar. In St. Mary's, Baldridge built himself a huge castle, kept warehouses full of the plunder he received from the various pirates that settled in St. Mary's, and made a fortune selling pirated goods in the colonies.

In response to the growing number of pirates making their home in Madagascar, England and several other European nations began sending warships to patrol the Indian Ocean and Red Sea. This turned out to be an effective move, making piracy much more difficult for the men living on the island. As a result, many accepted pardons that were extended to them, and moved on. Over the next two decades, Madagascar's population declined, as did its popularity with pirates. When Woodes Rogers drove the pirates out of New Providence in 1719, many settled in Madagascar, and for a brief time it once again became a popular base for pirates.

The Real Neverland

Many tales have been told over the years about a settlement on Madagascar known as Libertalia that was allegedly run as a utopian republic. According to legend, a man known simply as Captain Mission (or Misson) founded Libertalia as a place where "democracy would rule," where "the oppressed would fight the oppressors," and where "justice would be equally distributed." Here, men of all races lived together as equals, all treasure and food was shared equally among residents, and a delegation of pirates met at least once each year in order to deal with decisions on how things should be done within the settlement. While this sounds like a wonderful place, it never really existed, and neither did Captain Mission.

What is interesting is that the pirates chose to invent this particular fictional place with its very democratic attributes. Considering the violent nature of piracy, it may seem odd that pirates would readily choose to live in a democratic society. In reality, however, it's not that strange, given that most pirate ships were run in a democratic manner. In addition, many pirates and buccaneers were displaced from their homelands, had served on naval and merchant ships where they often worked long hours for little to no pay, faced floggings and other terrible punishments, and had little or no control over their daily lives and how they went about them. The idea of a land-based home where they would all live as equals—sharing so that no one was wanting, electing trusted leaders to make decisions for the group, and joining together to overcome anyone who would stand in the way of their pleasant society—would have been an enticing goal for pirates. Had it been real, Libertalia would indeed have been a pirate utopia.

For the Love of Louisiana

In addition to its pirate havens in the Florida Keys, the United States boasted another renowned pirate lair called Barataria, made famous by privateer, pirate, and smuggler Jean Lafitte (see Chapter 13). The islands of Grand Terre, Grande Isle, and Cheniere Caminada, located in Barataria Bay in Louisiana, were ideally situated for a pirate's base of operations. Located south of New Orleans and west of the Mississippi Delta, the area offered easy access to rivers and bayous that could be used for illegal smuggling operations, particularly those dealing with slavery and contraband.

Operating during the early 1800s, Lafitte gathered up hundreds of buccaneers and several dozen ships that proceeded to target and plunder all ships crossing their paths, many of which belonged to Spain. Leading his pirates from Grand Terre, Lafitte, with the help of his brother Pierre, provided Louisiana plantation owners with as many slaves as they required—for a price.

PIECES of EIGHT

As Lafitte's profits grew, so did his kingdom of Barataria. So effective were his business dealings and the safe harbor he provided that the lair attracted plenty of fellow pirates, including Blackbeard, who took refuge on the island in 1718 while eluding the British Navy.

Flagrant or Fabulous?

No matter where in the world pirates came ashore, they always left their mark, whether it be from a night of drunken debauchery or plunderous murder. Pirate havens were notorious for their wild atmospheres and outrageous over-the-top scoundrels. Ports that welcomed these raucous rogues with open arms did so out of self-preservation. Pirates were good for a town's economy and could be used as a formidable defense if the need arose. But how much truth is in the reports about pirates and their antics and exploits? Are the creative distortions of literature, film, oral history, and hearsay ultimately responsible for the overblown image one has of pirates? Pirate havens were a breeding ground, one that has done much to exaggerate the legendary stereotypical rogue, and that stereotype bears closer examination.

Chapter 17

Yo Ho Ho and a Bottle o' Rum

Most people usually think of pirates as gruff, smelly seamen who stomp about screaming "Arrgh" while sporting a fancy hat, gold earrings, an eyepatch, a pegleg, and a parrot on their shoulder. While some of these stereotypes may be true, the majority of pirates were dressed and used vernacular more like the merchant and naval seafarers of their day. Like many historical figures, pirates suffer a romanticized stereotype of themselves, from their scruffy beards to their spyglasses to the alleged treasure maps they prized where the inevitable "X" marked the spot.

The Stereotypical Pirate

The word *pirate* often conjures up images of pristine tall ships sailing majestically across the sea, manned by a host of swarthy men intent on terrorizing and robbing all passing ships of their worldly riches. While onboard, these pirates allegedly gambled among themselves for high stakes, shot each other if they didn't like their odds, and staggered across decks yelling "Yo ho ho and a bottle o' rum." When ashore, they'd do the same thing, only with a wench (or two) on their arm, and an ego to match the size of their booty. And it didn't stop there.

Legend dictates that pirates were flamboyant dressers, elegantly clad in expensive and exotic silk and velvet finery, flashing gold bejeweled rings and necklaces. In a show of power, they carried long shiny cutlasses, and pistols fit for any duel on command, and they wore eyepatches, carried parrots, and continued their criminal careers undaunted by something as trivial as a pegleg. But how much of this imagery is true? Were pirates really dressed to the nines? Did they dramatically swing from a ship's rigging with cutlass in hand and drop to the deck in a valiant display of victorious swordsmanship?

History by its very nature is highly speculative, and where pirates are concerned there is, in most cases, very little substantiated information about their personal habits and manner of exotic dress. As with all good legends, however, rumors and speculation have been embellished over the centuries primarily due to literature, film, and various accounts of pirate life written by individuals who claimed to have possessed firsthand knowledge. How much of the pirate legacy is true is anyone's guess, but one thing is certain—no matter how one approaches the study of piracy, it's guaranteed to provide a colorful journey through maritime history.

Lore and Legend

The legendary status of pirates is something most of us learned when we were kids. Literature and film gave birth to the savvy and sometimes savage image of pirates, whose scarcely believable tales of high seas adventures and pillaging often culminated in treasure chests overflowing with jewels and gold doubloons. The stereotypes created in works such as *Treasure*

Island, *Robinson Crusoe*, *Peter Pan*, *Captain Blood*, and even *Blackbeard's Ghost* remain fresh in the hearts and minds of everyone who has read books or watched films about pirates (see Chapter 18).

While the lure of the sea will always remain a romantic notion, so perhaps will the swashbuckling Errol Flynn pirate remain stereotypically unscathed. The truth, however, is that pirates didn't look or act like Errol Flynn, and their lives were anything but romantic. A pirate's life was hard, and depending on a pirate's ship, circumstance, era, and captain, his career was often only a few years long and fraught with danger, disease, and, more often than not, destitution (see Chapter 11). Yet popular culture continues to feed the image of a pirate being a flamboyant rogue who successfully wins epic and justifiable battles, who attracts women as smooth as the finest rum, and who wouldn't be caught dead without a bird on his shoulder.

SEA ROVER

It's said that notorious pirate Bartholomew Roberts was the best-dressed villain on the high seas. Captain Johnson's book described Roberts during a particular battle as "dressed in a rich crimson damask waistcoat and breeches, a red feather in his hat, a gold chain round his neck, with a diamond cross hanging to it, a sword in his hand, and two pairs of pistols hanging at the end of a silk sling slung over his shoulders."

Dressing the Part

Anyone who has seen *Captain Blood*, a version of *Treasure Island*, either of the current *Pirates of the Caribbean* movies, or any other popular pirate films no doubt recalls the flouncy blouses, breeches, elegant hats, and huge gold earrings worn by legendary pirates from Dr. Peter Blood to Long John Silver to Jack Sparrow. Of course, real pirates didn't have stylists, wardrobe designers, or dry cleaners to assure that their duds were *en vogue*, clean, and neatly pressed. On occasion, they did dress up, particularly if they were going ashore or needed to disguise themselves as naval men. Fine clothing was a prize. When plundering a ship, excess clothing was considered booty and was shared or auctioned among the crew. If a victim was wearing something a pirate fancied, the poor man might find his clothing commandeered.

Literature and film have definitely added to the romanticized notion of pirate attire, and while some of it is true, there's nothing to suggest that anyone dressed as Peter Pan's outrageously bewigged Captain Hook or paraded aboard ship dressed like a monarch at his inauguration. A pirate's clothing was nothing if not practical. They lived and breathed the ocean the majority of the time, and this meant dealing with harsh elements. Clothes had to be sturdy, given that pirates usually worked and slept in the same attire until every bit of cloth disintegrated. It also meant that most pirates simply retained the attire they wore when joining the crew, be it standard seaman or naval issue attire.

In general, no matter the era, what sailors traditionally wore differed from clothes worn by landlubbers. Most men of the sea wore short thick woolen jackets or overcoats called *fearnoughts* that were usually gray or blue in color. Often they were made of canvas and painted with wax or tar to make them waterproof. White or off-white shirts were usually made of cotton or linen or even a calico print of blue and white. The majority of the time aboard ship, assuming the weather was pleasant, pirates went shirtless and without shoes. Canvas pants, knee breeches, or so-called "petticoat breeches" or "sailor's petticoats" were worn, the last being shorter trousers that were secured just above the ankle. *Long clothes*, meaning clothing that was loose or blousy, weren't generally worn aboard ship given that they could become snagged or get hung up in the ship's rigging. Shorter coats, however, were safer in regard to movement as they were more tightly fitted to a seaman's body.

SHIVER ME TIMBERS

Captains in the British Royal Navy were allowed to outfit their crew and officers in any uniform of their choosing. The navy blue jackets of the *HMS Blazer* were the most highly revered attire. The "blazer" continues to be a popular addition to the well-dressed man's wardrobe.

A pirate captain's everyday attire was usually no different than that of his crew. Depending on a situation or a ruse a captain was planning, he would often wear his best sea coat, waistcoat, shirt, and *tricorn*, or three-cornered hat. Given that many former naval men served aboard pirate vessels, it wasn't uncommon for passing ships to make the unfortunate assumption that the rogues were simply merchant seamen. That is, until the Jolly Roger was raised and they were captured.

Pirate Eccentricities

Pirates were most definitely known for their outlandish style, especially when it came to flaunting themselves while in port. Unless a person belonged to royalty or had a particular public stature, certain dress codes were often in effect, and that meant normal, practical attire. Obviously, pirates had no intention of following the rules of any given nation or government, and therefore took great pleasure in dressing up for trips ashore, often arriving in splendid coats, tricorn hats, fine linen shirts, and gold earrings. The better a pirate dressed, the more likely it was that local populations were both in awe and fear of him.

Hooks and Peglegs

Pirates who lost a limb either by accident or in battle were lucky if they even survived their bout with their ship's "surgeon," who was typically the crew's carpenter (see Chapter 9). Given that useful artificial limbs were non-existent at the time, a disabled sailor had very few options. The idea of having a hook instead of a hand or arm likely evolved from J.M. Barrie's 1904 novel *Peter Pan* and his villainous Captain Hook. Historic accounts suggest that some pirates did indeed have hooks after losing a hand or arm. It's uncertain whether pirates would have cheaply fashioned their own hooks out of available materials or whether the only hook worthy of being a prosthetic device needed to be expensively made.

Surviving the loss of one's leg wasn't that common for a pirate or any seafarer. If the loss of blood didn't kill them, inevitable diseases such as gangrene likely would. Long John Silver is, of course, the classic one-legged pirate, and it's probably because of *Treasure Island* that pirates are stereo-typically assumed to have peglegs.

SCUTTLEBUTT

Who was *Jambe de Bois*?
One-legged French privateer Francois Le Clerc was known throughout the Caribbean as *Jambe de Bois*, or leg of wood. One of his more famous exploits took place in 1553 in Santiage de Cuba's harbor off the coast of Hispaniola. With over 300 men, Le Clerc conquered the port and proceeded to pillage the town for over a month.

Another infamous pegleg was Captain Cornelis Jol, a Dutch privateer for the Dutch West Indies Company during the 1630s and 1640s. Feared by the Spanish, he was given the Spanish name for wooden leg, *Pie de Palo*. Together with Captain Diego de los Reyes, a mulatto and former Cuban slave, Jol's rampages in 1635 included almost a dozen Spanish ships. It wasn't until 1636, after a brief time served as a Spanish prisoner, that he returned to privateering. Five years later, however, Jol's luck ran out and he died while attempting to overrun a West African Portuguese slave station.

Earrings and Eyepatches

Eyepatches are another stereotypical fact of piracy. Indeed, it is said that some pirates did wear eyepatches, if for no other reason than to hide the loss of one eye. Others might have worn them strictly for intimidation. One logical use was that gauging the sun's horizon while onboard ship meant staring into the sun either with or without a sextant. This would eventually lead to loss of sight in an eye that the pirate would then cover with a patch. Also, if a pirate were attacking a ship and needed to fight both on deck and below deck, it could be argued that wearing an eyepatch would help him adjust to the sudden change of light to dark. Of course, it could also act as a hindrance when it came to swordplay.

Pirates wearing gold earrings could have meant several different things, and there are more than a few amusing theories floating about. If a pirate wore a large gold earring, it was arguably a show of wealth. It also could have been for the simple reason that various taxation laws allowed pirates or privateers to keep whatever jewelry was on their body at the time. It has also been said that piercing one's ear and wearing a large gold hoop would provide a bit of acupressure necessary to help prevent seasickness. Further speculations surmise that pirates could even have worn earrings to gain an edge during battle. If the sun hit his earring at just the right spot, the glint could provide distraction, allowing him to defeat his enemy.

PIECES of EIGHT

Many speculate that a pirate who wore an earring was investing in his afterlife. Gold having such high value meant that if the pirate was killed, his earring could provide enough money to secure a proper burial complete with ceremony, coffin, and final resting place.

Hats Off!

Some form of headgear was extremely important to pirates, whether it was a small brimmed hat or a type of scarf or bandanna, primarily to keep their head safe from the beating sun as well as limit sweat from running into their eyes. They also might have worn a type of linen neck cloth or sash to curtail sweat around their neck. Sailors and pirates alike also typically wore knitted or woolen caps, called *monmouths*, that fit tightly on their head. The most commonly recognized pirate hat is a *tricorn* or *tricorne*, which hit the peak of its popularity during the eighteenth century. The tricorn is a three-cornered hat that has a trio of upturned brims, one on either side and one in the back. Today, tricorns are commonly worn during formal occasions and military re-enactments.

Wine, Wenches, and Song

It's no secret that pirates enjoyed carousing during their precious time ashore at any number of pirate havens including Port Royal, Tortuga Island, New Providence, and Madagascar (see Chapter 16). Their riotous behavior while imbibing in various on-land exploits is part of what has earned them their wild reputation over the centuries. Pirates worked hard and played hard, and the mere thought of setting two feet on solid ground with their pockets heavy with coin sent most pirates into a feeding frenzy.

Pirates didn't often save their riches, instead choosing to splurge on food, excessive drink, and prostitutes—luxuries that were obviously lacking aboard a pirate ship. More often than not, what ensued on-land was rampant drunkenness, whoring, gambling, fighting, and even the occasional duel, and there were plenty of career gamblers, tavern owners, and whores who were happy to exploit pirates primed for debauchery. Unfortunately for most pirates, once their hard-earned money was spent on what most God-fearing people would consider evil deeds, they would be forced to once again take to the seas in search of plunder.

SCUTTLEBUTT

Didn't pirates smoke pipes?

Given that smoking carried the inherent risk of fire or explosion, pirates were usually limited to chewing tobacco while onboard unless they had a covered pipe that could be safely enjoyed away from any munitions. When ashore at a tavern or punch house, they commonly smoked long-stemmed clay pipes called *churchwardens*. Up to 16 inches long, these pipes provided a cooler smoke than shorter traditional pipes.

Eat, Drink, and Be Merry

As described in Chapter 9, pirate cuisine while onboard ship was something only a starving individual could possibly desire. When a pirate ship put to shore, proper food was a high priority, especially anything that was insect-free with nary a maggot in sight. Given that pirates were typically desperate for a hot meal, they were often happy with whatever food, or *belly timber*, a tavern or inn might be serving at the time. After months of drinking fetid water aboard ship, pirates were primed for proper drink, and this included wine, beer, and liquors such as rum and gin served in tankards. The oft-heard term *grog* typically refers to alcohol, usually rum or watered-down rum. The modern-day act of feeling groggy finds its origins in pirate vernacular, especially in regard to the morning after a night of drinking.

In the Caribbean during the seventeenth and eighteenth centuries, a popular concoction was *Bumboo*, or *Bombo*, a sweet and potent mixture of water, nutmeg, sugar, and rum that was favored by many sailors given that it was much tastier than the grog provided by the British Navy. Another pirate favorite was *rumfustian*, which featured sugar, beer, gin, sherry, and raw eggs blended together and served hot.

The pirate haven of Port Royal was known for a particularly lethal rum punch appropriately called *kill-devil*. Yet another mind-bender was *flip*, a hot mixture of a small or light beer combined with sugar and brandy. With all of these drinks at a pirate's disposal, it would seem appropriate that after long drinking binges a pirate would have a bad taste in his mouth. This unfortunate by-product of drunkenness was aptly described as "the cat has kittened in my mouth."

SHIVER ME TIMBERS

A pirate who had too much to drink would often be *three sheets to the wind* or *loaded to the gunwalls*. Wasting hard-earned booty on drink would be to *piss money against a wall*. By contrast, a pirate who went overboard in regard to boasting would be *pissing more than he drinks*, or be known as a *windbag*, which was once a term for a sailing ship.

Girl Crazy

Most pirate havens were swarming with prostitutes who were more than happy to take money from pirates and sailors who'd spent months at sea with nary a wench in sight. The act of *catting*, or pursuing these sexual mavens, was high on a pirate's list of priorities. This meant visiting taverns, any low-class areas that served drink, or brothels disturbingly known as *punch houses*. In Port Royal, one visitor famously touted that these establishments featured "such a crew of vile strumpets and common prostitutes that 'tis almost impossible to civilise."

Port Royal was particularly overrun by working girls. One whorehouse teeming with treachery was that owned by John Starr, who featured twenty-one Caucasian women and two African-American women. Among Port Royal's wenches was the infamous Englishwoman Mary Carleton, dubbed

"The German Princess." Her self-proclaimed status as a German princess came about as a result of fraud, after she married John Carleton in London during the 1660s. After a trial and subsequent acquittal, she wrote and acted in a London theatrical play about herself.

Carleton's ruses, however, endured for the next decade as she continued her fraudulent portrayals in order to lure and rob various men of their money. Eventually sentenced for bigamy and various thefts, she was transported to Port Royal in 1671. Not a woman to sit still for long, she found pirates and other scoundrels to be easy prey. Sources describe Mary as "common as a barber's chair: no sooner was one out, but another was in." Carleton's wicked ways eventually caught up with her and after returning to England without permission in 1673, she was finally captured and summarily hanged.

Polly Wanna Cracker?

There certainly was no practical need for a pirate to possess animals other than to sell them or use them as food if supplies became scarce. Long John Silver's fictional parrot, affectionately named Captain Flint after Silver's former captain, is easily the most recognizable of pirate parrots given his constantly squawking "pieces of eight!" To pirates, exotic animals such as parrots and even monkeys were much like everything else a pirate liberated—commodities. Little is known about the status of parrots as pirate pets, but it would seem unlikely that any pirate working aboard his ship would do so with a bird gripping onto his shoulder offering nonstop commentary.

PIECES of EIGHT

As a commodity, however, parrots did sometimes prove highly valuable as word spread of their exotically colorful plumage and their ability to whistle and mimic words and phrases. In London newspapers during the 1700s, parrots that were up for sale were advertised and were often sold at a very high price.

Walking the Plank

The somewhat dramatic punishment of walking the plank has become one of the great pirate myths. In truth, there is very little evidence that any pirate captain or crew forced one of their own or their captives to be blindfolded, walk across a plank hanging from the side of the ship, and plunge themselves to a watery grave. One of the only known accounts of such an occurrence was the unfortunate crew of the *Vhan Fredericka*, a Dutch brig that was captured by pirates in 1829. Pirates fastened shot, or projectiles such as cannon or musket balls, to the victims' legs and then forced them to walk the plank one at a time.

Pirate Phraseology

Aside from their larcenous ways and general villainy, pirates are perhaps best known for their colorful vocabulary. Phrases such as *Shiver me timbers*, *Avast ye!*, *Dead men tell no tales*, and *Davy Jones' Locker* are typically associated with pirates. So did average pirates really skulk about yelling "Arrrgh" and calling each other *bilge rats*? No one knows for sure, but it's fair to say that these are just a few of the many phrases that legendary pirates and everyday culture have adopted. Real pirates spoke just as other individuals did during various eras. Medieval vocabulary differs from that of the ancients or those who lived during the Dark Ages or during piracy's Golden Age. In general, almost all pirates were fluent in maritime language.

Come Hell or High Water

The majority of the terminology pirates used was vernacular specific to ships, sailing, equipment, and onboard routines. Sailors were often referred to as *tars*, or *Jack tar*, and comrades often referred to each other as *mate* or *matey*. (The actual job of mate included overseeing the sailors aboard a ship, organizing work, and making sure orders were carried out.) Pirate crews often held the same positions one would find aboard naval vessels—captain, quartermaster, first mate, lieutenant, navigator, and so forth (see Chapter 9), so in many regards the vocabulary heard onboard a ship was universal. For example, the term *fire in the hole*, which indicated that a cannon was about to be fired, is still a common military term.

A few recognizable modern-day sailing terms that pirates used include:

Cut and run: If a pirate needed to make a hasty retreat, he would cut the sail lashings or anchor cables, which would enable his ship to escape. This would often damage the sails, but if it was an emergency it might be his only choice.

Hit the deck: A phrase still commonly used when firepower is imminent. This was especially crucial for pirates, given that they typically fought in cramped areas. This meant avoiding swivel guns, small cannon at the rail of a ship, or artillery coming from an opponent.

In the same boat: When out to sea, there was no easy return for a pirate who fancied land over the open ocean. Therefore, all pirates were in the same boat and situations together. The phrase is often interchangeable with *grin and bear it*.

Know the ropes: The process of sailing a ship involves the use of hundreds of ropes and their configurations. Experienced sailors know how all the ropes and riggings work. Inexperienced sailors don't yet *know the ropes*.

Landlubber: The word *lubber* refers to an awkward or clumsy individual. A sailor who is just getting his sea legs or people who don't sail are often referred to as *landlubbers*.

Rub salt into the wound: A process that would occur after a man had been flogged. As additional punishment, salt would be rubbed into the wound.

Square meal: Often used in the present day, a square meal was a big deal to pirates who literally ate their meals off square platters made of wood. If they were lucky, they could eat a proper meal that filled the plate, which would later be turned over to accommodate dessert if it was available. It's said that *fair and square* also originated from the platters, meaning that each sailor received his fair share of sustenance.

Stay the course: A commonly heard term meaning that if a ship travels in the right direction it will ultimately arrive at its final destination.

Holy Mackerel!

Piratespeak contained many phrases that are still used today, although in some cases the meanings may be slightly different. Pirates in general used rough language, and swearing was the mainstay of many a crewmember. A study of pirate vocabulary, however, is a fantastic and amusing journey through pages of colorful prose. Many phrases typically in use in the present day were pirate favorites. These include *chew the fat*, *clear the decks*, *miss the boat*, and even *minding your Ps and Qs*, which refers to a pirate's bar tab. Given that pirates visiting taverns swilled their ale in pints and quarts, it was to their benefit to keep close count of their Ps and Qs, lest the barkeep cheat by adding additional drinks to the pirate's ongoing bill.

Other commonly recognized pirate phrases include:

Bite the bullet: Often depicted in film, the process of biting a bullet was used when pirates or captives were being flogged by the cat o' nine tails. Biting a bullet would presumably keep them from screaming.

Holy mackerel!: A common phrase now often used as exclamations of surprise such as "holy cow!" and "holy smoke!" During the seventeenth century, mackerel was in abundance, but once caught it went bad quickly. Because of this, exceptions were made so that merchants could sell them on Sunday despite it being a holy day.

Let the cat out of the bag: In modern vernacular, "letting the cat out of the bag" is akin to divulging a secret. In pirate times, however, it was something to be feared. Cat o' nine tails were kept in leather bags. Pirates or captives guilty of an offense would be secured to an inanimate object, and the cat o' nine tails would be removed from the bag. A sailor's imminent punishment at that point was no longer a secret.

Loose cannon: These days, a *loose cannon* is usually someone of independent nature who causes potential damage. Aboard a pirate ship, a loose cannon literally meant an unsecured cannon. During storms or other catastrophic events, a loose cannon that moved about could prove lethal to a ship and its crew.

On an even keel: An *even keel* denotes steadiness in present day terminology—a person or project, for example, that is steady and on course toward a goal. For pirates, an even keel meant much the same as it applied to their ship. A vessel on an even keel was sailing steady without any disaster or threat of "keeling over."

Over a barrel: Having someone *over a barrel* is commonly used today, but it wasn't a happy phrase for pirates, as it applied to flogging. Offenders were typically tied to inanimate objects prior to their whipping, and that often meant being tied to the gun barrel of the ship. To kiss, hug, or marry the "gunner's daughter" also indicated a whipping.

Scraping the bottom of the barrel: The excess grease that resulted from frying salt pork aboard ship was added to what was called a *slush fund.* Pirate cooks scraped the perennial bottom of the barrel to retrieve the grease that was ultimately sold for use in candlemaking or tanning.

Under the weather: A modern phrase meaning that someone is feeling sick, *under the weather* could also have applied to pirates who were manning the bow of the ship keeping watch on the weather. This meant standing amid a constant barrage of spray, waves, and heavy rains.

Piratespeak is something that became further embellished through literature and most certainly as a result of motion pictures. Published accounts of piracy have shown that pirates spoke in similar fashion to sailors of their day. Novels and films have definitely made use of maritime phraseology, but they've also added a lexicon of colorful terms that will forever be associated with the fictional pirates or actors who said them. The next chapter explores those works, and the impact that literary and celluloid piracy has had on the public's imagination.

Literary and Celluloid Pirates

18

For generations, pirates have captured the public's imagination through literature, theater, and motion pictures that have immortalized their adventurous, romantic, and treacherous exploits. Whether it's children giggling over swarthy Long John Silver and Captain Hook, or men entranced by the swordplay of *Captain Blood* and the *Crimson Pirate*, or women swooning over Captain Jack Sparrow, pirates and their audacious seafaring lives continue to fascinate and entertain, and likely will for generations to come.

Famous Pirate Literature

For centuries, people have been absolutely fascinated with pirates and have remained mesmerized since the earliest published accounts of maritime piracy. In 1684, Alexandre Exquemelin's book, *The Buccaneers of America* (first published in 1678 in the Netherlands), was published in its first English edition. It went to a second printing in three months. Exquemelin's depiction of the buccaneers included firsthand reports from when he sailed with Henry Morgan and took part in Morgan's raid on Panama. Classics as *Treasure Island*, *Peter Pan*, *Captain Blood*, and William Goldman's *The Princess Bride* continued feeding the public's appetite for piracy. Some of the tales were more accurate than others, and a majority created stereotypes of pirates that would last forever, but regardless of the facts or fantasy that pirate literature showcased, all have left an indelible mark on pirate history.

Treasure Island

Robert Louis Stevenson wrote *Treasure Island* in 1881, while on holiday with his family. It was originally published in serialized fashion in *Young Folks* magazine and was alternately titled *The Sea Cook* or *Treasure Island*. In 1883, it was finally published as a novel. Many of the currently held pirate stereotypes originated as a result of *Treasure Island*, which immediately became immensely popular with readers of all ages. A classic hero's journey, the novel tells the tale of young lad Jim Hawkins, who comes into possession of a map leading to the buried treasure of the fabled Captain Flint. Allowed to join a crew that goes in search of the elusive treasure, Hawkins becomes friendly with ship's cook Long John Silver, a one-legged pirate who has on his shoulder a parrot aptly named Captain Flint. Initially, Silver becomes a father figure to young Jim, but is later discovered to be a mutineer who plans on stealing the legendary loot.

Stevenson's story is absorbing, and written with such convincing detail that it appears to be true. In fact, it heavily influenced public perception about pirates and their lives more than any other book. Film and literature have taken Stevenson's fictional adventure and made it part of popular culture's beliefs. Many of the most common pirate myths such as treasure maps and walking the plank can be traced directly back to his adventurous tale.

PIECES of EIGHT

The charming and dastardly Long John Silver eventually saves Jim's life, but in the end slips off with a portion of the treasure, never to be seen again. It's said that Silver was based on William Henley, a friend of Robert Louis Stevenson, whose larger-than-life personality and physical disabilities enhanced the legendary fictional pirate.

Blood and Water

One of the most engaging authors of pirate fiction is Rafael Sabatini, who was born in Italy in 1875. During his career he penned thirty-one novels and numerous short stories, but is revered for his swashbuckling tales of romance and adventure. Two of his best known works are *The Sea Hawk*, published in 1915, and *Captain Blood*, published in 1922. *The Sea Hawk*, set in the late 1600s, is the story of Sir Oliver Tressilian, who is betrayed and sold into slavery by his own brother. Sir Oliver is later freed by Barbary pirates who invite him to join their ranks. Taking on the Muslim name *Sakr-el-Bahr*, which means "hawk of the sea," Sir Oliver sets out to command his own band of pirates and exact revenge on his evil brother.

Even more popular than *The Sea Hawk*, *Captain Blood* became an international bestseller and made Sabatini a household name. Following a similar formula as his earlier works, *Captain Blood* is the story of Peter Blood, a doctor who is enslaved for treating a rebel in Barbados. He escapes and steals a warship with a band of fellow prisoners, turning to a life of piracy and revenge. The story is filled with sea battles, treasure, romance, and politics, and helped popularize and romanticize the lore of piracy. The stories Sabatini wrote are thrilling and colorful, despite the fact that they bear little resemblance to reality.

Hook, Line, and Sinker

James Matthew "J.M." Barrie was a Scottish playwright and author who, much like the central character of his most famous story, would never truly grow up. *Peter Pan* first appeared on the London stage as a 1904 play, and seven years later was released as a novel entitled *Peter and Wendy*. In the book, Peter—the boy who will never grow up—takes the Darling children to Neverland, where he lives with the Lost Boys. His nemesis in Neverland is Captain Hook, an evil pirate who's determined to bring Peter and the Lost Boys to their end.

Hook's legend in the story is that he was Blackbeard's boatswain and was the only man Long John Silver ever feared. Hook lost his right hand when Peter cut it off and fed it to a crocodile, who loved the taste so much that he followed Hook around hoping for a chance hors d'oeuvre. In both the play and novel, Hook is a much crueler character than the Disney film. He kidnaps Wendy and the boys, then challenges Peter to a duel to the end to save them. When Hook loses the duel, he commits suicide by jumping into the crocodile's waiting mouth. With Captain Hook's hook for a hand, and with his plan to make Wendy and the Lost Boys walk the plank, Barrie's tale succeeded in further perpetuating pirate stereotypes.

SEA ROVER

Captain Hook is thought to be based on English privateer Christopher Newport. Known as an impeccable dresser, Newport had long dark hair, and though his hand hadn't been mauled by a crocodile, he once gave King James I a pair of baby crocs. Newport later sailed for the Virginia Company of England, bringing supplies and colonists back and forth between England and Virginia.

Jolly Good Tale

Author Daniel Defoe is renowned for his legendary novel *Robinson Crusoe*, which is said to have been loosely based on the story of Alexander Selkirk, a real pirate who spent four years marooned on a deserted island. Defoe had quite an interest in pirates, a fact that led to an ongoing debate about another book, *A General History of the Robberies and Murders of the Most Notorious Pyrates*, written by Captain Charles Johnson. The wildly popular *Pyrates* was first published in its Dutch incarnation in 1678 and in English in 1724. The stories in the book were taken from the transcripts of pirate trials and newspaper reports, but the great detail made it seem that Johnson was intimately familiar with sailing and the lives of pirates. There was a debate from the beginning about whether Johnson was a sailor himself, or if he was writing under a pseudonym.

Many editions of the book have been published, and questions about the identity of its author continue to this day. In 1932, John Robert Moore, an American scholar, claimed that *Pyrates* was written by Daniel Defoe. He published his theory, showing samples of Defoe's writing compared to Johnson's. Moore was known as the leading Defoe scholar, and his arguments were so persuasive that most libraries recataloged the book under Defoe's name for the next fifty years. In 1988, two scholars, P.N. Furbank and W.R. Owens, published a book entitled *The Canonization of Daniel Defoe*. Their book pointed out the differences between Defoe's and Johnson's stories, and they argued that the works could not have been written by the same author. Although the books are available under both names, most libraries today again attribute the book to Captain Johnson, whoever he may be.

The Celluloid Pirate

Over the centuries literature has perpetuated the image of the stereotypical pirate. With the invention of motion pictures in the 1900s, that image was greatly enhanced, as actors ranging from Errol Flynn and Tyrone Power to Geena Davis and Johnny Depp portrayed pirates whose personalities and adventures appeared larger than life. In literature, seafaring rogues have pillaged, avenged, and raped their way across the oceans and ports of the world. On screen, they've done much the same, only their adventures have taken on a decidedly romanticized fervor. Among the many genres of film, pirates have held their own over the decades, though they haven't been particularly profitable. This changed during the twenty-first century, however, when a renewed interest in piracy led to the overwhelming success of the *Pirates of the Caribbean* franchise.

Have Sword, Will Travel

Pirate films have crossed all genres, from adventure, romance, and drama to science fiction, musical, and comedy. Despite the fact that the silver-screen versions of pirates have been greatly exaggerated from their historical originals, they've been some of the most memorable characters of all time. The list of actors who've portrayed pirates reads like a Who's Who list of Hollywood's Golden Age, including Charles Laughton, Errol Flynn, Douglas Fairbanks Sr., Tyrone Power, Robert Newton, Peter Ustinov, Fredric March, Yul Brynner, Randolph Scott, Robert Shaw, and Burt Lancaster.

Many classic pirate films such as *The Sea Hawk*, *Captain Blood*, *Peter Pan*, and *Treasure Island* were based on novels. Others are an amalgam of literature and fantasy that alternately personify pirates as either romantic heroes or mischievous peglegged devils of the sea. No matter the pirate captain, his crew, his vessel, or his adventure, one thing is for certain when it comes to piratical cinema—there's always a swashbuckling tale and there's always a hapless heroine who can't help but fall in love with a dastardly black-hearted seafarer.

SCUTTLEBUTT

Which pirate movie has been remade the most?
Treasure Island has been filmed many times over the decades. Orson Welles played Long John Silver in the 1972 film version, while Charlton Heston starred in the 1990 made-for-television production. *Return to Treasure Island* was also a popular remake. Tab Hunter starred in 1954, while Brian Blessed and Christopher Guard costarred in the 1985 Disney mini-series.

The Classic Rogue

Over the years, the motion picture industry has never abandoned the pirate genre. Some films, like director Renny Harlin's 1995 *Cutthroat Island* starring Geena Davis, turned out to be box office bombs, while others like *Pirates of the Caribbean: Dead Man's Chest* have given new meaning to the term blockbuster. The staying power of the pirate genre is undeniable, given that it began during Hollywood's Silent Era with the release of *The Black Pirate* in 1926, starring swashbuckling legend Douglas Fairbanks Sr. A year later, John Barrymore took to the sword in *The Beloved Rogue*, and by 1934 the first of many adaptations of *Treasure Island* hit the big screen. It wasn't until the following year, however, that audiences would begin flocking to theaters to witness the gallant and charming escapades of what have come to be known as true cinematic pirates.

Errol Flynn

In 1935, Warner Bros. studios took a chance on a relative newcomer when they cast twenty-six-year-old Australian actor Errol Flynn in the lead role of *Captain Blood*. Adapted from Rafael Sabatini's novel, *Captain Blood* epitomized the image of the romantic rogue with Dr. Peter Blood's tragic and ultimately triumphant journey from doctor to slave to pirate captain. Added to the chivalrous mix was another unknown, actress Olivia de Havilland, who at age nineteen began a legendary on-screen chemistry with Flynn that would last for another seven films. As a doctor and Irish gentleman unjustly found guilty of treason, Dr. Blood was forced aboard a slaving ship headed for the West Indies, and was eventually sold as a slave to the captivating Arabella Bishop. As one might predict, the rebellious Blood endures the trauma of slavery before managing to liberate a Spanish pirate ship and become the notorious Captain Blood.

Sabatini's novel and the subsequent film based on it brought to life a wildly popular adventure that appealed to all generations of audiences. *Captain Blood* was a hero's journey, enveloped in romance and punctuated with exciting cannon fire and fight scenes pitting Blood against French pirate Captain Levasseur, aptly played by Basil Rathbone. Considered by many to be one of the best pirate films ever made, *Captain Blood* set the stage for dozens of high seas adventures, each of which portrayed pirates in a variety of manners from brave and cunning to outrageous and cutthroat.

Errol Flynn continued his adventure career as Robin Hood in the 1938 film *The Adventures of Robin Hood*, with Basil Rathbone and Olivia de Havilland. But by 1940 Flynn once again took to the high seas, playing buccaneer turned pirate Captain Geoffrey Thorpe in an adaptation of Sabatini's *The Sea Hawk*. Flynn's classic good looks and charisma made Thorpe the perfect charmer of Queen Elizabeth I, and a valiant pirate who fought for England against the Spanish Armada. In true celluloid pirate fashion, Flynn also swashbuckled his way into the heart of Spanish royalty and a stunning beauty played by Brenda Marshall.

Evolution of the Cinematic Rogue

The popularity of *Captain Blood* and *The Sea Hawk* brought audiences to the theaters in the 1930s and 1940s for all types of pirate and adventure films and high seas epics. In 1937, Laurence Olivier, Flora Robson, and Vivian Leigh starred in *Fire Over England*. The following year Cecil B. DeMille brought Fredric March to the big screen as Jean Lafitte in *The Buccaneer*, a film that would be remade in 1958 with Yul Brynner, Claire Bloom, and Charles Boyer. Not to be outdone, Tyrone Power sailed onto the silver screen in 1942, using his unflinching piratical tactics to woo Maureen O'Hara in Sabatini's adapted novel *The Black Swan*.

Other popular films of the era include:

- *Frenchman's Creek* (1944) with Joan Fontaine and Basil Rathbone
- *The Spanish Main* (1945) with Paul Henreid and Maureen O'Hara
- *Captain Kidd* (1945) with Charles Laughton
- *Three Little Pirates* (1946) with The Three Stooges
- *Sinbad the Sailor* (1947) with Douglas Fairbanks Jr., Maureen O'Hara, and Anthony Quinn

Black Dots and Acrobats

By the 1950s, cinematic piracy and swashbuckling was all the rage, with a wide variety of rogues and scallywags swinging from rigging with cutlasses in hand and searching for elusive buried treasure. The 1950 remake of *Treasure Island* featured Robert Newton as Long John Silver in what is arguably one of the best portrayals of the stereotypical pirate. A one-legged trickster complete with parrot on his shoulder and a complex vocabulary of piratespeak, Newton is quite simply unforgettable. Equally enthralling was the infamous black dot, which pirates soberly issued to their mates as warning of their impending death. So good a pirate was Newton that he starred in *Blackbeard the Pirate* in 1952, and two years later reprised his legendary alter ego in *Long John Silver*.

ȘEA ȚOVER

The character of Dr. Peter Blood also made a comeback, with Louis Hayward and Patricia Medina teaming up in the 1950 film *Fortunes of Captain Blood* and *Captain Pirate* in 1952. Captain Blood even had his own personal legacy when Errol Flynn's son, Sean, set sail in the 1962 adventure *The Son of Captain Blood*.

One of the more memorable films of its time featured a very dashing and highly acrobatic Burt Lancaster in the 1952 film *The Crimson Pirate*. Featuring Lancaster and his longtime sidekick Nick Cravat, the film is a send-up of classical pirate films of the day, with pirates swinging from rigging and staving off evil Spaniards in true Keystone Cop fashion. Unlike most cinematic pirates, Lancaster and Cravat were acrobatic partners before they were actors, and their antics, stunts, and swordplay throughout the tale makes *Crimson* a fun family adventure.

Other popular pirate, swashbuckler, and high seas adventure films of the 1950s include:

- *Double Crossbones* (1951) with Donald O'Connor, Helena Carter, and Will Geer
- *Last of the Buccaneers* (1951) with Paul Henreid and Jack Oakie
- *Abbott and Costello Meet Captain Kidd* (1952) with Bud Abbott, Lou Costello, and Charles Laughton
- *Against All Flags* (1952) with Errol Flynn, Maureen O'Hara, and Anthony Quinn
- *Yankee Buccaneer* (1952) with Jeff Chandler and Scott Brady
- *Port Sinister* (1953) with James Warren and Lynne Roberts
- *Raiders of the Seven Seas* (1953) with John Payne, Donna Reed, and Lon Chaney Jr.
- *Prince of Pirates* (1953) with John Derek and Barbara Rush
- *The Master of Ballantrae* (1953) with Errol Flynn and Roger Livesey
- *Captain Kidd and the Slave Girl* (1954) with Anthony Dexter, Eva Gabor, and Alan Hale Jr.
- *Pirates of Tripoli* (1955) with Paul Henreid and Patricia Medina

Singing and Swinging Seafarers

For the next three decades piracy would continue to grace the silver screen in a variety of genres from adventure to comedy to musicals. Films of the 1960s ranged from Steve Reeves as Henry Morgan in *Morgan the Pirate* to Ricardo Montalban in *Rage of the Buccaneers* and Christopher Lee in *The Devil-Ship Pirates*. One of the more acclaimed pirate films of the era was *Swashbuckler*, starring Robert Shaw, James Earl Jones, and Peter Boyle.

Still a popular pirate family film is Peter Ustinov's unforgettable turn as Blackbeard in Disney's 1968 adventure *Blackbeard's Ghost*. Equally revered is William Goldman's screen adaptation of his classic fairy tale novel *The Princess Bride*, which found the Dread Pirate Roberts desperate to return to his beautiful love, Buttercup. The 1987 film, starring Cary Elwes, Robin Wright, and Mandy Patinkin, remains a cult classic.

SCUTTLEBUTT

Have there ever been any pirate musicals?
Pirate musicals made their first appearance in 1982, when Kristy McNichol and Christopher Atkins starred in the frivolous adventure *The Pirate Movie*. The following year, Gilbert and Sullivan's Broadway comic operetta *The Pirates of Penzance* was adapted for the silver screen, featuring performances by Kevin Kline, Angela Lansbury, and Linda Ronstadt.

Piratical comedy also took center stage with the 1983 film *Yellowbeard*, a satirical treasure hunt overloaded with the humor of Monty Python's Graham Chapman, John Cleese, Eric Idle, Cheech Marin and Tommy Chong, Marty Feldman, Peter Boyle, and the irrepressible Madeline Kahn as Yellowbeard's wenchy wife. The following year audiences saw the campy futuristic pirate comedy, *The Ice Pirates*, starring Robert Urich, Mary Crosby, and one unforgettable space herpe.

Other popular pirate films include:

- *The Boy and the Pirates* (1960) with Charles Herbert and Susan Gordon
- *Pirates of Tortuga* (1961) with Ken Scott and Leticia Roman

- *The King's Pirate* (1967) with Doug McClure and Jill St. John
- *The Island* (1980) with Michael Caine and David Warner
- *Nate and Hayes* (1983) with Tommy Lee Jones and Michael O'Keefe
- *Pirates* (1986) with Walter Matthau and Cris Campion
- *Shipwrecked* (1990) with Stian Smestad and Gabriel Byrne
- *Magic Island* (1995) with Lee Armstrong and Abraham Benrubi
- *Cutthroat Island* (1995) with Geena Davis and Matthew Modine

A Cinematic Treasure Trove

Several pirate films were released during the 1990s that began a renewed interest in the genre. The 1991 film *Hook*, staring Robin Williams, Julia Roberts, Bob Hoskins, and Dustin Hoffman as the flamboyant and bewigged Captain Hook once again brought Peter Pan to the limelight, reminding audiences why they love pirates. Five years later came Jim Henson's adored Muppets for a piratical turn in *Muppet Treasure Island*, featuring a dastardly Tim Curry as Long John Silver. Curry would later further his pirate career in the 1999 fantasy adventure *Pirates of the Plain*.

PIECES of EIGHT

As a result of the tremendous success of *Pirates of the Caribbean: The Curse of the Black Pearl* and the appeal of Jack Sparrow, Disney redesigned portions of the Pirates of the Caribbean ride, adding animatronic figures of Sparrow in two different places.

It wasn't until 2003, however, that the tide would forever turn on the pirate genre with the release of director Gore Verbinski's *Pirates of the Caribbean: The Curse of the Black Pearl*. A highly publicized and anticipated film based in part on Disneyland's renowned ride of the same name, *The Curse of the Black Pearl* grossed over $45 million in its opening weekend and as of February 2007 has grossed over $650 million worldwide. As it turned out, those numbers would pale in comparison to the July 2006 sequel, *Pirates of the Caribbean: Dead Man's Chest*, which set records for its opening weekend take of over $135 million and its astonishing worldwide gross of over $1 billion by the beginning of 2007. The latter figure has made *Dead Man's Chest* one of the top three grossing films of all time, and it's quickly encroaching on *Titanic* and *The Lord of the Rings: The Return of the King* to become the all-time grossing film.

There's no telling why *Pirates of the Caribbean* has become such a commercial success. Perhaps it's in part due to its action-packed tale, sweeping cinematography, and swashbuckling sequences. Or it could be the exceptional allure of scallywag pirate Jack Sparrow, brilliantly played by actor Johnny Depp. Part sympathetic rogue, part Keith Richards after a week-long bender, Depp brought a quirky and irresistible appeal to piracy, an effort that garnered him an Oscar nomination for Best Actor. With classic pirate style and panache, the *Pirates of the Caribbean* franchise has brought piracy to the forefront and gone where no pirate film has gone before—straight to the bank and the record books. If luck be a lady, or in this case a wench, the adventures of Jack Sparrow and his motley crew will continue their cinematic plundering of audiences the world over with the Spring 2007 release of *Pirates of the Caribbean: At World's End*.

The current renewed interest in piracy has done much to shed light on the true stories of legendary pirates, especially those who allegedly buried vast fortunes in cleverly chosen areas that have yet to be discovered. A handful of elite treasure hunters have hit pay dirt in regard to maritime archeology, while at the same time uncovering fortunes in gold, silver, and jewels. This group of dreamers—driven by the same quest for treasure as the pirates were—made discoveries that are nothing short of astonishing.

Chapter 19

"X" Marks the Spot

The lure of finding treasure is an impenetrable part of human nature, whether one is a pirate or a modern-day treasure hunter. Spanish galleons were an enviable target for pirates, as their heavily laden cargoes included vast quantities of gold, silver, jewels, and other New World riches. Pirates and hurricanes were a galleon's biggest enemy and if a vessel managed to elude both, it was lucky. For centuries, individuals have been hunting for treasure lost at sea and legendary wealth buried on land, and when that treasure is found, it's nothing less than spectacular.

Modern-day Treasure Hunting

Contemporary treasure hunters who stay within the confines of the law are not pirates indulging in criminal activity and murderous behavior. The lure of finding and ultimately possessing great treasure, and the quest for securing that treasure, however, are as compelling as they were to the pirates of legend. Spanish galleons bursting at the seams with gold, jewels, and other commodities plundered from the territories and peoples of the Spanish Main, such as the Incas and Aztecs, often fell victim to Atlantic hurricanes and pirates while sailing to or from Spain. These galleons and their treasure troves have proven elusive over the centuries, but remain of supreme interest to treasure hunters, historians, scholars, and maritime archeologists. Inherent in the hunt is the difficulty in finding reliable information about the ships, their cargoes, and the exact locations where vessels met their fate.

Over many decades, ships have been and continue to be recovered throughout the world. The Spanish galleons *Atocha*, *Maravilla*, and *Concepcion*, and the infamous pirate ship the *Whydah Gally*, are spectacular finds in regard to history, to say nothing of the millions of dollars' worth of gold, silver, jewels, gems, and myriad implements that were recovered. Work also continues to the present day on Blackbeard's infamous flagship *Queen Anne's Revenge* and the sunken pirate haven of Port Royal. While many treasure galleons and pirate ships have been found over the years, and some measure of wealth recovered, the vast majority continue to tempt maritime experts and diving fanatics. One example of this is the "money pit of Oak Island," where for over two centuries many individuals have tried and died while searching for alleged treasure hidden at the bottom of the pit.

Black Sam's Whydah Gally

Barry Clifford grew up along the coast of Massachusetts and spent many of his early years listening to stories told by his uncle, Bill Carr. One of Carr's favorite stories to tell was about the night when pirate Black Sam Bellamy and his ship, the *Whydah Gally*, were lost in a storm just off the coast of Cape Cod, Massachusetts (see Chapter 11). The tales of this real pirate ship—lost off the shore of his home and loaded with treasure that had gone down with the vessel—filled young Clifford with excitement. He never forgot his uncle's tales. In fact, he grew up to become a diver and wreckage salvor who often put himself in great danger. Eventually he decided to become a treasure hunter, and set his sights on bringing up the *Whydah*, following Carr's advice to him when Clifford confidently proclaimed he would find her: "You'll never know unless you try, Boy."

Truth or Dare

Locating the wreckage of the *Whydah* wouldn't be an easy task. For more than 250 years the ship remained hidden under shifting sands off the shores of Cape Cod. Because the ocean floor is composed almost entirely of sand, and because of the strong surf, the topography off the Cape changes constantly. Even sandbars shift in strong currents. Clifford knew that the sunken ship would've quickly been covered with sand, and while it was certain that locals collected much of the wreckage that floated to the shore, it was highly unlikely that anyone could have located the ship itself, or the treasure of gold, silver, and gems that Bellamy reportedly had onboard. During the early years, diving technology didn't exist for uncovering the vessel.

SEA ROVER

The son of a British naval lieutenant, Captain Cyprion Southack lived in the Boston area in the early 1700s, where he was a cartographer and commander of ships that patrolled the coast of New England defending merchant ships against pirates and privateers. He was the ideal person to search for the wreckage, and was able to locate much of what was found on shore, but was unable to locate and salvage the ship.

In 1974, Clifford used a combination of actual accounts of the shipwreck taken from the surviving pirates' trials. He also studied written accounts and maps drawn by Captain Cyprion Southack, who was appointed by Massachusetts Bay governor Samuel Shute to investigate the wreck of the *Whydah* and locate its remains and cargo. In addition, Clifford absorbed newspaper articles and stories passed on by area residents. Once he had a good idea of the general area where the ship likely sunk, Clifford had to convince the Massachusetts Board of Underwater Archeological Resources to issue a permit for his crew to dive the specific area and search for a shipwreck. This was easier said than done, as Clifford had endured a run-in with the Board in the past and they weren't too pleased with him. In fact, they required him to provide artifacts showing that the area was the likely site of a wreck, but at the same time he had no permit to dive and so couldn't bring any artifacts to the surface. Clifford solved the problem by having someone search the shoreline just off his desired dive area with a metal detector. Old coins dating from the time of the 1717 shipwreck were located onshore and ultimately convinced the Board to allow Clifford's team to dive the suspected wreck site.

Saving the Whydah

Clifford began diving for the *Whydah* in the summer of 1982. Two years later, with about four dollars left in his pocket, a single tank of fuel, and a camera crew from a news station riding along hoping for footage of a whale, Clifford's electronic sensors made out something beneath the ship. Diving down, the crew discovered an old cannon, covered in *concretions*, which are masses of rock and minerals that form around items underwater, protecting them from the elements. Shortly thereafter, Clifford brought up another concretion found near the cannon and chipped away the stone to reveal a piece of eight dated 1684. The crew believed they'd discovered the *Whydah*, though they wouldn't officially prove that until October 1985, when they would retrieve the ship's bell and remove the concretions to discover it was imprinted with the words: *The Whydah Gally 1716*.

Over twenty years later, the *Whydah* salvage operation continues. More than 200,000 artifacts have been discovered to date, including not just coins and gold and silver bars, but items used by real pirates—tools, cannons, firearms, swords and blades, navigational equipment, jewelry, barrels, kitchenware, tableware, clothing, pipes, candle holders, chains, and ship components. Some of the more interesting items found were an ornate gun including the intact satin ribbons used to hold it around a pirate's neck, a leather ammunition pouch tied with a silk ribbon and containing twenty-eight lead bullets, and a shoe, sock, and human leg bone that were found together in a concretion. The shoe size and the length of the bone show that they belonged to a man who was likely no more than five feet four inches tall. In order to share the *Whydah*'s pirate treasure and artifacts with the public, Clifford and his organization established the Expedition Whydah Sea Lab and Learning Center in Provincetown, Massachusetts, where a selection of artifacts are on permanent display. They have also joined with other supporters to form the Center for Historic Shipwreck Preservation, which aids in *Whydah*-related recovery, conservation, research, and display, and helps other archeological shipwreck projects.

Atocha, Maravilla, *and* Concepcion

Few treasure hunters have reached the legendary status of Mel Fisher, Bob Marx, and Burt Webber, whose underwater exploits and discoveries far surpass what most treasure hunters only dream of. At their prime as underwater salvors, dive technology wasn't nearly what it is today, which makes their discoveries of the Spanish galleons *Atocha*, *Maravilla*, and *Concepcion* all the more amazing. What drove these men was not only the lure of treasure, but the quest for a small piece of maritime history—a glimpse into an age when pirates prowled the seas in search of the same Spanish treasure fleets that Fisher, Marx, and Webber ultimately found.

"Today's the Day!"

In 1985, iconic treasure hunter Mel Fisher ended his unwavering sixteen-year pursuit for treasure when he found the *Santa Margarita* and its sister ship, the *Nuestra Señora de Atocha*, two of the vessels that were part of the ill-fated convoy of the 1622 Spanish treasure fleet. Having served as part of the team exploring the shipwrecks of the 1715 fleet, Fisher, along with fellow treasure hunter Kip Wagner, recovered an estimated $20 million in treasure. What Fisher found between the *Santa Margarita* and the *Atocha* was nothing less than astonishing—treasure estimated at over $400 million, including gold and silver bars and coins, silverware, gems and gold jewelry, and an amazing assortment of what is assumed to be contraband emeralds.

Of equal value was the historical information that was uncovered in the form of five bronze cannon, various armaments, navigational tools, and other implements that shed light on seventeenth century maritime experiences. Fisher's treasure trove was arguably one of the greatest finds since Howard Carter's discovery of King Tutankhamen's tomb in Egypt in 1922.

Both the *Santa Margarita* and the *Atocha* were part of the Spanish *Tierra Firme* flotilla, a convoy of twenty-eight ships that on September 4, 1622 departed from Havana loaded with a huge cargo of wealth meant to fill Spanish coffers. At over 500 tons and more than 100 feet in length, and with a crew of 265 men, the *Atocha* sailed at the rear of the fleet, its decks heavily fortified should the convoy be attacked. Within its beams, the holds were bursting with riches from Mexico and South America, including over 24 tons of silver bullion, silver and copper ingots, over 100 gold bars, over a ton of silverware, and a massive quantity of contraband jewels and gemstones.

Two days after its journey began, the flotilla encountered a hurricane off the coast of Florida and eight of the fleet were decimated, including *Atocha* and *Santa Margarita*. A mere five individuals survived the *Atocha* catastrophe. Efforts were made to secure the ship's position for future salvage operations, but to no avail. A second hurricane a month later scattered her on the ocean floor across the Dry Tortugas and the lower Florida Keys. For the next half-century, the Spanish attempted to recover treasure from their lost ships, but it wasn't until Mel Fisher took on the hunt in earnest in 1969 that the wreckage would slowly be found.

The first hint of treasure in the form of several silver bars was salvaged in 1973. Two years later, the bronze cannon were recovered by Fisher's son, Dirk, who tragically died with his wife and another diver several days later when their boat capsized. The *Margarita* and her treasure were uncovered in 1980, but it was on July 20, 1985 that Fisher's other son, Kane, informed his father that the motherlode of the *Atocha* was now in their grasp. The vivacious and determined Fisher began each day with the catch phrase "Today's the day," and finally that day had arrived. Sadly, Fisher passed away in 1999, but his legacy continues. Treasure and artifacts from the *Atocha* and other wrecks are still being salvaged and sold today, with the rest on display at Fisher's nonprofit Maritime Heritage Society Museum in Key West, Florida.

Time Raider

Treasure hunter, historian, and renowned maritime archeologist Bob Marx is one of the most famous and prolific treasure seekers alive today. Throughout his colorful career, in true Indiana Jones fashion, Marx has created a virtual historical lineage with his finds both on land and at sea. Since the early 1950s, he's explored and discovered numerous sites and shipwrecks all over the world, from American civil war vessels and Mayan temples to fourth century Phoenician shipwrecks and the sunken city of Port Royal. Amid his explorations of over 3,000 wrecks is perhaps his most famous discovery—the *Nuestra Señora de la Maravilla*, a Spanish galleon which sunk in 1656 off the Bahamian coastline. At 900 tons, the *Maravilla* was loaded with gold, silver, and emeralds, which Marx and his team found in 1972.

Immaculate Conception

For seventeen years, treasure hunter Burt Webber had trekked back and forth from his native Pennsylvania to the Florida Keys and the Caribbean. At home, he would take a job at a car dealership or selling encyclopedias, all the while spending his spare time raising money and researching possible sunken treasure ships. Once he'd raised sufficient cash and discovered a viable location for a ship, he would head south, returning home to his wife and children months later with empty pockets. But his perseverance paid off on November 30, 1978, when Webber and his crew brought up the first handfuls of pieces of eight from the Spanish treasure ship *Nuestra Señora de la Concepcion*.

When the Spanish treasure fleet had made its journey to the Spanish Main in early 1641, the *Concepcion* had been the flagship. However, during their stay in Mexico the captain had died, and the newly appointed captain of the fleet, Juan de Campos, made his own vessel the lead ship for the return voyage. The *Concepcion* still held an important position, being designated as the *Almiranta*, the second most senior ship whose job it was to guard the rear of the fleet and direct battle if the fleet was attacked. The *Concepcion* wasn't in the best condition at the time—she was massively overloaded and had numerous leaks, but de Campos was unwilling to wait for her to be repaired. On the morning of September 20, 1641, the fleet began its journey, sailing straight into a storm that quickly transformed into a hurricane. After three days of hurricane-force winds, the storm abated, and the fleet found that nine ships had been sunk and numerous others run aground.

SCUTTLEBUTT

What was Burt Webber's first discovery as a treasure hunter?

Webber's first underwater find was seven slot machines he discovered in Pennsylvania's Millardsville Quarry when he was eighteen. The machines were dumped there years earlier by an illegal casino operator, and they contained about ten dollars' worth of coins. Webber was allowed to keep the coins as his salvage.

The *Concepcion* was still afloat but badly damaged. With a jury-rigged sail and a still-functioning rudder, the *Concepcion* limped along for three weeks, running short of food for its crew and passengers; it was uncertain whether she was headed in the direction of Grand Bahamas Island, where the crew hoped to make repairs. In late October the ship ran aground on a reef, and sank late that evening. The survivors split into two groups, with one group staying on the exposed reef and a second heading out on rafts for help. The raft group met up with a pirate ship, were robbed of what little they had brought with them, and were put ashore on Santa Domingo, where they were eventually rescued. Those on the reef died a slow and unpleasant death.

William Phipps, an American colonist, led a successful salvage attempt of the *Concepcion* in early 1687 for the British, which yielded over 450,000 pieces of eight, 459 silver bars, 374 pounds of silver plate, and 25.7 pounds of gold objects. The treasure he salvaged was only a small portion of what the *Concepcion* had carried, but would be worth more than $30 million today. When Phipps later returned to the wreckage, he found that others had been in the area salvaging. As it turned out, he couldn't locate the main portion of the ship, nor could anyone else for over 300 years. When Webber located the wreckage in 1978, his dream of finding treasure at last came true. The yield from his salvage efforts brought forth another $14 million in coins and artifacts.

The 1715 Fleet

In July of 1715, a Spanish treasure fleet of twelve vessels left Havana for Spain loaded with treasure and contraband. Most of the illegal cargo consisted of silver bullion and coins that were omitted on the official ship logs, and would subsequently not be reported to, or completely paid to, Spanish King Phillip V. Much like the *Concepcion* seventy-four years earlier, the fleet was struck by a terrible hurricane only six days into their voyage. More than 1,000 sailors drowned, and only one ship escaped. The rest of the fleet was scattered and sunk along a 50-mile stretch of Florida coastline.

PIECES of EIGHT

Despite their best efforts, the Spanish were able to salvage only a portion of the lost treasure. Pirate attacks on the salvagers became more frequent, and as sand covered the wreckage, the Spanish eventually abandoned all efforts to recover the remainder of the fleet's treasure.

In 1948, Kip Wagner found Spanish coins that had washed ashore on Sebastian Beach in Florida, so he began beachcombing in his spare time, finding more and more coins, and becoming convinced that the seas off the coast held his fortune. During the sixties he formed the Real Eight Corporation, and they began diving in the area. The first wreck they located was affectionately named "The Cabin Wreck" as it was very close to Wagner's beach home. From this wreck, they recovered a number of silver coins and ingots. This success helped Wagner convince Mel Fisher and his team to join them in their diving, so they worked out an agreement with the state of Florida that allowed the treasure hunters to keep 75 percent of what they found in Florida waters.

Not long after, the group discovered the "Gold Wreck," named for the carpet of gold coins lying around it, and the "Wedge Wreck," named for the silver wedges that were recovered. The Gold Wreck alone yielded a treasure valued at about $5 million. No further large treasures were found, although salvagers continued to work the area through the 1970s. In 1989, the Wedge Wreck, which is believed to be the remains of the Spanish ship *Urca de Lima*, was made into an underwater archaeological preserve and museum open to all interested divers.

The Money Pit of Oak Island

The most famous treasure trove of the past two centuries is what has come to be known as The Money Pit of Oak Island. Located off the coast of Nova Scotia, the area first came to be noticed in 1795 by teenager Daniel McGinnis and his friends Anthony Vaughn and Jack Smith. Roaming around the eastern side of the island, the trio noticed a clearing and an area of ground that bore an intriguing circular depression. Hovering over the area was a large oak tree that had one of its limbs partially sawed off. The limb, which hung conspicuously over the depression, appeared to have been used for a pulley system. After a bit of digging, the trio realized that the depression was a shaft that in some areas showed marks made by picks.

Continuing their dig, they reached a level of 10 feet, where they found an oak plank. By the time they reached 30 feet they noticed that markers had been made every 10 feet. Proving to be too much for the young lads, their search for what they hoped was pirate treasure was eventually abandoned and left undisturbed until they could feasibly return to their search years later. Around 1802, Dr. Simeon Lynds visited the island, and, after hearing the boys' story, decided to form a company and begin excavations. Little did Lynds or the boys know that this effort would launch a quest for a goal that continues to elude treasure hunters to this day.

Much has been written and speculated about the Oak Island treasure over the past two centuries, but what's known is that many individuals lost their bank accounts and their lives when attempting to force the pit to give up its mysteries. Lynds' Onslow Company was able to reach 90 feet into the pit through layers of putty and what appeared to be coconut fiber, only to have it flood with water. This would be a consistent problem that all future treasure hunters would have with The Money Pit. What would be retrieved from the pit over the decades, as a result of various companies and individuals taking on the endeavor, would be more coconut husk, wood perceived to be from oak casks, concrete, pieces of metal, gold links thought to be part of a chain, parchment with bits of writing, and even a stone with a mysterious inscription.

What exactly is the treasure of Oak Island and who buried it?
The Money Pit's origin remains a mystery, though over the years many rumors have circulated. The most popular theory is that the treasure was buried there by Captain Kidd. Another rumor has it that the French crown jewels, which disappeared in 1791, were smuggled and eventually buried for safekeeping. Some have even suggested that Shakespeare's original works or the Holy Grail are hidden in the pit!

$\mathcal{S}$CUTTLEBUTT

During one drilling expedition it was discovered that the water that inevitably flooded the pit and its surrounding areas during an excavation was salt water, and that the water level rose and fell to correspond with the tide at a nearby beach at Smith's Cove. This eventually led to the infuriating speculation that The Money Pit was somehow meticulously engineered as a booby trap, designed with an intricate system of drains and waterways that would make it seemingly impossible to recover what so many treasure seekers could never quite grasp. A variety of machinery and devices from dams to explosives were used over the decades, but The Money Pit refused to succumb. Everyone from Franklin Delano Roosevelt to the famed Woods Hole Oceanographic Institute that found *Titanic* have taken a stab at finding the alleged treasure, but in true pirate fashion, the pit refuses to give up without a significant fight.

City under the Sea

The devastating earthquake and subsequent tidal wave that destroyed the majority of Port Royal, Jamaica, in 1692 resulted in a modern-day maritime archeologist's dream. Port Royal still exists and houses a sparse population, and remains home to an underwater museum that rivals the historic significance of areas such as Italy's famed city of Pompeii and Egypt's city of Alexandria. A keen interest in Port Royal led Bob Marx to the sunken town in 1964, and he began excavating the area under a four-year agreement with the Jamaican government. A challenge, to be sure: Marx and his team survived two dozen cave-ins during their excavation, which ultimately produced over two million artifacts that account for a mere 5 percent of the site's potential area of discovery. A strong advocate of preventing future dredging of the site, Marx eventually was able to work with the Jamaican government to preserve Port Royal and its underwater archeology.

Sea Rover

Marx's exploration of Port Royal mapped only a small portion of what has yet to be discovered. The two acres he focused on, however, revealed a number of taverns, homes, and markets and a trio of ships. The Nautical Archeology Institute of Texas' A&M University excavated the site for almost a decade, finding historically significant implements such as pewter plates bearing the name of their craftsman, Simon Benning.

The time Marx spent in what was once deemed "the wickedest city in the world" proved invaluable not only to maritime archeology but to pirate history in general. Recovered items painted a portrait of the haven's seventeenth century residents, merchants, and especially pirates who frequented the port. Over a dozen acres in area, with depths of up to 40 feet, the site remains a constant source of education and history for nautical archeologists who over the decades continue to catalog artifacts and map out the structural remains of the original Port Royal. One artifact of particular interest was found in 1960 by Edwin Link. It was a pocket watch that showed 11:43 a.m., the exact time the town was swallowed into the sea.

Hunt for the Queen Anne's Revenge

Blackbeard, who consistently sailed off the coast of the Carolinas, had a base set up at Ocracoke Island, North Carolina. In 1718, following his blockade of Charleston, South Carolina, he abandoned his flagship, the *Queen Anne's Revenge*, as he sailed through Carolina's Outer Banks (see Chapter 12). In 1997, the nonprofit Maritime Research Institute (MRI) began exploring the wreckage site of *Queen Anne's Revenge*. The MRI worked with the North Carolina Office of State Archaeology to ensure that the site was designated a protected state archeological preserve. The agreement between the MRI and the state allowed North Carolina to retain ownership of all artifacts found at the site, with the MRI granted exclusive rights to sell artifact replicas and commercial accounts of the story of the salvage.

Queen Anne's Revenge was located in 1996 off the coast of Beaufort, North Carolina. She lay in shallow waters approximately 20 feet deep, her remains covered in a fine layer of silt, and scattered over an area measuring approximately 200 by 100 feet. The only items removed to date have been for diagnostic purposes—to help determine that the wreckage was indeed *Queen Anne's Revenge*. Thus far, the yearly field expeditions have shown eighteen cannons, the ship's bell dated 1709, anchors, wine bottles, tableware, a large number of guns, and even a syringe.

PIECES of EIGHT

It's assumed that the syringe could be a by-product of Blackbeard's siege of Charleston, during which the majority of his ransom demands included medical supplies. As syphilis was allegedly a huge problem among his crew, the presence of the syringe helped point toward the ship being *Queen Anne's Revenge*.

Each year since the wreck's discovery, field expeditions have been held to monitor the condition, nature, and age of the site. With the exception of the diagnostic items, only a portion of the hull and the related items around it have been removed, and these were taken as a precautionary measure to avoid damage during catastrophic Atlantic storms. The expeditions are ongoing, with divers continuing to document exposed items, record annual environmental changes, and explore the buried remains by using remote sensors before excavating any items.

Legends of the Fallen

Every day of the year, somewhere in the world, someone is searching for pirate treasure. The thrill of the chase, the quest for historical knowledge, and the potential for unimaginable wealth drive these treasure hunters to meticulously hunt for decades at a time. The research surrounding their particular shipwreck, individual, or treasure includes considerable measures of myths and legends. These tales, no matter how far-fetched, are an unavoidable aspect of the pirate realm. The next chapter explores a few of these legends, and the circumstances and conclusions surrounding them.

Chapter 20

Pirate Fact or Fiction

For as long as piracy has existed, so too have myths and legends about various pirates and their adventurous and often outrageous behavior. The exploits of a pirate often seem larger than life—some of them wiping out dozens of men in a single swordfight, others burying secret piles of booty that are still sought today. Many well-known pirates became famous long after their deaths, and in some cases—like steamboat terrorist Gunpowder Gertie, husband and wife pirates Eric and Maria Cobham, Captain Kidd, and the infamous Half-Arse—their legends continue to grow.

20

Dead Men Make Good Tales

Myths and legends are intrinsically linked to history and have been since the dawn of man. When it comes to piracy, there are arguably more fables than fact, especially in regard to famed pirates ranging from Blackbeard to Captain Kidd. Ghosts, secret spoils, and epic battles of the sword are woven throughout the pirate realm, and with each passing generation the tales of treachery, torment, and even the identity of pirates themselves become more elaborate and exceedingly grandiose. Was there really a pirate called Half-Arse? Did Captain Kidd really bury a fabulous treasure trove? Who are Gunpowder Gertie and the Cobham pirates?

Gunpowder Gertie

Gertrude Imogene Stubbs was a female pirate in the Canadian province of British Columbia. Her story is an intriguing one, and is well-known throughout the province where people love hearing about the exploits of Gunpowder Gertie. From 1898 until 1903, Gertie traveled up and down the rivers of the Kootenay Rockies and surrounding areas, launching raids and robbing any steamboats that were unfortunate enough to cross her path. Traveling in her ill-begotten boat, *The Witch*, she would ambush her prey and start wildly waving her Gatling gun. After liberating all the valuables onboard a steamer, she would hop aboard *The Witch* and sail off into the sunset. The Canadian Provincial Police searched desperately for her, but she knew the rivers of the Kootenays better than the police, and she would always make good on her escape.

How Gertie Got Her Gun

Gertrude Stubbs was born in England in 1879 and moved to Canada in 1895 when her father took a job with the K&S Railway. It was during the long voyage across the Atlantic that Gertrude fell in love with sailing, a love that would remain with her throughout her life. The family settled in the town of Sandon, but tragedy would soon befall them. Within a month of their arrival Gertrude's mother was killed in an avalanche, and her heartbroken father took to drinking and gambling to ease his depression. As a result, he was unable to carry out many of the duties of his job on the railroad, so Gertrude would ride with him, shoveling coal and keeping the engine running for her drunken father. When he died a year later, Gertrude was left penniless and unemployed, given that the railway wouldn't hire a woman.

Gertrude did her best to make ends meet, taking whatever jobs she could, but her father had left large debts to pay off. Times were hard, so she decided on drastic measures—she cut her hair short, dressed like a man, and took a job shoveling coal on a sternwheeler. Gertrude was good at her job, and her work was appreciated as long as her employers and co-workers thought she was a man. Unfortunately, her secret was uncovered after the sternwheeler engaged in a race with another ship. During the contest there was an explosion in the boiler room and Gertrude was rushed to the hospital, blinded in one eye and unconscious. The doctor quickly shared her secret, and she was immediately fired. Angry that she was denied a job because she was a woman, Gertrude swore she would get revenge on the steamship lines. At that moment, Gertrude Stubbs ceased to exist and Gunpowder Gertie was born.

SEA ROVER

Gertie's first act of piracy was to take a police patrol boat that had been specially fitted with a new type of propeller that enabled it to reach a speed of twenty-two knots. This was the fastest boat on the water at the time, and the police were mortified when Gertie managed to steal it from a railcar before they'd even taken possession of it.

Pirate Queen of the Kootenays

Gertie decorated her slick new ride with her own handsewn version of a Jolly Roger, and began racing along the rivers of the Kootenays, robbing steamships at will. In time, she soon picked up a small crew to help her with her piracy, but that act would prove to be her downfall. One of her crew, Bill Henson, decided that Gertie was not sharing their booty fairly, and he turned her in to the Provincial Police. In return he received a large reward and a promise of clemency for his piratical acts. With a trap set, Henson told

Gertie that a ship carrying a huge payroll would be traveling down Redfish Creek. Gertie stopped the boat, but instead of plunder found herself facing the police. She attempted escape, but Henson had damaged a gasket on *The Witch*, which slowed the boat considerably, allowing the authorities to capture her after a diligent struggle. Gertie was sentenced to life in prison, and she died in 1912 from pneumonia, without revealing where she'd hidden the treasure she'd accumulated during her years of pirating. Over the years, many have searched but no one has discovered where Gertie hid her gold.

April Fools

Gunpowder Gertie's tale is a fascinating one, but it isn't true. Gertie was the brainchild of Carolyn McTaggert, who concocted the tale when leading a group of schoolchildren on a tour of the Kootenay Lake area where she lived. McTaggert decided that a treasure hunt would pique the children's interest in local history. During the tour, she told them Gertie's story (as well as other true local stories), and the group ended their day digging for Gertie's treasure at the beach. The local paper, *The Kootenay Review*, picked up the story and ran it as an April Fools' joke. A few years later, someone sent the story to the Canadian Broadcasting Center, and they ran it as a true piece on their *This Day in History* television show. McTaggert now makes a living as a historical storyteller, and has added several Gertie tales to the original story she made up. To this day, there are still people who firmly believe that Gunpowder Gertie was real.

Half-Arse

French pirate Louis le Golif became known by the descriptive French name *Bourgnefesse* ("one buttock") as well as Half-Arse when his left buttock was shot off by a cannonball during a battle on Lake Nicaragua. A self-described valiant buccaneer, le Golif wrote a book detailing his many adventures: *Memoirs of a Buccaneer: Being a Wondrous and Unrepentant Account of the Prodigious Adventures and Amours of King Louis XIV's Loyal Servant, Louis Adhamer Timothy le Golif, as Bourgnefesse, Captain of the Buccaneers.* Despite its amusing title, or perhaps because of it, the book was not published in le Golif's lifetime. The manuscript was discovered in the rubble of a building that was bombed in France during World War II; it was subsequently published in 1954.

As the title of the book suggests, le Golif was very taken with himself, and his tales of bravery, wit, and cunning are exceptionally detailed and likely embellished. His story begins when he escaped indentured servitude to join the buccaneers. For a time, he was used as a sex slave, but later began sailing as a pirate. He became a pirate captain after the ship he was on was fiercely attacked by a Spanish ship. Amid the chaos, the ship's captain was killed. Le Golif immediately assumed command, and devised a plan to trick the Spanish into believing that they'd mistakenly attacked a Spanish merchant ship and the crew were in desperate need of assistance from their "brothers."

Using the only man onboard who spoke Spanish, le Golif succeeded in his ploy, and after killing the men sent to assist them, the pirates dressed in the dead Spaniards' clothes and rowed over with the intention of capturing the vessel. It is said that a bloody battle ensued and le Golif himself was forced at times to fight four or five men at once, firing a pistol from one hand while swinging his sword with the other. When the battle ended victoriously, le Golif's men elected him captain, and they sailed the Spanish ship, renamed the *Santa Clara*, back to the port of Tortuga. Upon their arrival le Golif was greeted by the governor and officials of the West Indian Trading Company, who gave him "a thousand embraces and civilities."

SHIVER ME
TIMBERS

Pirates love to recount a good tale, often creatively embellishing details as a story passed from person to person. Spreading gossip among a ship's crew or in the taverns of a pirate haven was known in the pirate realm as *telling it to the parrot.*

Le Golif continues to describe his many adventures throughout his memoir, all of which were filled with danger and gallantry. While his tales are a fun read, it's very likely that Half-Arse never really existed. There's no mention of him in any other stories of that era, which would seem unlikely considering his extraordinarily daring exploits. Much of the information that he reveals in his book fails to mesh with confirmed historical facts, which leads one to believe that Half-Arse is a fictional character ghostwritten by an unknown author who took great care in writing a cheeky adventure.

Ocean Born Mary

In 1720, Irish immigrants James and Elizabeth Wilson headed from Londonderry, Ireland, to Londonderry, New Hampshire. Their voyage turned out to be a tumultuous one, as Elizabeth gave birth to a daughter and their ship was captured by pirates led by young Captain Don Pedro. Deciding his captives were to be murdered, Pedro gave his orders, only to be interrupted by the sound of an infant crying. In an odd turn of events, Pedro insisted on seeing the little girl and was immediately taken with her. Addressing Elizabeth he informed her that all lives aboard the ship would be spared if she named her daughter Mary, in honor of his mother. When she agreed, Pedro ordered one of his crew to go to their ship. Upon his return, green silk brocade fabric was given to Elizabeth to be used as a wedding dress when her daughter came of age. After the exchange, Pedro and his crew sailed away, leaving Elizabeth and the rest of the passengers to continue on their journey.

Home Is Where the Hearthstone Is

Unfortunately for Elizabeth and Mary, James Wilson died shortly after reaching Boston, but they managed to settle in Londonderry, New Hampshire, as planned. In 1742, at the age of twenty-two, the red-haired Mary, in a dress fashioned from the green silk brocade fabric, was wed to James Wallace, with whom she had five children before becoming a widow. As fate would have it, pirate Don Pedro gave up his plunderous ways and opted for a luxurious retirement in Henniker, New Hampshire. It is said that he sought the whereabouts of Mary and eventually the two were wed and living in his mansion in Henniker.

Sometime during the wedded years, Mary witnessed her husband and one of his former crew as they buried a large trunk behind their home. The incident was never discussed, but Pedro did insist that if he should die, he wished to be interred with his treasure inside the mansion. Under the heading of "Be careful what you wish for," Pedro was allegedly found by Mary a year later, stabbed to death. Abiding by his final wishes, Mary did indeed bury her piratical husband and his treasure beneath a hearthstone. Of course the story doesn't end there. Legend has it that after Mary's demise in 1814, her ghost took up residence in their home, where she can be seen to this day.

Heart of the Matter

The story of Mary Wallace is one that is steeped in piracy, romance, and fate enveloped in a cloud of paranormal activity. Various versions of the legend are plentiful, with individuals, names, circumstances, and outcomes changing depending on who is telling the tale. So the questions remain: Was there really an Ocean Born Mary, did she actually marry a pirate, and is her ghost still swirling about Henniker, New Hampshire?

New Hampshire historians confirm that there was indeed a Mary Wallace who was born while her parents were asea on the same day their ship was captured in 1720. The invading captain did hear her wail and further investigated by approaching the Wilsons and ultimately making his offer to spare everyone's lives if they would honor his mother or possibly wife by calling her Mary. The gifts he awarded the infant, including the green silk fabric, are also confirmed. On her wedding day in 1742 Mary did wed James Wallace and she did indeed wear a dress made of the silk fabric. What she didn't do was marry Don Pedro or any other pirate at any time during her long life. Records show that she was, in fact, married to James Wallace until his death at age eighty-one.

PIECES of EIGHT

At that time, Mary was seventy-one, which would have made for an interesting romance with Pedro given that he would have been in his nineties residing in the Sunshine Happy Home for Pirates. Mary herself passed away in 1814 at age ninety-four, having lived with one of her sons for almost her last twenty years.

As to the infamous Henniker mansion where Mary and her notorious rogue allegedly lived, it was purchased by Wisconsonite Louis Maurice Auguste Roy in 1917 despite its state of disrepair after many years of vacancy. Roy, who was searching for a historical home, embraced Mary's legendary tale and went to great lengths to make the home a tourist attraction. The house has become known as the Ocean Born Mary House despite the fact that her son's house is the true residence of ocean-born Mary Wallace. And since science has yet to catch up, the opinion of whether or not the mansion is haunted by Mary depends entirely on which version of her legend you believe and whether or not you believe in ghosts.

Kidd's Secret Stash

When Captain William Kidd was captured in Boston in 1699 and sent back to London to await his trial, it was rumored that he left behind a great treasure. Kidd was tried, found guilty, and hanged at Execution Dock the following year, but throughout the process he continued protesting his innocence, and declaring that if freed he would lead his captors to his treasure. Whether the treasure actually existed or not is anyone's guess, but people have been searching the rivers and shores of New England for Kidd's secret stash since the 1700s, and continue to do so to the present day. Benjamin Franklin even wrote about it in 1729, saying, "You can hardly walk half a mile out of the town on any side without observing several pits dug . . . there seems to be some peculiar charm in the conceit of finding money."

You've Hit It!

One of the areas where Kidd supposedly buried his treasure was Clarke's Island, located in the Connecticut River in Northfield, Massachusetts. According to legend, Kidd and his men buried a chest full of gold on Clarke's Island, choosing the spot because it was secluded but distinctive enough to be easily found. Burying treasure wasn't all glamour, as one of Kidd's men would quickly discover. During the process they drew lots to see which of them would be sacrificed, then buried that man on top of the chest so he could guard the treasure for all eternity. The legend later grew to say that the treasure could only be dug up by three men, standing in a triangle formation around the spot, digging at midnight in absolute silence, under a full moon. A man named Abner Fields and two of his friends claimed to have tried it in the early 1800s, but when they struck the chest, a mysterious voice cried out, "You've hit it!" and the chest sank out of sight.

SCUTTLEBUTT

What is the Flying Dutchman?

Pirates were very superstitious. Some pirates claim to have seen the *Flying Dutchman*, a ship that set sail in 1660 and met with an accident as it attempted to sail around the Cape of Good Hope off South Africa. Legend has it that the ship still sails back and forth along the Cape, its ghostly crew crying for help as they endlessly work the sails.

In Palmer, Massachusetts in 1849, two boys claimed to have found a bottle wedged in a ledge of rocks. Upon opening the bottle, they discovered a letter that appeared to have been written by Captain Kidd to John Bailey, Esquire, claiming that Kidd was being held as a pirate and was waiting to be taken to England. Kidd asked Bailey to come to Boston, but if Bailey did not arrive before he left, he wanted to let him know that his treasure was buried on Conant's Island, in Boston Harbor, in two chests that contained gold, silver, jewels, and diamonds. He continued on to say that they were buried about 4 feet deep, with a flat stone placed on top of them, and a pile of stones nearby to mark the place, which was about 60 rods up the side of the hill.

The letter, as it turned out, did appear to have been written around 1700, as the seal on the bottle appeared to have been that old, and the information contained in the letter as well as the style of the writing all pointed to it being an actual Kidd letter. Unfortunately, the area of Conant's Island 60 rods up the side of the hill had been washed into the sea during the 150 years between the writing of the letter and its discovery, so it seemed likely that the sea had claimed the treasure. In a dispute over ownership of the letter, however, the father of one of the boys who found it admitted that he had written it, and that everything was a hoax. What has been confirmed is that Kidd did bury a small amount of treasure on Gardiner's Island just off of Long Island in

New York. That treasure was dug up almost immediately after his arrest and was sent to England with Kidd to be used as evidence in his trial.

New Jersey also boasts several areas that claim to be the site of Kidd's buried treasure. The first is Cape May, which had abundant fresh water and was a popular pit stop for pirates. A second possible site is at the mouth of the Toms River, where pirates often hunkered down to avoid the open ocean during storms. Yet another popular choice is Sandy Hook, where Kidd is known to have anchored his ship during his final voyage. The most likely New Jersey burial site is near what was ironically called Money Island, located off the coast of Cliffwood Beach. Money Island has since eroded and disappeared, but a few gold coins were found there, and a few more found at nearby Treasure Lake. Although many have dug at all these places, no treasure has been discovered.

Whether there was even any treasure to be found is a matter of debate. Kidd was not a particularly successful pirate, and many of his men had left him in Madagascar in 1699, possibly taking more than their share of loot with them. At one point, in an effort to find Kidd's alleged treasure, the governor of New York had Kidd's New York City home searched. The family silverware was taken but nothing else was found, and the silver was returned to Mrs. Kidd after she complained.

PIECES of EIGHT

The peculiar charm of finding money that Benjamin Franklin noted over 300 years ago endures to the present day. On any given day, it's not unusual to find individuals with metal detectors scouring the shores of rivers and islands throughout New England looking for the treasure of Captain Kidd.

The Adventure Galley

In the year 2000, an expedition to Madagascar led by Barry Clifford, who had found Black Bellamy's *Whydah Gally* (see Chapter 19), located two shipwrecks near each other off the coast. After several difficult months of political issues and a confrontation with a jealous archeologist who was doing all he could to stop Clifford from excavating the wrecks, the group secured permits and dug the site. The two wrecks found were the *Fiery Dragon*, a pirate ship commanded by a pirate known as "Billy One-Hand," and the *Adventure Galley*, William Kidd's ship that he'd been forced to burn and scuttle shortly before returning to Boston. While the *Fiery Dragon* yielded a respectable load of treasure, the *Adventure Galley* did not. It is assumed that Kidd likely removed most of her contents before he scuttled her. Of the few artifacts that were recovered from the *Adventure Galley*, one was of particular interest. It was a large pewter beer tankard, the type that would have belonged to an officer, possibly even to Kidd himself.

The Cobhams: A Piratical Marriage

Eric Cobham was born in England sometime around 1700, and as a teenager was caught working in a gang that was smuggling brandy from France into England. After two years of incarceration, he stole some gold coins and used them to purchase a ship. True piracy, however, didn't emerge until Cobham and his crew captured a ship in the Irish Sea, drowned all the sailors onboard, and claimed a booty worth £40,000. When Cobham returned to Plymouth, England, he met Maria Lindsey. He reportedly confessed to her the atrocities he committed, and she was so enamored with him and his lifestyle that she married him the following day. Shortly thereafter, the couple set sail for the Americas and settled into the area around Newfoundland, Canada. From 1720 to 1740, the couple and their crew attacked vessels with a vengeance, securing plunder and murdering the unfortunate sailors they'd captured.

Both Eric and Maria were known for never giving quarter to those they attacked, and for their cruel and vicious methods of killing. Maria in particular found murder to be a very pleasurable exercise, sometimes tying men to the mast of their ship and using them for target practice. It took Eric some time to convince Maria to give up piracy, but eventually they did retire and purchased an estate in France.

SEA ROVER

Eric Cobham adjusted quite well to being a landlubber, becoming a magistrate and living respectably. Maria, on the other hand, couldn't handle the life of a "proper" lady, and is said to have either killed herself or was murdered by her husband, depending on what version of the story is being told.

As a husband and wife pirate team, Eric and Maria Lindsey Cobham were a rarity in the pirate realm, and while their tale is exciting, it is often cited as pure fiction. No mention of either individual was ever made until the 1920s, and Eric is an uncommon name for someone born in 1700s England. Their story was allegedly written by Eric to be published after his death, but his wealthy family purchased every copy and burned them—all except for one copy that is supposedly in the French National Archives. In addition, details of the story don't correspond to known facts of the era, so it's highly unlikely that this cruel husband and wife pirate team really existed.

Chapter 21

Epilogue: Modern-day Piracy

Over the centuries, piracy has endured in one form or another. Since the 1980s it has unfortunately been on the rise, with modern-day pirates continuing the practices established by their historic brethren. Vessels ranging in size from smaller fishing boats to yachts to oil tankers have fallen victim to contemporary pirates who have the advantages of technology and dangerous weaponry. In general, contemporary pirates tend to prey on unstable waters and ports where corruption and disorganization breed contempt for laws and law enforcement.

Worldwide Epidemic

Over the centuries, piracy has had many incarnations, and although during different eras it has been suppressed, it has never been entirely wiped out. A host of disciplines have fallen victim to piracy, which remains by definition any act of robbery or violence done independently without jurisdiction. One might think the oceans of the world are safer places, but in many modern waters, they're not. Maritime piracy continues to be a constant source of danger, whether it's small bands of individuals attacking private yachts or groups terrorizing and robbing commercial vessels and even luxury liners.

Pirates of the new world have much in common with, and are no less cruel than, their predecessors, especially in regard to their attack techniques, pillaging and ransoming, and disregard for human life. The main difference nowadays is that technology is more advanced and the pirates more technically astute. But that doesn't always work in their favor. Advances in technology can help track pirates, assuming governments are willing to dedicate time, money, and resources to capturing them. Unfortunately, piracy seems more prevalent in regions of the world that are unstable, and this fact alone makes it difficult to monitor and wipe out their numbers.

PIECES of **E**IGHT

Maritime piracy isn't the only problem facing the modern world. The arrival of the Internet has given birth to all manner of entertainment piracy in the film and music industries, and rampant software and computer piracy. An ongoing worldwide battle continues to rage in an attempt to stop these illegal activities, but with the sheer volume of piracy, cessation of all such acts is virtually impossible.

Rising Tide

Statistics from major reporting bureaus such as the International Chamber of Commerce (ICC), and the International Maritime Bureau (IMB) and its Piracy Reporting Centre, show that hundreds of acts of piracy are committed each year. In 2004 alone, the IMB listed 325 attacks by pirates, the majority of which took place in Indonesia and off the coast of Nigeria. Over thirty individuals died as a result of those acts. In 2005, 276 attacks were reported, with almost 30 percent occurring in Indonesian waters. While there were no deaths reported that year, over 440 people were taken hostage by pirates, and of those, a dozen are still listed as missing. Additionally, in 2005, Iraq became a new pirate "hotspot," with 10 attacks reported, while none had been reported in their waters in earlier years. In the first quarter of 2006, 61 reports of piracy were received by the IMB Piracy Reporting Centre, which was up 8 percent from the same quarter of 2005. Modern-day piracy obviously continues to be a serious problem.

Going on Record

The Piracy Reporting Centre, based in Kuala Lumpur, Malaysia, was begun in 1992 under the umbrella of the IMB. While IMB statistics strive for accuracy, the sad truth is that many more attacks actually occur but go unreported. Sometimes acts of piracy are done at the behest of rival governments; others remain unchallenged due to the nature of the piracy in question, which is typically drug-trafficking or smuggling. Many other incidents are swept away as a result of corrupt officials or governments and the fear they inspire in their victims. One particular benefit of organizations such as the IMB, the International Chamber of Shipping (ICS), and the International Shipping Federation (ISF) are the guidelines they've established for anyone traveling through a danger zone. Information about these organizations and their safety guidelines can be found at the following Web sites:

- **ICS, ISF, and Piracy Reporting Centre:** *www.marisec.org/index .htm*
- **General Guidelines:** *www.marisec.org/piracy/general%20 guidance.htm*
- **ICC International Crime Services:** *www.icc-ccs.org/main/index .php*
- **Yacht Piracy:** *www.yachtpiracy.org/en/index.htm*

Vietnamese Terror

When the Golden Age of piracy ended in the 1700s, many people assumed that worldwide piracy ended as well. While pirate attacks did decrease dramatically, there were sporadic attacks that continued on, especially in the Far East and along the western coast of Africa. During the American Civil War, the South used privateers to help them in their fight against the North, but beyond that piracy had fallen to a very small amount, and it would continue as a fairly rare event throughout most of the nineteenth and twentieth centuries.

In the 1980s, modern-day piracy emerged as a threat when a large number of attacks were carried out by pirates on the Vietnamese boat people. More and more attacks occurred, and local governments were clearly not able to cope with them. These attacks reached their peak in the first six months of 1990, when the boat people reportedly suffered thirty-three pirate attacks. Those attacks left nine victims dead and 266 missing, and were responsible for thirty-five reported rapes. Even as local governments managed to deal with that particular problem, piracy against commercial shipping in the region became a more common event, signifying that modern-day piracy had begun in earnest.

Maritime Law

Maritime law is defined as the body of law relating to maritime commerce and navigation, and to maritime matters in general. Each country generally controls the waters surrounding it, and their laws apply, but there are vast areas on the high seas that aren't owned or governed by any country. Because of this, the international community has often attempted to work together to form laws that would cover the world's oceans. In 1958, the United Nations Conventions on the High Seas was held, and in 1982 the Convention on the Law of the Sea was convened. These two groups defined piracy as "an attack mounted for private ends on a ship on the high seas that involves violence, illegal detentions of persons or property, or the theft or destruction of goods." The more recent United Nations Law of the Seas defines piracy as "any illegal acts of violence or detention, or any act of depredation, committed by individuals for private ends against a private ship or aircraft." They also specify that two vessels must be involved in the incident, otherwise the act is one of hijacking rather than piracy.

SCUTTLEBUTT

Why was there a need for a change in the definition of piracy?

There are problems with the first definition, including the fact that it states that the attack must occur "on the high seas." Many pirate attacks are much closer to shore, some even occurring on docked boats and rivers. Also, this definition said that the attack had to occur for private gain, and this is difficult to prove given that pirate's identities are typically unknown and the individuals can't be shown to be acting for their own private gain.

The majority of modern pirates operate out of a specific homeland, and piracy is most common near areas where authorities tend to turn a blind eye to their acts. Most countries have differing levels of laws and law enforcement, and local governments may condone or even participate in acts of piracy. For example, in 1995 the Philippine Coast Guard boarded the merchant ship *Kafu Maru*, allegedly searching it for illegal firearms. They found no firearms, but did commandeer the ship's cargo of cigarettes and liquor, which was worth over 4,500,000 pesos. The coast guard officers neglected to report that they'd taken the cargo, despite the fact that it was later found in their homes.

Outside of local waters, international maritime laws prevail in any instance of piracy. If a ship on the high seas is suspected of being a pirate ship, it can legally be boarded and seized by any official government vessel. The pirates can then be arrested, and subjected to the laws and penalties of any country that apprehends them.

Yacht Piracy

Yacht piracy is more prevalent and more violent than the general public may realize. While attacks on yachts have increased dramatically, they're often unreported, partially because those who sail yachts for pleasure don't feel that being attacked by pirates fits their image. Many private yacht owners don't report incidents either because of trauma or embarrassment, or because they feel that authorities can't or won't help them. Over the decades, many yachts have simply vanished and no one knows what happened to them. They could have been lost to an accident, or they could have fallen victim to piracy, but there's no way to know for certain.

To pirates, a yacht can be a relatively easy ship to attack. Yachts generally have only a few people onboard, the sailors are usually wealthy folks, and the yachts themselves are very expensive. In addition, they often travel alone, can be expected to be out of touch with family and friends back home for lengthy periods of time, don't have to file plans with any agency, and often sail for a destination on a whim. While some yacht owners have taken to carrying weapons, many do not, and a number of those who were attacked and had available firearms never had a chance to arm themselves in time.

PIECES of EIGHT

While the adventure and excitement of sailing the high seas can be a great incentive for yachtsmen, they need to be cautious and keep in close contact with foreign consulates, travel agencies, cruising clubs, and other sailors via ham radios or satellite telephones.

New Victims, Old Tactics

Modern-day pirates enlist many of the same plundering techniques as traditional pirates, especially swift surprise attacks and rule-by-fear tactics. Like their historic counterparts, many pirates, especially smaller bands, lay in wait in small inlets or island hideaways and quickly strike when their target approaches. A major difference is that modern pirates have the advantage of much faster speed boats complete with technological conveniences, such as communication devices, navigation equipment, and tracking devices including radar and sonar.

Areas such as the South China Sea, Malaysia, Indonesia, Singapore, Colombia, Venezuela, Brazil, Nigeria, Somalia, and areas of the Philippines and the Caribbean continue to be plagued by maritime piracy. Smaller groups of pirates tend to prey on fishing vessels or cargo ships if given the opportunity. In general, they'll rob victims of anything they have onboard or even steal their vessel. The fact that they work independently, much like traditional pirates, means they can operate and thieve at will. Larger groups of pirates tend to be more organized, and their targets loaded with valuable cargo. These groups are more willing to take risks by hijacking, kidnapping, and ransoming crews, cargo, and vessels. Sophisticated operations such as these may require sponsorship from a government or corrupt officials or warlords. Pirates who are extremely well-organized and funded opt for sheer terrorism, their minds set on destruction, or at the very least, disruption of trade and commerce. No captive is ever safe from pirates, especially those pirates who are desperate and armed to the teeth.

The Information Highway

Because of advances in technology, today's pirates can intercept e-mails, radio and satellite transmissions, or any number of communication methods to ascertain what a vessel might be carrying and when it will be sailing. This is especially true of more sophisticated groups of pirates, who tend to operate under the guidance of a more powerful entity or in some cases officials or governments. These pirates set their sights on much bigger fish; their prey includes large oil tankers and merchant and cargo vessels. Piracy of this sort takes organization and planning, and often includes bribery of officials or insiders who can provide crucial information.

Armed and Dangerous

Pirates who aren't using knives or machetes generally carry heavier automatic weaponry such as rifles, AK-47s, and even grenade launchers, machine guns, and rocket launchers. They may wear ski masks, bandannas, or some type of head covering or clothing to hide their identity. They might also wear stolen uniforms and pose as officials or the military. They could attack in broad daylight, or raid ships in the dead of night when crews are asleep. When ships aren't as heavily manned, pirates have ample opportunity to strike. Quite often, pirates continue the traditional use of grappling hooks to pull their vessel closer to their target, giving them easier boarding access. The methods and madness of modern pirates vary from general robbery of small-cargoed boats to oil tankers that can be ransomed to their owners.

SEA ROVER

Some pirate operations involve stealing from smugglers, a dangerous business that is commonplace in major ports the world over, especially in Brazil, Bangladesh, Indonesia, and Nigeria. Commodities in this case can involve anything from narcotics to various technologies to exotic animals.

The River Wild

Piracy that occurs on major rivers is also prevalent. China's Yangtze River had long suffered from pirate attacks, but more recently, pirates have taken to the Amazon River, and as a result it has become one of the most dangerous waterways on the planet. Most people didn't recognize river piracy as a particular problem, but that changed in 2001 when pirates murdered New Zealander Sir Peter Blake. Blake was one of yachting's most accomplished and famous sailors, whose races and accolades are legendary. During his final expedition, the fifty-three-year-old Blake and his crew spent several months on the Amazon immersed in environmental research. His fateful night came at the end of their journey.

Aboard his 119-foot yacht, the *Seamaster*, Blake and his crew were anchored off Macapa, an area where the Amazon merges with the Atlantic Ocean. After going ashore to celebrate the end of their journey, the crew returned to the *Seamaster* to await the next day's trip to Venezuela, where they were to meet other members of Blakexpeditions. Little did they know that they were about to be attacked by a gang of Brazilian pirates called the Water Rats. Composed primarily of young twenty-something criminals, the pirates didn't expect any resistance, but Blake and his crew fought back and chaos ensued. In the struggle, Blake was fatally shot and died. The pirates proceeded to steal camera equipment, money, and the crew's watches—including Blake's—before leaving the *Seamaster*. The pirates were eventually apprehended and convicted, but the damage was done. Despite tragically falling victim to pirates, however, Blake's legacy and environmental research continue through the Sir Peter Blake Trust.

Strait to Hell

Another of the most dangerous and feared waterways is the Strait of Malacca, located between the Indonesian island of Sumatra and the Malaysian peninsula. With over 600 miles of waterways, Malacca serves as the primary shipping lane between the Pacific and Indian Oceans, where literally hundreds of ships—including oil tankers—sail its waters on a daily basis. Over a third of the world's trade is carried through the Strait, its waterway as narrow as two nautical miles in some areas. In addition to being a bottleneck of maritime commerce traffic, Malacca is an irresistible lure to modern pirates. A persistent haze in the area coupled with numerous islands and potential hiding places has resulted in all manner of pirate attacks including general robbery, terrorism, and the kidnapping of crews and vessels in exchange for ransom.

PIECES of EIGHT

Captains of oil tankers must be vigilant while maneuvering through narrow areas such as Malacca, in order to avoid running aground and causing catastrophic oil spills. Pirates capturing tankers have been known to tie up entire crews and leave a ship running full steam ahead while they escape.

As a result of pirate activity, international governments have been forced to work together to curtail attacks on their ships and personnel. Some nations, like the United States, refuse to negotiate or pay ransom to terrorists, a practice which in this case serves to further complicate matters. Adding to the mix are the natural disasters that the Malacca area has suffered in the past, including Indonesia's 2004 tsunami and various earthquakes in the

Sumatra region. After initial recovery from those disasters, piracy returned with a vengeance once international security forces protecting the regions dissipated. Many of the area's indigenous security forces and military aren't technologically equipped to handle the onslaught of pirates in the Strait, an issue that is in urgent need of resolution given the number of nations whose vessels sail through the area.

History, Horror, and Homage

Piracy is a subject that runs the gamut from perceived glamour to disgusting depravity. In the scale of human history, pirates aren't the worst groups of people who've dominated and abused individuals and entire civilizations, but as an entity it's fair to say that pirates have left and continue to leave an indelible mark on history. What remains undisputed is that pirates will forever be a source of entertainment, mystery, fantasy, and controversy wrapped in a cloak of myths and legends that will no doubt continue to enhance their personalities, careers, and reputations as consummate rogues of the sea.

Appendix A

Glossary

Articles:
Codes of conduct agreed upon and signed by all crewmembers of a pirate ship. Articles varied depending on the ship and her captain.

Atocha:
Nuestra Señora de Atocha. A Spanish galleon from the 1622 treasure fleet found by renowned treasure hunter Mel Fisher.

Barataria:
Renowned pirate lair in Louisiana made famous by French privateer, pirate, and smuggler Jean Lafitte.

Barbary Coast:
An area of northern Africa that ran along the Atlantic and Mediterranean coastlines of what are now Algeria, Morocco, Tunisia, and Libya.

Barrie, J.M.:
Author of the 1911 novel *Peter Pan*.

Bilge:
The lowest deck of a ship, often filled with rats, where stagnant water (called bilge water) that couldn't be pumped out of the ship became utterly toxic.

Bireme:
An ancient Greek vessel with two rows of oarsmen stacked one deck above the other.

Blackbirders:
Another name for slave ships. The act of slave trading was called blackbirding.

Blake, Sir Peter:
Famed New Zealand yachtsman who in 2001 was murdered by Brazilian pirates on the Amazon.

Bloody Mary:
Nickname of England's Queen Mary I who reigned from 1553 to 1558.

Boatswain:
The individual responsible for the ropes, lines, cables, sails, and every functional piece of equipment on a ship.

Boucan:
A wooden frame of green sticks and boughs that was used to smoke meat. The word buccaneer is derived from *boucan*.

Bow:
The front of a ship.

Brethren of the Coast:
Caribbean pirates, also referred to as buccaneers, who swore allegiance to each other.

Brigantine:
A double-masted ship usually rigged with a square-rigged *foresail* (the lowest sail on a mast) and a fore-and-aft rigged mainsail.

Buccaneers:
Hunters and survivalists who turned to piracy in the 1600s.

Buccaneers of America, The:
Infamous account of the adventures of the buccaneers. See Alexandre Exquemelin.

Cannons:
The primary weapons aboard pirate ships, initially made of bronze, then of cast iron. Sometimes referred to as "guns."

Captain:
A pirate who was voted leader of a ship by his crew, chosen for his leadership, tactical skills, and knowledge of trade routes and potential booty they could acquire.

Captain Blood:
Famous novel by Rafael Sabatini and 1935 film starring Errol Flynn.

Caravel:
A large but narrow Spanish vessel featuring a double or triple mast, flat stern, and lanteen sails.

Careening:
Process where a wooden ship is taken to shallow waters, the masts pulled to the ground, and the ship placed on its side so it can be repaired and cleaned.

Carpenter:
The crewmember who attended the ship's repair work and who also served as crew surgeon.

Carrack:
Light, fast ships that had three or four masts and a high-rounded stern.

Cartagena:
Modern-day Colombia.

Charts:
Maps drawn by cartographers or other individuals who sailed particular routes.

Clinker:
A Viking-style ship with hulls made of overlapping planks secured by iron nails, with tarred waterproofing wedged between the planks.

Cog:
A single-masted square-sailed vessel with high sides and raised bow and stern.

Concepcion:
Nuestra Señora de la Concepcion. A Spanish galleon found off the coast of Manila by Burt Webber in 1978.

Corsairs:
Barbary Coast pirates who were the European and American version of privateers.

Defoe, Daniel:
Author of *Robinson Crusoe.*

Doubloons:
Gold coins minted by Spain that were originally called *escudos.*

Drakar (Dragon):
Large Viking longship with over seventy oars and a length of over 150 feet.

Earrings:
Often gold, pirates and privateers wore them primarily as a show of wealth, to avoid taxa-tion, or as security to pay for their funeral.

Elizabeth I:
The Queen of England who reigned from 1558 to 1603, and issued letters of marque to privateers including Francis Drake, John Hawkins, Walter Raleigh, and Richard Grenville.

Escudos:
See Doubloons.

Eyepatch:
Used by pirates to cover the loss of an eye or blindness, or to intimidate foes.

Execution Dock:
Gallows located in the Wapping district of London, where many famous pirates were hanged.

Exquemelin, Alexandre:
Renowned buccaneer, pirate, and surgeon during the mid- to late 1600s. Author of *The Buccaneers of America.*

Fearnought:
A short thick woolen jacket or overcoat usually gray or blue in color, often made of canvas and painted with wax or tar for waterproofing.

Flogging:
A common punishment involving whipping or lashing a victim with a cat o' nine tails. Additional pain was sometimes inflicted by pouring salt into the open wounds.

Flotilla:
A large fleet of ships sailing together.

Fore-and-aft Rigged:
Sails lined up with a ship's hull, rather than being set at right angles to the hull as when they were square-rigged.

Forecastle:
The portion of a ship located ahead of the tallest mast, or *mainmast,* which generally holds the sailors' quarters.

Galleon:
A 400-ton cargo- and treasure-bearing warship built by the Spanish that was the supreme target of pirates.

Galley:
Ancient single-deck vessels powered by sails and oars.

German Princess, The:
Nickname of Englishwoman Mary Carleton, the most infamous prostitute in Port Royal during the 1670s.

Gibbet:
An iron cage designed specifically to display the bodies of executed criminals.

Gokstad Ship:
Famed Viking warship excavated in Norway in 1880.

Golden Age:
An era of piracy estimated to have lasted between thirty and fifty years, with its heyday being from 1714 to 1722.

Granado (or Granada) Shell:
A primitive grenade made of hollow balls of iron or wood that could be filled with gunpowder and set with a fuse. Also called powder flasks.

Hanseatic League:
A Germanic guild of naval and merchant ships during the 1200s that gained riches through extensive commerce while attempting to suppress piracy.

Helmsman:
The individual who operated the wheel that controlled a ship's rudder. Worked closely with the ship's master and boatswain.

Hispaniola:
Present-day Haiti and the Dominican Republic, claimed by Christopher Columbus for Spain in 1492.

Hook:
A prosthetic device used by pirates who lost a hand or arm.

Huguenots:
French Protestants, some of whom were pirates, who challenged Spain for New World dominance during the 1500s.

Hull:
The frame or body of a ship.

International Maritime Bureau (IMB):
A modern-day organization that oversees the Piracy Reporting Centre based in Kuala Lumpur, Malaysia.

Jib:
A triangular sail attached to the bow of a ship.

Johnson, Captain Charles:
Author of the renowned 1678 book *A General History of the Robberies and Murders of the Most Notorious Pyrates.*

Jolly Roger:
An all-encompassing description of pirate flags, most typically showing a skull and crossbones.

Keelhauling:
A punishment where victims were tied to a rope hanging from a yardarm, then tossed into the sea and dragged under the ship's keel.

Knarr:
A Viking merchant vessel over 50 feet long that could carry heavy cargo of up to fifteen tons.

Langrel:
A type of cannon shot favored by privateers and pirates made of canvas bags filled with musket balls or bits of scrap iron and chain.

Lanteen:
A triangular sail suspended by a long arm, or yardarm.

Letter of Marque:
Commissions, licenses, or other documents that authorized the holder to attack enemy merchant ships in the name of the government that had issued the letter.

Letter of Reprisal:
An uncommon privateering commission, valid during war or peace, that allowed the holder to seize goods from a ship in order to right a wrong that could not be corrected in the legal system.

Libertalia:
A fictional pirate haven deemed to be the perfect pirate utopia where "democracy would rule."

Lieutenant:
The second in command of a ship, under the captain.

Long Clothes:
Clothing worn by pirates that were loose and blousy. Typically worn while not aboard ship.

Longship:
A distinctively narrow craft, designed for speed, pillage, warring, and exploration. The most recognizable Viking vessel.

Madagascar:
Notorious haven and tropical utopia where pirates established "kingships."

Mainmast:
The tallest mast of a ship, usually located at the center of the ship.

Mainsail:
The largest sail of a mainmast.

Maracaibo:
A Spanish port in Venezuela.

***Maravilla*:**
Nuestra Señora de la Maravilla. A Spanish galleon that sunk in 1656 off the Bahamian coastline and was found by treasure hunter Bob Marx.

Marooning:
A pirate punishment that involved abandoning an individual or group on an uninhabited island with few or no natural resources.

Master Gunner:
The individual in charge of the cannon during attacks, and of directing the crew in aiming, firing, and reloading the cannon.

Maynard, Robert:
English lieutenant who in 1718 was credited with killing Blackbeard.

Mizzenmast:
Typically the shortest mast of a ship, and in all but the largest sailing ships is the mast farthest from the bow.

Mock Trials:
A favorite pastime of pirates while at sea, where they would pretend to be criminals and hold a trial.

Money Pit of Oak Island:
Located off the coast of Nova Scotia, the most famous and elusive treasure trove of the past two centuries.

Monmouths:
Knitted or woolen caps typically worn by sailors and pirates.

Monoreme:
A long, narrow ancient Greek vessel that relied on a single row of as many as fifty oars for propulsion.

Mutiny:
When men in the service of a particular captain turned against him and took over the ship.

Navigator:
The most important member of a crew, often pressed into pirate service from captured merchant vessels.

New Providence:
An island in the Bahamas that served as a pirate haven until it was reformed by governor Woodes Rogers.

New Spain:
See Hispaniola.

Ocean Born Mary:
New Hampshire resident Mary Wallace, who allegedly married the pirate who had invaded the ship she was born on and spared the crew's lives because of her.

Ocracoke Island:
Blackbeard's hideout off the coast of North Carolina.

Oseberg Ship:
Famed Viking clinker-style karve ship excavated in Norway in 1904.

Parrots:
A commodity pirates occasionally sold for high prices.

Pegleg:
A prosthetic device often made of wood worn by pirates who had survived the loss of a leg.

Philip II:
The King of Spain who married England's Mary I in 1554 for political reasons.

Pieces of Eight:
Silver coins minted by Spain that were originally called *reales*.

Pinnace:
A small, fast, maneuverable vessel with two square-rigged masts. Typically 40 feet long, it could carry up to 15 tons of cargo.

Pirate:
Someone who without government authorization steals from another party while at sea or who plunders goods on land, having made their approach from an ocean or body of water.

Pirate Code:
See Articles.

Pompey the Great:
Famed Roman naval leader who wiped out Mediterranean piracy in 67 B.C., an act that virtually eliminated the practice for 400 years.

Portholes:
Small square windows cut into the hull through which pirates could shoot guns.

Portobello:
Port city of Panama that was attacked by Henry Morgan in 1668.

Port Royal:
Notorious Jamaican pirate haven that fell into the sea during a 1692 earthquake and tidal wave.

Powder Monkeys:
Boys serving on pirate ships who prepared cartridges, filled canisters with gunpowder, and transported and loaded them into muskets and cannons.

Privateer:
An individual who engaged in privateering.

Privateering:
Legal piracy that gave the bearer of a government commission the right to board any ship and seize its contents.

Quartermaster:
The individual responsible for keeping track of ship stores and inventory. Also the arbiter for crew disputes and liaison between crew and captain.

Reales:
See Pieces of Eight.

Renegados:
European seamen who converted to Islam and preyed on European merchant ships in the company of the Barbary pirates.

Rigging:
The systems of ropes and lashings used to secure a ship's sails and masts.

Sabatini, Rafael:
Renowned author who wrote *The Sea Hawk* (1915) and *Captain Blood* (1922).

Sailor's Petticoats:
Sometimes called petticoat breeches. Shorter trousers secured just above the ankles.

Salvo:
A simultaneous discharge of two or more guns as a salute.

Schooner:
A double-masted ship with fore-and-aft rigging.

Scurvy:
A life-threatening disease caused by a lack of vitamin C.

Sea Dogs:
Queen Elizabeth I's nickname for England's famed privateers. Sometimes called sea rovers.

Sextant:
Navigational device used to measure the angle of the sun or stars above the horizon.

Ship's Master:
The individual who oversees the actual sailing of a ship and the coordination of all functional aspects of a ship.

Shipwright:
A carpenter who designs, constructs, and launches wooden vessels.

Skull and Crossbones:
The image most associated with pirates, usually on their flag. See also Jolly Roger.

Slaver:
Another name for a slave ship.

Sloop:
A common pirate ship with a single mast and usually a fore-and-aft rigged mainsail.

Slush Fund:
Excess grease that resulted from frying salt pork aboard ship that was sold for use in candlemaking and tanning.

Spanish Main:
Spanish-controlled lands that included areas of the Caribbean and Central and South America.

Square Meal:
Literal meaning referring to the square wooden platters pirates often ate from while onboard ship.

Square-Rigger:
A powerful three-masted ship with square rigging and jib sails.

Square-Rigged Sails:
Rectangular sails draped from horizontal bars called *yards*, or *yardarms*, which are attached to the mast.

Stern:
The back of a ship.

Sterncastle:
The upper portion of the sailing deck located behind a short mast, or *mizzenmast*. Typically used as an onboard fortress.

Stevenson, Robert Louis:
Author of *Treasure Island*, published in 1883.

Stinkpots:
A container filled with any vile-smelling item pirates could find. Usually tossed onto a potential victim's deck.

Strait of Malacca:
An over 600-mile-long waterway between Sumatra and the Malaysian peninsula plagued by modern-day pirates.

Tar:
Another name for sailor. Sometimes called Jack tar.

Tricorn or Tricorne:
A three-cornered hat often worn by pirates and seamen.

Trireme:
An ancient Greek vessel with three rows of oarsmen stacked one deck above the other.

Tortuga:
Famous pirate haven. A small turtle-shaped island at the northwest corner of Hispaniola (present-day Haiti). Often called Turtle Island.

Wallace, Mary:
See Ocean Born Mary.

Woolding:
A form of torture that involved tying a cord around a prisoner's head and around a stick. The stick would be twisted until the victim's eyes popped out.

Yardarm:
A long arm that is set at a forty-five-degree angle to a ship's mast. Sometimes called a yard.

Appendix B

Famous Pirates

Adventure Galley:
Captain William Kidd's ship.

Barbarossa Brothers:
Greek brothers Aruj and Hizir. Two of the most famous Barbary Corsairs who pirated against the Christians during the early 1500s.

Bellamy, Samuel:
See Black Sam Bellamy.

Black Bart:
Prolific Welsh pirate who terrorized the Caribbean during the Golden Age. Known for his successful plundering and flashy attire. See Bartholomew Roberts.

Blackbeard:
Also known as Edward Teach. Notorious Golden Age pirate renowned for his devilish appearance and rule-by-fear tactics.

Black Sam Bellamy:
British pirate active in the Caribbean during the Golden Age. Captain of the *Whydah Gally*.

Bonnet, Stede:
Plantation owner turned pirate who purchased his own ship. He was hanged in 1718.

Bonny, Anne:
Irish pirate who was partnered with Calico Jack in the Caribbean during the Golden Age.

Braziliano, Roche (Rock or Rok):
Cruel Dutch pirate who sailed with Francois L'Ollonais through-out the Spanish Main during the 1660s.

Breakes, Hiram:
Dutch sailor turned pirate who allegedly murdered his mistress's husband and later killed himself after she murdered their infant son.

Captain Hook:
Evil villain of J.M. Barrie's 1911 novel *Peter Pan*.

Cheng, I Sao:
Asian pirate during the early 1800s who took command of over 50,000 pirates when her husband died. Often called Mrs. Cheng.

Choi San, Lai:
Known as Queen of the Macao Pirates, she commanded pirates and a dozen junks in the waters surrounding Hong Kong during the 1920s.

Cilician Pirates:
Mediterranean pirates who primarily sailed off the southern coast of Turkey during the first century B.C.

Cobham, Eric and Maria:
Mythical husband and wife pirates whose acts over two decades were particularly outrageous and violent.

Cutlass Liz:
British housewife turned pirate during the late 1500s.

Dampier, William:
English buccaneer and navigator during the 1600s, who circumnavigated the world three times.

Danziger, Simon:
Dutch pirate of the early seventeenth century who was known as "Captain Devil."

Davis, Howell:
Welsh pirate during the early 1700s, whose career lasted only a year.

De Soto, Benito:
Exceptionally cruel Portuguese pirate during the 1820s and 1830s.

De Veenboer, Suleyman Reis:
Dutch Barbary Corsair during the 1600s.

Drake, Sir Francis:
Privateer to Elizabeth I during the 1500s. A vice-admiral in the British navy, he later sailed around the world. Cousin to Sir John Hawkins.

England, Edward:
Irish pirate during the 1700s who captained the Fancy, was marooned, and died a beggar.

Eustace the Monk:
A Medieval monk turned pirate during the 1200s.

Every, Henry:
Prolific and brutal English pirate during the late 1600s, who had a London stage play based on his exploits.

Flail of the Spaniards:
See Francois L'Ollonais.

Frobisher, Martin:
Privateer for Elizabeth I who turned to piracy against the Spanish. Known for returning to England with "fool's gold."

Gilbert, Don Pedro:
American pirate during the 1830s known for his cruelty and for being the last pirate to commit acts of piracy in the Atlantic.

Greaves, Red Legs:
Well-respected Scottish pirate of the Golden Age who in later years was known for his charitable deeds.

Grenville, Sir Richard:
Privateer for Elizabeth I during the late 1500s who plundered Spanish towns and galleons in the Azores.

Gunpowder Gertie:
Gertrude Imogene Stubbs. A mythical Canadian pirate who preyed upon steamboats in British Columbia in the early 1900s.

Half-Arse:
Possibly mythical French buccaneer turned pirate Louis le Golif, who lost one buttock to cannon fire and who may or may not have penned his own memoirs.

Hawkins, Sir John:
British slaver and pirate who served under Elizabeth I during the mid- to late 1500s in the Spanish Main and the Caribbean. Cousin to Sir Francis Drake.

Hawkins, Sir Richard:
Son of John Hawkins and privateer for Elizabeth I during the late 1500s.

Heyn, Pieter (Piet):
Dutch pirate who in 1628 at age fifty-one captured an entire treasure convoy off Cuba.

Hook, Captain:
Renowned fictional bewigged pirate featured in J.M. Barrie's legendary *Peter Pan*.

Hornigold, Benjamin:
Privateer turned pirate during the 1700s who served as mentor to Edward Teach.

Jol, Cornelis:
One-legged Dutch privateer for the Dutch West Indies Company during the 1630s and 1640s. Nicknamed *Pie de Palo*, or wooden leg, by the Spanish.

Kidd, William:
Scottish privateer turned pirate during the 1700s, whose alleged buried treasure has never been found.

Killigrew, Lady Mary:
English pirate and wife of the Vice-Admiral of Cornwall during the late 1500s.

Lafitte, Jean:
French pirate and smuggler of the 1800s who based his operations in New Orleans.

Le Clerc, Francois:
French privateer known throughout the Caribbean as *Jambe de Bois*, or leg of wood, for the pegleg he wore.

Le Golif, Louis:
See Half-Arse.

L'Ollonais, Francois:
Born Jean David Nau. One of the most cruel and sadistic pirates known. Based in Tortuga, he was dubbed *Flail of the Spaniards* by the Spanish.

Low, Edward:
English pirate during the 1720s who is known for being one of the most sadistic pirates on record.

Lowther, George:
Scottish pirate active during the 1720s.

Lukka:
One of the earliest groups of sea raiders, active around the fourteenth century B.C.

Menendez, Pedro de Avilles:
Spanish nobleman and pirate hunter active in the Spanish Main during the 1500s.

Morgan, Henry:
Notorious Welsh buccaneer of the 1600s who became the "greatest of the Brethren of the Coast."

Myngs, Christopher:
English naval officer and buccaneer during the 1600s who mentored Henry Morgan.

Nau, Jean David:
See Francois L'Ollonais.

O'Malley, Grace:
Irish pirate during the mid- to late 1500s, she was nicknamed "Mother of All Rebellions."

***Queen Anne's Revenge*:**
Blackbeard's revered flagship, which has been found off the North Carolina coast.

Rackham, Calico Jack:
Golden Age pirate who was noted for having two women aboard his ship—Anne Bonny and Mary Read.

Raleigh, Sir Walter:
Tumultuous privateer who served under Elizabeth I during the late 1500s. Half-brother to Sir Humphrey Gilbert.

Read, Mary:
Notorious Golden Age pirate who served with Calico Jack Rackham and Anne Bonny during the 1700s. Her alter ego was Mark Read.

Roberts, Bartholomew:
See Black Bart.

Rogers, Woodes:
Former English privateer who served as governor of New Providence starting in 1718.

Rupert, Prince of the Rhine:
German royal turned pirate during the 1600s who survived his career to become an English governor.

Schouten, Peter:
Dutch privateer who fought against the Spanish during the 1620s.

Sea Peoples:
Tribes who banded together as pirates and terrorized the east coast of the Mediterranean sea during the twelfth and thirteenth centuries B.C.

Shirland, Elizabeth:
See Cutlass Liz.

Silver, Long John:
One-legged fictional pirate of Robert Louis Stevenson's *Treasure Island* who walked with a crutch and sported a parrot on his shoulder.

Spriggs, Francis:
Notoriously brutal pirate who committed torturous acts in the 1720s aboard his ship, *Delight*.

Stubbs, Gertrude Imogene:
See Gunpowder Gertie.

Teach, Edward:
See Blackbeard.

Tew, Thomas:
American pirate who became a privateer for Bermuda in the early 1690s.

Van Haarlem, Jan Janszoon:
Also known as Murad Reis. Ruthless Dutch Barbary Corsair during the 1600s.

Vane, Charles:
British pirate during the 1700s who was known for his cruelty.

Victual Brothers:
A maritime guild of pirates that wreaked havoc in the Baltic Sea from the late twelfth century until the mid-fourteenth century.

Vikings:
Norse pirates who ruled the Baltic and Mediterranean Seas starting in 789 A.D.

Wall, Rachel:
American pirate active during the late 1700s.

Whydah Gally:
Samuel "Black Sam" Bellamy's ship, and the first known pirate vessel in U.S. waters to be salvaged.

Appendix C

Piratespeak

Belly Timber:
Another name for food.

Bilge Rat:
Rats that swarmed in the bilge of a ship. Also a derogatory aspersion pirates cast upon one another.

Bite the Bullet:
Pirates or captives being flogged would be given a bullet to bite on to keep them from screaming.

Booty:
Any goods, money, or supplies obtained illegally.

Bumboo or **Bombo:**
A sweet and potent mixture of water, nutmeg, sugar, and rum.

Burgoo:
A watery gruel flavored with sugar, salt, and butter, often serving as a pirate's breakfast.

Catgut Scrapers:
Fiddlers who served aboard pirate ships.

Cat o' Nine Tails:
A short wooden stick or handle with nine knotted ropes, each 18 inches long, secured to its end and used for flogging.

Catting:
The act of pursuing prostitutes.

Churchwarden:
A long-stemmed clay pipe up to 16 inches long, typically smoked by pirates visiting taverns or punch houses.

Cut and Run:
Pirates in need of a hasty retreat would cut the sail lashings or anchor cables to enable a ship to speed away.

Davy Jones' Locker:
Pirate term for someone ending up at the bottom of the ocean. Also used as a threat of death or when speaking of a pirate nearing death.

Flip:
A hot mixture of a small or light beer combined with sugar and brandy.

Give Quarter:
A term pirates used as an offer for their victims to surrender.

Grog:
A typical reference to alcohol, usually rum or watered-down rum.

Hard Tack:
Biscuits eaten aboard a pirate ship, typically infested with weevils and other critters.

Hit the Deck:
A literal term which meant avoiding swivel guns, or small cannon at the rail of a ship or artillery coming from an opponent.

In the Same Boat:
Often interchangeable with "grin and bear it." A phrase meaning that pirate crews were in the same boat and situations together.

Kill-devil:
A lethal rum punch enjoyed by pirates who visited Port Royal, Jamaica.

Know the Ropes:
Being familiar with all the ropes and riggings of a ship.

Landlubber:
Term for a sailor getting his sea legs or individuals who don't often sail.

Let the Cat Out of the Bag:
The removal of the cat o' nine tails from a leather bag prior to flogging.

Loaded to the Gunwalls:
Pirate term for excessive drinking.

Loose Cannon:
Literal term aboard a pirate ship that meant an unsecured cannon.

On an Even Keel:
Term meaning a vessel that sailed steady without any threat of "keeling over."

On the Account:
Once a pirate signed a ship's articles he would have to account for his own illegal actions if caught, and would be paid only when there was booty to share.

Over a Barrel:
Term describing victims of flogging who were often tied to inanimate objects, like a gun barrel, prior to whipping.

Pissing More than He Drinks:
Pirate term for someone who boasts too much. Sometimes called a *windbag*.

Piss Money Against a Wall:
Pirate term for spending booty on alcohol.

Prostitutes:
A favorite pastime of all pirates. Also called whores and strumpets.

Punch House:
Another name for a brothel.

Rub Salt into the Wound:
The practice of pouring salt over victims' wounds after they've been flogged.

Rumfustian:
A favorite pirate drink, usually served hot, which contained a blend of sugar, beer, gin, sherry, and raw eggs.

Salamagundy:
A mix-and-match meal consisting of boiled onions and salt fish. Often added were available meats, anchovies, eggs, oil, wine, and various types of marinated shellfish.

Sun Dried:
A term used to describe the body of a hanged pirate that was left hanging as a warning to other pirates.

Swung Off:
A piratical reference describing the way the body of a hanged man tended to swing back and forth.

The Cat Has Kittened in My Mouth:
A pirate's description of the bad taste in his mouth after a night of drinking.

Three Sheets to the Wind:
Pirate term for excessive drinking.

Walking the Plank:
One of the great pirate myths. An alleged punishment in which victims were blindfolded, then forced to walk across a plank hanging from the side of the ship.

Appendix D

Recommended Reading

Bawlf, Samuel. *The Secret Voyage of Sir Francis Drake 1577–1580*. New York: Walker & Company, 2003.

Botting, Douglas. *The Pirates*. Alexandria, Virginia: Time-Life Books, 1976.

Breverton, Terry. *The Pirate Dictionary*. Gretna, LA: Pelican Publishing, 2004.

Cawthorne, Nigel. *Pirates: An Illustrated History*. Edison, NJ: Chartwell Books, 2005.

Clifford, Barry, with Peter Tuchi. *The Pirate Prince*. New York: Simon & Schuster, 1993.

Clifford, Barry, with Paul Perry. *Return to Treasure Island and the Search for Captain Kidd*. New York: HarperCollins, 2003.

Cordingly, David. *Life among the Pirates: The Romance and the Reality*. London: Abacus, 1995.

———. *Pirates: Terror on the High Seas from the Caribbean to the South China Sea*. Atlanta: Turner Publishing, 1996.

———. *Under the Black Flag: The Romance and the Reality of Life among the Pirates*. New York: Random House, 1996.

Cordingly, David, and John Falconner. *Pirates: Facts and Fiction*. New York: Abbeville Press, 1992.

Davis, William C. *The Pirates Lafitte: The Treacherous World of the Corsairs of the Gulf*. New York: Harcourt, 2005.

Day, Jean. *Blackbeard: Terror of the Seas*. Newport, North Carolina: Golden Age Press, 1997.

Defoe, Daniel. *A General History of The Robberies and Murders of the Most Notorious Pyrates*. New York: Dover Publications, 1972.

Defoe, Daniel. *Robinson Crusoe*. London, 1719.

Downie, Robert. *The Way of the Pirate*. New York: ibooks, inc., 1998.

Druett, Joan. *She Captains: Heroines and Hellions of the Sea*. New York: Simon & Schuster, 2000.

Earle, Peter. *The Pirate Wars*. New York: Thomas Dunne Books, 2003.

Eastman, Tamara, and Constance Bond. *The Pirate Trial of Anne Bonny and Mary Read*. Cambria Pines by the Sea, California: Fern Canyon Press, 2000.

Exquemelin, A.O. *The Buccaneers of America*. Mineola, New York: Dover Publications, 1969.

Grissim, John. *The Lost Treasure of the Concepcion: The Story of One of the World's Greatest Treasure Finds and Burt Webber, the Man Who Never Gave Up*. New York: William Morrow, 1980.

Johnson, Captain Charles. [1724]. *A General History of the Robberies & Murders of the Most Notorious Pirates*. London: Conway Maritime Press, 1998.

Jones, Gwen. *A History of Vikings*. London: Oxford University Press, 1973.

Kemp, P. K., and Christopher Lloyd. *Brethren of the Coast: Buccaneers of the South Seas*. New York: St. Martin's Press, 1960.

Konstam, Angus. *Blackbeard: America's Most Notorious Pirate.* New York: John Wiley & Sons Books, 2006.

———. *The History of Pirates.* Guilford, CT: The Lyons Press, 1999.

———. *The History of Shipwrecks.* Guilford, CT: The Lyons Press, 1999.

———. *Pirates 1660–1730.* Oxford, UK: Osprey Publishing, 1998.

———. *The Pirate Ship 1660–1730.* Oxford, UK: Osprey Publishing, 2003.

———. *Privateers & Pirates 1730–1830.* Oxford, UK: Osprey Publishing, 2001.

Lewis, Jon E. *The Mammoth Book of Pirates.* New York: Carroll & Graf Publishers, 2006.

Marx, Robert. *Pirate Port: The Story of the Sunken City of Port Royal.* Cleveland, Ohio: The World Publishing Co., 1967.

Meltzer, Milton. *Piracy & Plunder: A Murderous Business.* New York: Dutton Children's Books, 2001.

Nesmith, Robert I. *Dig for Pirate Treasure.* New York: Devin-Adair Company, 1958.

Parry, Dan. *Blackbeard: The Real Pirate of the Caribbean.* New York: Thunder's Mouth Press, 2006.

Pickering, David. *From Blackbeard to Walking the Plank.* New York: HarperCollins Publications, 2006.

Pringle, Patrick. *Jolly Roger: The Story of the Great Age of Piracy.* Mineola, New York: Dover Publications, 2001.

Rediker, Marcus. *Between the Devil and the Deep Blue Sea.* New York: Cambridge University Press, 1997.

———. *Villains of All Nations.* Boston: Beacon Press Books, 2004.

Rieseberg, Lieut. Harry E. *Fell's Complete Guide to Buried Treasure, Land & Sea.* New York: Frederick Fell, Inc., 1970.

Rogozinski, Jan. *Honor among Thieves: Captain Kidd, Henry Every, and the Pirate Democracy in the Indian Ocean.* Mechanicsburg, Pennsylvania: Stackpole Books, 2000.

Stephens, John Richard. *Captured by Pirates.* Cambria Pines by the Sea, California: Fern Canyon Press, 1996.

Stevenson, Robert Louis. *Treasure Island.* London, 1883.

Thubron, Colin. *The Ancient Mariners.* Alexandria, Virginia: Time-Life Books, Inc., 1981.

Time-Life Books. *Time Frame 800–1000: Fury of the Northmen.* Richmond, Virginia: Time-Life Books, Inc., 1998.

Tompkins, B. A. *Treasure: Man's 25 Greatest Quests for El Dorado.* New York: Times Books, 1979.

Wagner, Kip, as told to L. B. Taylor Jr. *Pieces of Eight: Recovering the Riches of a Lost Spanish Treasure Fleet.* New York: Dutton, 1968.

Wernick, Robert. *The Seafarers: The Vikings.* Alexandria, Virginia: Time-Life Books, Inc., 1979.

Index

THE EVERYTHING SERIES!

BUSINESS & PERSONAL FINANCE

Everything® Accounting Book
Everything® Budgeting Book
Everything® Business Planning Book
Everything® Coaching and Mentoring Book
Everything® Fundraising Book
Everything® Get Out of Debt Book
Everything® Grant Writing Book
Everything® Guide to Personal Finance for Single Mothers
Everything® Home-Based Business Book, 2nd Ed.
Everything® Homebuying Book, 2nd Ed.
Everything® Homeselling Book, 2nd Ed.
Everything® Improve Your Credit Book
Everything® Investing Book, 2nd Ed.
Everything® Landlording Book
Everything® Leadership Book
Everything® Managing People Book, 2nd Ed.
Everything® Negotiating Book
Everything® Online Auctions Book
Everything® Online Business Book
Everything® Personal Finance Book
Everything® Personal Finance in Your 20s and 30s Book
Everything® Project Management Book
Everything® Real Estate Investing Book
Everything® Retirement Planning Book
Everything® Robert's Rules Book, $7.95
Everything® Selling Book
Everything® Start Your Own Business Book, 2nd Ed.
Everything® Wills & Estate Planning Book

COOKING

Everything® Barbecue Cookbook
Everything® Bartender's Book, $9.95
Everything® Cheese Book
Everything® Chinese Cookbook
Everything® Classic Recipes Book
Everything® Cocktail Parties and Drinks Book
Everything® College Cookbook
Everything® Cooking for Baby and Toddler Book
Everything® Cooking for Two Cookbook
Everything® Diabetes Cookbook
Everything® Easy Gourmet Cookbook
Everything® Fondue Cookbook
Everything® Fondue Party Book
Everything® Gluten-Free Cookbook
Everything® Glycemic Index Cookbook
Everything® Grilling Cookbook

Everything® Healthy Meals in Minutes Cookbook
Everything® Holiday Cookbook
Everything® Indian Cookbook
Everything® Italian Cookbook
Everything® Low-Carb Cookbook
Everything® Low-Fat High-Flavor Cookbook
Everything® Low-Salt Cookbook
Everything® Meals for a Month Cookbook
Everything® Mediterranean Cookbook
Everything® Mexican Cookbook
Everything® No Trans Fat Cookbook
Everything® One-Pot Cookbook
Everything® Pizza Cookbook
Everything® Quick and Easy 30-Minute, 5-Ingredient Cookbook
Everything® Quick Meals Cookbook
Everything® Slow Cooker Cookbook
Everything® Slow Cooking for a Crowd Cookbook
Everything® Soup Cookbook
Everything® Stir-Fry Cookbook
Everything® Tex-Mex Cookbook
Everything® Thai Cookbook
Everything® Vegetarian Cookbook
Everything® Wild Game Cookbook
Everything® Wine Book, 2nd Ed.

GAMES

Everything® 15-Minute Sudoku Book, $9.95
Everything® 30-Minute Sudoku Book, $9.95
Everything® Blackjack Strategy Book
Everything® Brain Strain Book, $9.95
Everything® Bridge Book
Everything® Card Games Book
Everything® Card Tricks Book, $9.95
Everything® Casino Gambling Book, 2nd Ed.
Everything® Chess Basics Book
Everything® Craps Strategy Book
Everything® Crossword and Puzzle Book
Everything® Crossword Challenge Book
Everything® Crosswords for the Beach Book, $9.95
Everything® Cryptograms Book, $9.95
Everything® Easy Crosswords Book
Everything® Easy Kakuro Book, $9.95
Everything® Easy Large Print Crosswords Book
Everything® Games Book, 2nd Ed.
Everything® Giant Sudoku Book, $9.95
Everything® Kakuro Challenge Book, $9.95
Everything® Large-Print Crossword Challenge Book

Everything® Large-Print Crosswords Book
Everything® Lateral Thinking Puzzles Book, $9.95
Everything® Mazes Book
Everything® Movie Crosswords Book, $9.95
Everything® Online Poker Book, $12.95
Everything® Pencil Puzzles Book, $9.95
Everything® Poker Strategy Book
Everything® Pool & Billiards Book
Everything® Sports Crosswords Book, $9.95
Everything® Test Your IQ Book, $9.95
Everything® Texas Hold 'Em Book, $9.95
Everything® Travel Crosswords Book, $9.95
Everything® Word Games Challenge Book
Everything® Word Scramble Book
Everything® Word Search Book

HEALTH

Everything® Alzheimer's Book
Everything® Diabetes Book
Everything® Health Guide to Adult Bipolar Disorder
Everything® Health Guide to Controlling Anxiety
Everything® Health Guide to Fibromyalgia
Everything® Health Guide to Postpartum Care
Everything® Health Guide to Thyroid Disease
Everything® Hypnosis Book
Everything® Low Cholesterol Book
Everything® Massage Book
Everything® Menopause Book
Everything® Nutrition Book
Everything® Reflexology Book
Everything® Stress Management Book

HISTORY

Everything® American Government Book
Everything® American History Book, 2nd Ed.
Everything® Civil War Book
Everything® Freemasons Book
Everything® Irish History & Heritage Book
Everything® Middle East Book

HOBBIES

Everything® Candlemaking Book
Everything® Cartooning Book
Everything® Coin Collecting Book
Everything® Drawing Book
Everything® Family Tree Book, 2nd Ed.
Everything® Knitting Book
Everything® Knots Book
Everything® Photography Book

Everything® Quilting Book
Everything® Scrapbooking Book
Everything® Sewing Book
Everything® Soapmaking Book, 2nd Ed.
Everything® Woodworking Book

HOME IMPROVEMENT

Everything® Feng Shui Book
Everything® Feng Shui Decluttering Book, $9.95
Everything® Fix-It Book
Everything® Home Decorating Book
Everything® Home Storage Solutions Book
Everything® Homebuilding Book
Everything® Organize Your Home Book

KIDS' BOOKS

All titles are $7.95
Everything® Kids' Animal Puzzle & Activity Book
Everything® Kids' Baseball Book, 4th Ed.
Everything® Kids' Bible Trivia Book
Everything® Kids' Bugs Book
Everything® Kids' Cars and Trucks Puzzle
   & Activity Book
Everything® Kids' Christmas Puzzle
   & Activity Book
Everything® Kids' Cookbook
Everything® Kids' Crazy Puzzles Book
Everything® Kids' Dinosaurs Book
Everything® Kids' First Spanish Puzzle and
   Activity Book
Everything® Kids' Gross Cookbook
Everything® Kids' Gross Hidden Pictures Book
Everything® Kids' Gross Jokes Book
Everything® Kids' Gross Mazes Book
Everything® Kids' Gross Puzzle and
   Activity Book
Everything® Kids' Halloween Puzzle
   & Activity Book
Everything® Kids' Hidden Pictures Book
Everything® Kids' Horses Book
Everything® Kids' Joke Book
Everything® Kids' Knock Knock Book
Everything® Kids' Learning Spanish Book
Everything® Kids' Math Puzzles Book
Everything® Kids' Mazes Book
Everything® Kids' Money Book
Everything® Kids' Nature Book
Everything® Kids' Pirates Puzzle and Activity Book
Everything® Kids' Presidents Book
Everything® Kids' Princess Puzzle and Activity Book
Everything® Kids' Puzzle Book
Everything® Kids' Riddles & Brain Teasers Book
Everything® Kids' Science Experiments Book
Everything® Kids' Sharks Book
Everything® Kids' Soccer Book
Everything® Kids' States Book
Everything® Kids' Travel Activity Book

KIDS' STORY BOOKS

Everything® Fairy Tales Book

LANGUAGE

Everything® Conversational Japanese Book with
   CD, $19.95
Everything® French Grammar Book
Everything® French Phrase Book, $9.95
Everything® French Verb Book, $9.95
Everything® German Practice Book with CD,
   $19.95
Everything® Inglés Book
**Everything® Intermediate Spanish Book with
   CD, $19.95**
**Everything® Learning Brazilian Portuguese
   Book with CD, $19.95**
Everything® Learning French Book
Everything® Learning German Book
Everything® Learning Italian Book
Everything® Learning Latin Book
**Everything® Learning Spanish Book with
   CD, 2nd Edition, $19.95**
Everything® Russian Practice Book with CD, $19.95
Everything® Sign Language Book
Everything® Spanish Grammar Book
Everything® Spanish Phrase Book, $9.95
Everything® Spanish Practice Book
   with CD, $19.95
Everything® Spanish Verb Book, $9.95
Everything® Speaking Mandarin Chinese Book
   with CD, $19.95

MUSIC

Everything® Drums Book with CD, $19.95
**Everything® Guitar Book with CD, 2nd
   Edition, $19.95**
Everything® Guitar Chords Book with CD, $19.95
Everything® Home Recording Book
Everything® Music Theory Book with CD, $19.95
Everything® Reading Music Book with CD, $19.95
Everything® Rock & Blues Guitar Book
   with CD, $19.95
**Everything® Rock and Blues Piano Book
   with CD, $19.95**
Everything® Songwriting Book

NEW AGE

Everything® Astrology Book, 2nd Ed.
Everything® Birthday Personology Book
Everything® Dreams Book, 2nd Ed.
Everything® Love Signs Book, $9.95
Everything® Numerology Book
Everything® Paganism Book
Everything® Palmistry Book
Everything® Psychic Book
Everything® Reiki Book

Everything® Sex Signs Book, $9.95
Everything® Tarot Book, 2nd Ed.
Everything® Toltec Wisdom Book
Everything® Wicca and Witchcraft Book

PARENTING

Everything® Baby Names Book, 2nd Ed.
Everything® Baby Shower Book
Everything® Baby's First Year Book
Everything® Birthing Book
Everything® Breastfeeding Book
Everything® Father-to-Be Book
Everything® Father's First Year Book
Everything® Get Ready for Baby Book
Everything® Get Your Baby to Sleep Book, $9.95
Everything® Getting Pregnant Book
Everything® Guide to Raising a One-Year-Old
Everything® Guide to Raising a Two-Year-Old
Everything® Homeschooling Book
Everything® Mother's First Year Book
**Everything® Parent's Guide to Childhood
   Illnesses**
Everything® Parent's Guide to Children
   and Divorce
Everything® Parent's Guide to Children
   with ADD/ADHD
Everything® Parent's Guide to Children
   with Asperger's Syndrome
Everything® Parent's Guide to Children
   with Autism
Everything® Parent's Guide to Children with
   Bipolar Disorder
**Everything® Parent's Guide to Children with
   Depression**
Everything® Parent's Guide to Children
   with Dyslexia
**Everything® Parent's Guide to Children with
   Juvenile Diabetes**
Everything® Parent's Guide to Positive Discipline
Everything® Parent's Guide to Raising a
   Successful Child
Everything® Parent's Guide to Raising Boys
Everything® Parent's Guide to Raising Girls
Everything® Parent's Guide to Raising Siblings
Everything® Parent's Guide to Sensory
   Integration Disorder
Everything® Parent's Guide to Tantrums
Everything® Parent's Guide to the Strong-Willed
   Child
Everything® Parenting a Teenager Book
Everything® Potty Training Book, $9.95
Everything® Pregnancy Book, 3rd Ed.
Everything® Pregnancy Fitness Book
Everything® Pregnancy Nutrition Book
Everything® Pregnancy Organizer, 2nd Ed., $16.95
Everything® Toddler Activities Book
Everything® Toddler Book

Everything® Tween Book
Everything® Twins, Triplets, and More Book

PETS

Everything® Aquarium Book
Everything® Boxer Book
Everything® Cat Book, 2nd Ed.
Everything® Chihuahua Book
Everything® Dachshund Book
Everything® Dog Book
Everything® Dog Health Book
Everything® Dog Obedience Book
Everything® Dog Owner's Organizer, $16.95
Everything® Dog Training and Tricks Book
Everything® German Shepherd Book
Everything® Golden Retriever Book
Everything® Horse Book
Everything® Horse Care Book
Everything® Horseback Riding Book
Everything® Labrador Retriever Book
Everything® Poodle Book
Everything® Pug Book
Everything® Puppy Book
Everything® Rottweiler Book
Everything® Small Dogs Book
Everything® Tropical Fish Book
Everything® Yorkshire Terrier Book

REFERENCE

Everything® American Presidents Book
Everything® Blogging Book
Everything® Build Your Vocabulary Book
Everything® Car Care Book
Everything® Classical Mythology Book
Everything® Da Vinci Book
Everything® Divorce Book
Everything® Einstein Book
Everything® Enneagram Book
Everything® Etiquette Book, 2nd Ed.
Everything® Inventions and Patents Book
Everything® Mafia Book
Everything® Philosophy Book
Everything® Pirates Book
Everything® Psychology Book

RELIGION

Everything® Angels Book
Everything® Bible Book
Everything® Buddhism Book
Everything® Catholicism Book
Everything® Christianity Book
Everything® Gnostic Gospels Book
Everything® History of the Bible Book
Everything® Jesus Book

Everything® Jewish History & Heritage Book
Everything® Judaism Book
Everything® Kabbalah Book
Everything® Koran Book
Everything® Mary Book
Everything® Mary Magdalene Book
Everything® Prayer Book
Everything® Saints Book, 2nd Ed.
Everything® Torah Book
Everything® Understanding Islam Book
Everything® World's Religions Book
Everything® Zen Book

SCHOOL & CAREERS

Everything® Alternative Careers Book
Everything® Career Tests Book
Everything® College Major Test Book
Everything® College Survival Book, 2nd Ed.
Everything® Cover Letter Book, 2nd Ed.
Everything® Filmmaking Book
Everything® Get-a-Job Book, 2nd Ed.
Everything® Guide to Being a Paralegal
Everything® Guide to Being a Personal Trainer
Everything® Guide to Being a Real Estate Agent
Everything® Guide to Being a Sales Rep
Everything® Guide to Careers in Health Care
Everything® Guide to Careers in Law Enforcement
Everything® Guide to Government Jobs
Everything® Guide to Starting and Running a Restaurant
Everything® Job Interview Book
Everything® New Nurse Book
Everything® New Teacher Book
Everything® Paying for College Book
Everything® Practice Interview Book
Everything® Resume Book, 2nd Ed.
Everything® Study Book

SELF-HELP

Everything® Dating Book, 2nd Ed.
Everything® Great Sex Book
Everything® Self-Esteem Book
Everything® Tantric Sex Book

SPORTS & FITNESS

Everything® Easy Fitness Book
Everything® Running Book
Everything® Weight Training Book

TRAVEL

Everything® Family Guide to Cruise Vacations
Everything® Family Guide to Hawaii
Everything® Family Guide to Las Vegas, 2nd Ed.
Everything® Family Guide to Mexico
Everything® Family Guide to New York City, 2nd Ed.
Everything® Family Guide to RV Travel & Campgrounds
Everything® Family Guide to the Caribbean
Everything® Family Guide to the Walt Disney World Resort®, Universal Studios®, and Greater Orlando, 4th Ed.
Everything® Family Guide to Timeshares
Everything® Family Guide to Washington D.C., 2nd Ed.

WEDDINGS

Everything® Bachelorette Party Book, $9.95
Everything® Bridesmaid Book, $9.95
Everything® Destination Wedding Book
Everything® Elopement Book, $9.95
Everything® Father of the Bride Book, $9.95
Everything® Groom Book, $9.95
Everything® Mother of the Bride Book, $9.95
Everything® Outdoor Wedding Book
Everything® Wedding Book, 3rd Ed.
Everything® Wedding Checklist, $9.95
Everything® Wedding Etiquette Book, $9.95
Everything® Wedding Organizer, 2nd Ed., $16.95
Everything® Wedding Shower Book, $9.95
Everything® Wedding Vows Book, $9.95
Everything® Wedding Workout Book
Everything® Weddings on a Budget Book, $9.95

WRITING

Everything® Creative Writing Book
Everything® Get Published Book, 2nd Ed.
Everything® Grammar and Style Book
Everything® Guide to Magazine Writing
Everything® Guide to Writing a Book Proposal
Everything® Guide to Writing a Novel
Everything® Guide to Writing Children's Books
Everything® Guide to Writing Copy
Everything® Guide to Writing Research Papers
Everything® Screenwriting Book
Everything® Writing Poetry Book
Everything® Writing Well Book